Planning Your Pension

Jonquil Lowe

CONSUMERS' ASSOCIATION

Which? Books are commissioned by
Consumers' Association and published by
Which? Ltd, 2 Marylebone Road, London NW1 4DF
Email address: books@which.net

Distributed by The Penguin Group:
Penguin Books Ltd, 27 Wrights Lane, London W8 5TZ

First edition June 1993
Revised edition August 1994
Second edition April 1997
Third edition June 1999
Reprinted December 2001
Fourth edition July 2002
Fifth edition September 2004
First three editions published as *The Which? Guide to Pensions* and next three as
The Which? Guide to Planning Your Pension
Copyright © 1993, 1994, 1997, 1999, 2002, 2004 Which? Ltd

British Library Cataloguing-in-Publication Data
A catalogue record for this book is available from the British Library

ISBN 0 85202 998 5

For a full list of Which? books, please write to Which? Books, Castlemead,
Gascoyne Way, Hertford X, SG14 1LH, or access our website at
http://www.which.net

Typeset by WPG Ltd, Welshpool, Powys, Wales
Printed and bound in Wales by Creative Print and Design

Contents

Part 4 Your options when there is no occupational pension scheme

Part 5 Boosting your pension

Part 6 Reaching retirement

Part 7 Complaints

★ An asterisk next to the name of an organisation in the text indicates that the address can be found in this section

Introduction

Which? first published a guide to saving for retirement in 1983. Since then, pensions have been in a constant state of flux. With every change to the rules, the system has become more complex. With every mis-selling scandal and scheme closure, the public has lost a little more confidence. The authorities talk of a massive pensions gap with a generation of workers heading for old age poverty. To tackle the crisis, comes the most ambitious change yet to the pension system.

From April 2006, the many sets of rules about what you can pay into and draw out of pension schemes and plans are being swept away and replaced by a single, new, simplified regime. Whether this will be enough to tempt savers and pension providers back into the water remains to be seen. The fundamental problem of pensions remains: they are very long-term investments that require someone in the chain to take some risk.

Tens of thousands of occupational scheme members have seen their pension schemes close with gaping holes in the pension fund. As a result, workers who thought they were on track for a comfortable retirement have disastrously seen their pensions vanish. They belonged to a type of pension arrangement called a salary-related scheme. The key characteristic of such schemes is that members are promised a certain level of pension according to their pay and years of membership. The members often pay something, but the bulk of the cost borne by the employer. This is an open-ended cost for two reasons:

- if investments perform badly – as they did over the period 2000 to 2003 – the employer needs to pump extra money into the pension fund to make good the resulting shortfall
- if people start to live longer than originally expected, the cost of paying each pension over a whole retirement rises. This is precisely

what has been happening with average life expectancy increasing by one or two years every decade.

The extra money the pension fund needs has in some cases become so large that employers can't afford to make good the scheme shortfalls. Hence scheme closures and broken pension promises. But the picture needs to be put in perspective. Some 9.1 million people belong to salary-related schemes. Only a small proportion are in schemes that have collapsed. And 4.5 million are in public sector salary-related schemes where the government can fall back on tax revenues to meet the cost.

Moreover, it is important to be clear that the problems with salary-related schemes arise because of the pension promise. With the main alternative – a money purchase arrangement – there is no promise to be lost or broken. You might imagine this means there is no crisis. But pity the members of this type of scheme who planned or had to retire between 2000 and 2003 and found with the falling stock market that their pension fund had plummeted. There was no employer sheltering them from investment risk. And people retiring now are getting only half the pension they would have done 15 years ago because the rate at which you can convert a pension fund into pension (the annuity rate) has fallen dramatically in large part because people are living longer. Members of money purchase schemes retire on wildly different pensions according to how fate deals with them as they reach retirement.

So don't be in too much of a hurry to condemn salary-related occupational schemes. They are still, for the majority of people, the best way of building up retirement savings.

You might wonder whether it's worth saving for retirement at all. But set against the difficulties of building up a pension is the near certainty that you will have an impoverished old age if you don't. *Planning your Pension* helps you systematically to consider how much income you will need, how to check what state pension and other savings you have built up so far and the steps you can take to fill any gap. Throughout it explains the pros and cons of each way to save in clear and objective terms so that you can understand and manage the risks and make balanced decisions to put you firmly on the road to a happy retirement.

This guide reflects measures passed in the Finance Act 2004 and proposed in the 2004 Pensions Bill. The latter was still being debated by Parliament and could be subject to further changes.

Part 1

Building a retirement plan

Chapter 1

Planning for retirement

This book is about planning to make sure that you can enjoy a comfortable lifestyle when you eventually retire. Retirement may seem a long way off, but you need to build up savings now if you are to finance the years after work.

Planning ahead

The earlier you start to save, the easier it will be to build up enough money. But during some stages of life – particularly when you have family commitments – it may be hard to give pension planning top priority. And pension savings are tied up for the long term – that could be problematic if you are not sure whether you'll need access to your savings at some time before retirement. So, while pension planning is very important, you'll have to weigh it against your other financial commitments, such as protecting your family, clearing debts and running a home.

New-age retirement

In order to gauge how much money you should salt away for your pension, you need some idea of what life in retirement might be like.

Retirement used to be the twilight of life. The terms 'old-age pensioner' and 'senior citizen' once seemed apt descriptions of people who had traded their smart suits and crowded desks for slippers and the fireside. But these days retirement has taken on a completely different character.

New-age retirees are busy and active, often still working part-time, taking up new sports and hobbies, making frequent trips abroad and even living overseas for all or part of the year. Retirement is also ceasing to happen at a distinct point in time. Instead, people are tending gradually to ease back from work, reducing their hours and taking longer holidays, often from a relatively young age – perhaps from their fifties.

Two major factors have transformed retirement:

- improved health and longevity. As Table 1.1 shows, retirement can easily last for 20 or 30 years. Most people can expect to be reasonably healthy and active during much of that time. Government figures show that, at birth, men can expect just under eight years of ill health during their lifetime and women about 11. But these are average figures, and actual experience will vary from person to person

- greater affluence. Many people retiring today have the security of better state pensions than in the past, as well as good company pensions.

Table 1.1: How long is retirement?

If you retire at age:	On average, you can expect these many years in retirement:	
	Women	Men
50	32	28
55	28	24
60	23	20
65	19	16
70	15	12
75	12	10
80	9	7
85	6	5
90	4	4

Source: *Government Actuary's Department. Data for UK*

Sources of retirement income

If you are to enjoy yourself for 20 or 30 years without working, you will clearly need to build up a very substantial fund of savings. In fact, retirement planning can easily cost as much as, if not more than, buying a house.

The importance of building up these savings is underlined by the stark contrast between the richest and poorest pensioners today. A government survey of incomes and spending in 2002–3 shows that the poorest fifth of pensioners have a before-tax income of just £100 a week (single pensioner) and £170 a week (couples). The richest fifth have £392 a week (single) and £855 a week (couples). As Table 1.2 shows, the difference is mainly due to the impact of receiving an occupational pension and, to a lesser extent, earnings and investment income. The poorest fifth of households rely on state pensions and other state benefits for 85 to 90 per cent of their income. (Note that the next poorest and next wealthiest fifths have been omitted from the table.)

Table 1.2: Income of the poorest and wealthiest pensioner households

| | Type of pensioner household | | | | | |
| | Single pensioner | | | Couples | | |
	Poorest fifth	Middle fifth	Wealthiest fifth	Poorest fifth	Middle fifth	Wealthiest fifth
Before-tax weekly income	£100	£169	£392	£170	£292	£855
of which:						
State pensions and other state benefits	£90	£133	£141	£145	£188	£162
Occupational pensions	£5	£26	£138	£15	£71	£306
Personal pension income	£1	£2	£11	£4	£8	£41
Investment income	£3	£5	£49	£4	£11	£146
Earnings	£0	£2	£45	£2	£12	£183
Other income	£1	£1	£7	£1	£1	£15

Source: *The Pensioners' Incomes Series 2002–3*

How much you need to save

How much you need to set aside for retirement depends on a variety of factors, including:

- the income that you expect to need in retirement
- how much of that income you can expect from state pensions (see Chapter 3 for an overview and Chapters 4 to 7 for details)
- how much pension your savings will produce. Chapters 10 to 32 look at various ways of saving for retirement and the pensions (and other benefits) that they might give you
- how long you save for
- the allowance that you have to make for the effects of inflation.

The income that you will need

How much income you equate with a comfortable lifestyle is a personal decision. On the whole, it will depend on the spending patterns that you consider essential or desirable. Chapter 2 shows you how to work out what you might spend in retirement.

In the past, the maximum pension you can have from many pension schemes has been restricted to two-thirds of your pre-retirement pay, so many financial advisers have suggested that you work towards a target of two-thirds of your pay or sometimes half your pay. For example, if you earn £30,000, you might aim for a pension of £20,000 or £15,000. Alternatively, you can start with your likely spending needs, which may result in a lower or higher target pension.

How long you save for

The earlier you start to save for retirement, the easier it is to build up enough funds. When you are saving for something which is a long way off, the savings you make in the early days are more valuable than savings made later on. This is not simply because the savings have longer to grow. They also benefit from 'compounding' – this means that, as well as getting a return on your original capital, you also get a return on growth which has been reinvested. The case history of John shows the effect of compounding.

Once you have accumulated a sizeable pension fund, each year's growth will be a big addition to the pot. It follows that, if you retire early, the pot will be a lot smaller and, on top of that, the pension will have to be paid for longer. The impact that early retirement has on your pension depends on the type of savings arrangement you are using (see Chapters 6, 15 and 19 for details). But clearly, if you plan to retire at a relatively early age, you will need to save more.

Don't forget inflation

Another feature of saving over a long time period is changes in the value of money due to price inflation. What makes money worth having is the things you can buy with it. But, as prices rise, your money buys less. For example, £900 might buy you a stylish three-piece suite today, but if inflation averaged even 1 per cent a year, in 30 years' time your £900 would run to the sofa but no armchairs. To maintain your previous pattern of spending as prices rise, you need more money.

CASE HISTORY: John

John has been able to get a return of 5 per cent a year, year in, year out, on his savings. The £100 which he invested 20 years ago has grown by £165 (to £265) today, but the £100 invested five years ago has grown by just £28 (to £128).

Although 20 years is only four times five years, £165 is much more than four times £28. The 'extra' growth reflects compounding: in other words, the return on each year's reinvested growth.

To see how compounding works, look at what happened to the money that John invested 20 years ago:

- at the end of the first year, John had his £100 original capital plus 5% × £100 = £5 growth, a total of £105
- at the end of the second year, John had his £100 original capital plus 5% × £100 = £5 growth for the second year, plus £5 growth from last year *and* an extra 5% × £5 = 25p from reinvesting last year's growth, a total of £110.25
- at the end of the third year, John had his £100 plus £5 growth for the third year, plus £10.25 growth from earlier years *and* an extra 5% × £10.25 = 51p from reinvesting the previous years' growth, a total of £115.76
- and so on, year after year.

Some forms of saving for retirement automatically take inflation into account, ensuring that, as your pension builds up, its buying power is maintained or increased. But other forms of retirement saving don't do this automatically (throughout the book, we will tell you when this is the case), and you will need to make sure that you are saving enough to compensate for the effect of rising prices (see the case history of Helen and Jake).

The average rate of inflation between now and the time when you retire has a big impact on your target pension. There is no way of knowing what that rate will be: you can only guess. There is no reason why what happens in the future should follow the patterns of the past, but past experience might help you to make a reasoned guess. Chart 1.1 shows the peaks and troughs of inflation for every decade from 1940 to the present. Over the whole period, inflation has ranged from less than zero (that is, falling prices) up to nearly 27 per cent a year. The average inflation rate has varied from 2.6 per cent a year during

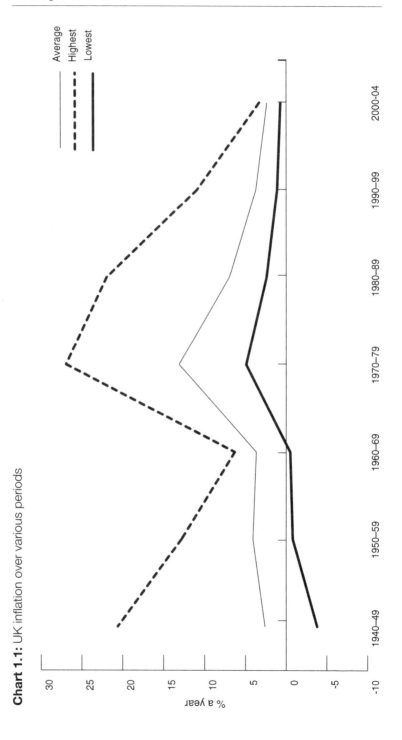

Chart 1.1: UK inflation over various periods

the 1940s to 13.1 per cent during the 1970s. Since the start of the new millennium, inflation has again been low, averaging 2.4 per cent a year.

CASE HISTORY: Helen and Jake

Helen and Jake jointly earn £39,000 a year. By the time they retire, in 23 years' time, demands on their finances will have changed, and they expect that an income of, say, £22,000 would be enough to support a reasonably comfortable retirement.

But, if inflation averages even a low rate of 2.5 per cent a year in the intervening 23 years, £22,000 at retirement would be worth only the same as £12,467 today. Rising prices would nearly have halved the buying power of the pension.

To retire on a pension which has the same buying power as £22,000 today, if Helen and Jake expect inflation to average 2.5 per cent a year, they need to aim for a pension of £38,821. If they think inflation will be higher, their target pension needs to be higher too.

The Calculator in Chapter 2 will help you to work out the target pension you need to aim for if it is to have the same buying power as a selected sum in today's money. But, before making that calculation, you should first take into account any pension that you might get from the state (see Chapters 3 to 7).

How much income?

You will probably need less to live on after retirement than during your working years. Depending on your age now, you may currently have some or all of the following heavy demands to meet:

- buying your own home, probably with a mortgage
- bringing up your children
- financing your children through university
- work-related expenses: for example, travel, smart clothing.

By the time you retire you are likely to have paid off your mortgage, the children will be grown up and independent, and you will no longer have all those work-related expenses.

Spending in retirement

Chart 2.1 compares average weekly spending according to the age of the head of the household. Before retirement, in total the average household spends £473 a week (head of household aged 30 to 49) or £416 (aged 50 to 64). After retirement this drops markedly to £263 (age 65 to 74) and even more to £169 a week in later retirement. The fall affects all areas but there is a particularly marked drop in spending on motoring and other travel, clothes and footwear. Retired households spend less in £s but proportionately more on food, fuel and power and household services than non-retired households.

As might be expected, spending on housing falls with age, largely as any mortgage is paid off. Spending on items like life insurance and pension contributions also falls sharply as the need for these items largely disappears. But, with increasing age, you might find a higher

Chart 2.1: Changes in spending after retirement

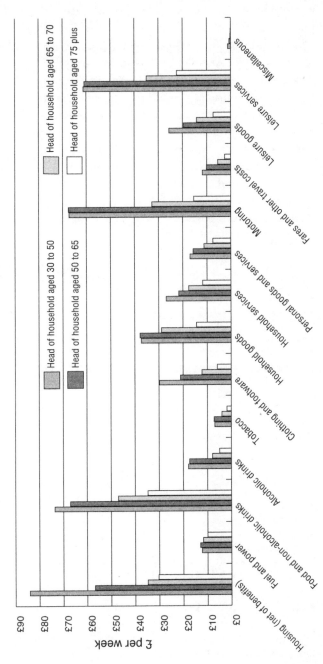

Source: *Family Expenditure Survey 2000–1*

19

proportion of your budget going on health-related spending. Table 2.1 illustrates how health problems tend to increase with age.

Anticipation of future health problems, or actual ill-health, in retirement may have several effects on your spending. For example, you may decide to adapt your home by building a downstairs bedroom or bathroom. You may plan ahead to cope with the costs of care in your own home or a care home by taking out long-term care insurance (see page 22). This will help if you need to employ homecare or nursing staff to help with, say, getting dressed and bathing, or you eventually decide to move into a residential or nursing home. But the state might help with some or all of these costs.

Table 2.1: How health tends to deteriorate with age

Health indicator	Women aged			Men aged		
	45–64	65–74	75 and over	45–64	65–74	75 and over
Percentage with a long-standing illness	44%	61%	72%	46%	65%	71%
Percentage with a limiting long-standing illness	28%	39%	53%	28%	43%	52%
Percentage consulting GP within last 14 days	17%	21%	27%	15%	22%	21%
Percentage attending outpatient or casualty department within last three months	16%	20%	25%	15%	24%	26%
Percentage receiving day patient treatment within last 12 months	8%	10%	10%	8%	11%	12%
Percentage receiving inpatient treatment within last 12 months	8%	8%	16%	8%	15%	18%
Number of people per 1,000 reporting arthritis and rheumatism	119	219	268	86	153	194
Number of people per 1,000 r eporting high blood pressure	74	132	140	65	119	84
Number of people per 1,000 reporting heart attack	15	58	90	26	70	118

Source: HMSO *Living in Britain 2004* (figures for 2002).

Retirement-spending calculator

Use the Expenses Calculator on pages 23–4 to estimate how much income you will need in retirement. Put in amounts as if you were retiring today: in other words, use today's money values. At this stage, do not worry about inflation: we will return to the problem of rising prices in Chapter 9. The notes below will help you to fill in the Calculator.

Day-to-day living

Include here all the basic household bills that you incur week in, week out, plus the extras that you may spend – on magazines, music and clothes, for example. Include any small items of household equipment (such as a kettle, shower curtain, laundry basket and so on) that you would expect to buy out of the normal household budget. Enter also gardening costs (for potting compost, plants and tools, for example). These are all the sorts of items that you'll buy on shopping trips or from catalogues.

Home-related

These are the major household bills which crop up monthly, quarterly or yearly. Include here any payments for help around the house (for example, a cleaner) and a sum to cover any tradespeople whom you contract to do repairs (such as fixing the washing machine) or odd jobs (putting up a greenhouse, fitting a new electrical socket and so on).

Living it up

This section is for non-essential spending.

Transport

Enter here all the expenses that you expect to run up during day-to-day travelling. Do not include out-of-the ordinary expenses, such as air fares for holidays or the cost of trips to visit relatives abroad: include those in 'Living it up', above. If you plan to use buses, trains and taxis, bear in mind that the over-65s often qualify for concessionary fares, which may cut costs by, say, as much as a third.

Health-related

You are likely to continue to make regular trips to the dentist. Unless your income is very low, you will have to pay for dental check-ups and treatment, or you may decide to take out dental insurance. Similarly, you may need to allow for the periodic costs of glasses or contact lenses, though eye tests are free for the over-60s.

There are various types of health insurance that you might consider though none of these is essential:

- **private medical insurance (PMI)** This pays the bills for private hospital treatment. However, it does not cover treatment for chronic health conditions, and, if you change insurer, any existing health problems are not covered either at all or for the first couple of years. On top of that, the cost of PMI escalates rapidly, especially as you get older. In the UK, around 7.6 million people (12.8 per cent of the population) are covered by PMI, but two-thirds get cover through an employer. Cost varies greatly depending on various factors, in particular, the degree of cover you choose. Age is also very important, with premiums increasing sharply. For example, a woman in her 60s can expect to pay around twice as much as a woman in her 40s and four times as much as one in her 20s. In retirement you could easily be paying over £1,000 a year for cover. An increasingly popular option, if you fancy neither NHS treatment nor paying for insurance, is to 'self-pay' – in other words, pay a hospital direct for private treatment either by dipping into savings or taking out a loan
- **hospital cash plan** This pays out cash benefits to you if you go into hospital (either NHS or private). Some plans also pay out if you need chiropody, a hearing aid and so on. Premiums are usually the same for all ages, so they can work out as good value for older people, but the cash pay-outs are relatively small, and there are often lots of restrictions in the small print
- **long-term care insurance** This pays towards the cost of care in your own home or towards fees for a nursing or residential home if you are no longer able to look after yourself. In 2004, in England the state picks up the nursing costs up to a limit but pays the other costs in full only if your income is low and you have capital of no more than £12,250. If your capital is in the region of £12,250 to £20,000, the state may pay part of the cost. If your income is high enough and/or you have capital of over £20,000, you have to pay these costs. (Different rules and capital limits apply in Scotland, Wales and Northern Ireland.) So taking out long-term care insurance, in essence, is a way of protecting your capital. This might be important to you if you are keen to leave an inheritance to your children, say.

Caring for others

Don't forget the grandchildren's pocket money and family birthdays!

If your family tends to be long-lived, you may find yourself continuing to support elderly parents even though you are yourself retired.

Expenses calculator

Item	Yearly total £
Day-to-day living	
Food shopping and household basics	
Newspapers/magazines/books	
Videos/music	
Dog/cat/other pets	
Clothes/shoes/cosmetics/hairdressing	
Small household items	
Gardening	
Home-related	
Mortgage/rent	
Repairs/service charge/decoration	
Buildings and contents insurance	
Council tax	
Water rates/gas/electricity/other fuel	
Telephone	
TV licence/satellite or cable charges	
Home help/window cleaner/other paid help	
Living it up	
Sports and hobbies: materials/lessons/other	
Dining out/takeaway food	
Theatre/cinema/concerts/exhibitions	
Holidays/holiday home/second home	
Smoking/drinking/other luxuries	
Transport	
Owning a car: tax/insurance/servicing/breakdown service/repairs	
Renting a car: rental charge/insurance	
Running a car: petrol/diesel/oil/anti-freeze	
Fares: train/bus/coach/taxi	
Health-related	
Dentist	
Optician	
Hospital cash plan/private medical insurance	
Long-term care insurance	
Other health-related	

Item	Yearly total £
Caring for others	
Spending on children/grandchildren	
Spending on elderly relatives	
Christmas/birthday/other presents	
Gifts to charity/church collections	
Protection-type life insurance	
Other caring expenses	
Saving and borrowing	
Saving to replace major household items/ home improvements/car and so on	
Saving for later retirement, for example, to cover health spending or cope with inflation	
Other regular saving	
Loan repayments (other than mortgage)	
Other	
All other expenses	
TOTAL	

Would anyone suffer financially in the event of your death (for example, a parent who lives with you)? You may have pension arrangements that would continue to pay a pension (though probably at a reduced rate) to a wife, husband or partner and maybe other dependants, too. If not, you may need to continue paying for life insurance after retirement. Starting a new policy at that time could be very costly.

Saving and borrowing

Consider how you would replace major household items or a car, say. You might dip into capital, buy on credit or plan ahead by saving regularly. (But don't include here any small items that you have already entered under 'Day-to-day living'.)

In the earlier years of retirement, you might decide to save part of your income to use later to fund health-related expenses or simply to counter inflation.

Other

Enter here any expenses which don't fit under the above headings.

Chapter 3

Where will your pension come from?

Before 1948, old age was viewed largely as a problem of poverty: those who could not provide for themselves had to look for support to family, charity, the poor laws and, eventually, a means-tested (and morals-tested) old-age pension introduced in 1908.

The state pension

The start in 1948 of a nation-wide contributory pension system (credited to William Beveridge, though first mooted as early as 1879) marked a break with the past. All working individuals were required to 'save' through compulsory National Insurance contributions and, in return, had the right to receive a pension once they reached retirement age. State pensions were no longer tainted with the stigma of poverty.

A contract between the generations

In fact, the state pension system is not a savings scheme. Instead it works on a 'pay-as-you-go' principle. Contributions paid in today fund the pensions paid out today. Similarly, future pensioners must rely on future taxpayers to foot the bill. It is a contract between the generations.

The cost of pensions today

Improvements in the state pension system – in particular, protecting pensions against inflation and the introduction of a second-tier pension – the state second pension (S2P), formerly the state earnings-related pension scheme (SERPS) – have made pensions a major component of central government spending. In 2003–4, spending on state retirement pensions, winter fuel allowance and means-tested top-ups for pensioners amounted to £55 billion compared with, for example, £6.9 billion spent on sickness benefits and £2.5 billion on Jobseekers' Allowance.

The cost of pensions to come

A pay-as-you-go system can work very well if there is a favourable balance between the people who are working and the people who are retired. But the cost to those in work can become unacceptable if the ratio of workers to pensioners (called the 'support ratio') falls too low. It is forecast that during the first half of the twenty-first century the number of people over state pension age will rise by about a third. This is due to the retirement of the 'baby-boom' generation that was born after the Second World War, as well as to increasing life expectancy. As a result, the number of people of working age per pensioner will fall from more than three today to around two by 2040.

If there had been no change to the current system, the cost of providing state pensions could have become unaffordable. In fact, state pensions have been progressively cut back over the last 20 years (see Chapter 7) with some of the changes being phased in over the years ahead. The future cost to the state is contained, but the consequence is that individuals are increasingly being required to make their own provisions for retirement.

The big divide

The dilemma faced by the state is that not all people are able and/or willing to make their own savings for retirement.

There is already a large rift between the poorest and the wealthiest pensioners (see page 13). Those most at risk from retiring on unacceptably low incomes are:

- people on earnings so low that they do not pay any National Insurance contributions (often women in part-time jobs). They are often not building up even a state pension
- people on low earnings who are contributing to a state pension but cannot afford to make their own savings for an extra pension
- people who can't work because they are either disabled or are full-time carers looking after, for example, young children, an elderly relative or a relative with a disability.

With this in mind, the government has made some major changes to the pension system in recent years: the pension credit, and the State Second Pension (see page 32).

The pension credit

The pension credit started in October 2003. It is designed to top up the resources of current pensioners whose income is low and has two parts: a guarantee credit and a savings credit. Depending on your circumstances, you might qualify for either or both of these elements.

The guarantee credit

This replaces and is basically the same as an earlier safeguard, the minimum income guarantee (MIG). Any person aged 60 or over whose income is less than a set amount called the minimum guarantee (£105.45 a week for a single person and £160.95 for a couple in 2004–5) is entitled to claim a top-up to bring their income up to that level. The minimum guarantee is higher for people who are severely disabled and for carers and can include extra to cover mortgage interest and certain other housing costs (but not rent, for which you might be able to claim housing benefit instead).

The minimum guarantee is increased each year in line with national average earnings.

Pension credit and couples

At the time of writing, 'couple' means either a married couple or partners living together as man and wife. In future (from a date as yet unknown), it will also include same-sex couples who have registered their relationship as a civil partnership and unregistered same-sex partners living together. Until the new law comes into effect, same-sex partners are treated as single people.

The savings credit

A problem inherent in the guarantee credit is that it discourages people who do not expect to have much income in retirement from saving anything at all. What is the point of saving enough to provide, say, £20 a week in retirement if it will simply replace money you could otherwise have claimed through the guarantee credit? To tackle this problem, pension credit also has a savings credit which is designed to reward you for making your own savings for retirement.

If you are aged 65 or over, you can claim a credit of 60p for each £1 of income that you have between two thresholds. The lower threshold at which savings credit starts is the same as the maximum state basic retirement pension (£79.60 a week for a single person and £127.25 for a couple in 2004–5). The upper threshold is the minimum guarantee described above (£105.45 a week for a single person and £160.95 for a couple in 2004–5). This gives a maximum savings credit of £15.51 a week in 2004–5 if you are single and £20.22 if you are a couple. But the savings credit is reduced by 40p for each £1 of income above the minimum guarantee. In this way, the savings credit is tapered away to nothing for single people with income of £144.22 or more and couples with income of £211.50 or more. Tables 3.1 and 3.2 show in detail how much you can get, depending on your retirement income.

Your income for working out pension credit

The rules are complicated and this description gives just a broad outline. Income from most sources is taken into account, including

---

Example

In 2004–5, Greg, who is 66, has a state pension of £75 a week and £7,800 in a building society savings account. He makes a claim for pension credit. The interest from his savings account is ignored but he is treated as getting £1 a week for each £500 (and part-£500) of savings above £6,000, so he has a deemed income from savings of £4 a week. This brings his income up to £79 a week. This is less than the minimum guarantee of £105.45 a week, so he gets a guarantee credit of £105.45 – £79 = £26.45 a week. Although he has some savings income, it is not enough to bring his income above the threshold (£79.60 a week in 2004–5) at which he would qualify for savings credit. In effect, his savings are wasted since they earn him no savings credit and, without the £4 a week deemed income, he would simply qualify for £4 more guarantee credit.

Example

In 2004–5, June has a state pension of £79.60 a week and a personal pension of £20 a week, making a total weekly income of £99.60. This is £5.85 less than the minimum guarantee for a single person of £105.45, so she qualifies for guarantee credit of £5.85. Her income is £20 more than the £79.60 threshold at which the savings credit starts, so she is also entitled to a savings credit of 20 x 60p = £12. The pension credit has boosted her weekly income to £99.60 + £5.85 + £12 = £117.45.

Example

In 2004–5, Joe and Betty together get state pensions of £140 a week plus £35 a week from Joe's occupational pension, taking their total weekly income to £175 a week. This is more than the minimum guarantee for a couple (£160.95), so they do not qualify for any guarantee credit. However, their income of £175 is £47.75 more than the threshold at which savings credit starts (£127.25 in 2004–5), so they may qualify for some savings credit.

Initially, the savings credit is worked out as the maximum amount of (£160.95 – £127.25) x 60p = £20.22. But, because their £175 income is £14.05 higher than the minimum guarantee (£160.95), they lose 14.05 x 40p = £5.62, reducing their savings credit to £20.22 – £5.62 = £14.60. This increases their weekly income to £175 + £14.60 = £189.60.

---

state pensions, occupational pensions, personal and stakeholder pensions, earnings if you carry on working, profits if you are self-employed, rent from lodgers, and so on. However, income from many state benefits does not count and neither does your actual income from any savings and investments, such as building society accounts and unit trusts. Instead, you are treated as receiving a deemed amount from savings and investments of £1 a week from every £500 of savings over £6,000 (or £10,000 if you live in a care home). The first £6,000 (or £10,000) of savings and investments is ignored. £6,000 (£10,000) is the limit in 2004–5 – it could be raised in future but is not normally increased every year.

Table 3.1: Pension credit if you are single

Your income from all sources	Income above threshold at which savings credit starts	Guarantee credit	Savings credit	Your income including pension credit
£0	£0	£105.45	£0.00	£105.45
£5	£0	£100.45	£0.00	£105.45
£10	£0	£95.45	£0.00	£105.45
£15	£0	£90.45	£0.00	£105.45
£20	£0	£85.45	£0.00	£105.45
£25	£0	£80.45	£0.00	£105.45
£30	£0	£75.45	£0.00	£105.45
£35	£0	£70.45	£0.00	£105.45
£40	£0	£65.45	£0.00	£105.45
£45	£0	£60.45	£0.00	£105.45
£50	£0	£55.45	£0.00	£105.45
£55	£0	£50.45	£0.00	£105.45
£60	£0	£45.45	£0.00	£105.45
£65	£0	£40.45	£0.00	£105.45
£70	£0	£35.45	£0.00	£105.45
£75	£0	£30.45	£0.00	£105.45
£79.60 [1]	£0	£25.85	£0.00	£105.45
£80	£0.40	£25.45	£0.24	£105.69
£85	£5.40	£20.45	£3.24	£108.69
£90	£10.40	£15.45	£6.24	£111.69
£95	£15.40	£10.45	£9.24	£114.69
£100	£20.40	£5.45	£12.24	£117.69
£105	£25.40	£0.45	£15.24	£120.69
£105.45 [2]	£25.85	£0.00	£15.51	£120.96
£110	£30.40	£0.00	£13.69	£123.69
£115	£35.40	£0.00	£11.69	£126.69
£120	£40.40	£0.00	£9.69	£129.69
£125	£45.40	£0.00	£7.69	£132.69
£130	£50.40	£0.00	£5.69	£135.69
£135	£55.40	£0.00	£3.69	£138.69
£140	£60.40	£0.00	£1.69	£141.69
£144.22 [3]	£64.62	£0.00	£0.00	£144.22

[1] Threshold at which savings credit starts (equal to full state basic pension).
[2] Minimum guarantee (and threshold at which savings credit starts to be lost).
[3] Income level at which all savings credit lost.

Table 3.2: Pension credit if you are a couple

Your income from all sources	Income above threshold at which savings credit starts	Guarantee credit	Savings credit	Your income including pension credit
£0	£0	£160.95	£0.00	£160.95
£5	£0	£155.95	£0.00	£160.95
£10	£0	£150.95	£0.00	£160.95
£15	£0	£145.95	£0.00	£160.95
£20	£0	£140.95	£0.00	£160.95
£25	£0	£135.95	£0.00	£160.95
£30	£0	£130.95	£0.00	£160.95
£35	£0	£125.95	£0.00	£160.95
£40	£0	£120.95	£0.00	£160.95
£45	£0	£115.95	£0.00	£160.95
£50	£0	£110.95	£0.00	£160.95
£55	£0	£105.95	£0.00	£160.95
£60	£0	£100.95	£0.00	£160.95
£65	£0	£95.95	£0.00	£160.95
£70	£0	£90.95	£0.00	£160.95
£75	£0	£85.95	£0.00	£160.95
£80	£0	£80.95	£0.00	£160.95
£85	£0	£75.95	£0.00	£160.95
£90	£0	£70.95	£0.00	£160.95
£95	£0	£65.95	£0.00	£160.95
£100	£0	£60.95	£0.00	£160.95
£105	£0	£55.95	£0.00	£160.95
£110	£0	£50.95	£0.00	£160.95
£115	£0	£45.95	£0.00	£160.95
£120	£0	£40.95	£0.00	£160.95
£125	£0	£35.95	£0.00	£160.95
£127.25 [1]	£0	£33.70	£0.00	£160.95
£130	£2.75	£30.95	£1.65	£162.60
£135	£7.75	£25.95	£4.65	£165.60
£140	£12.75	£20.95	£7.65	£168.60
£145	£17.75	£15.95	£10.65	£171.60
£150	£22.75	£10.95	£13.65	£174.60
£155	£27.75	£5.95	£16.65	£177.60
£160	£32.75	£0.95	£19.65	£180.60
£160.95 [2]	£33.70	£0.00	£20.22	£181.17
£165	£37.75	£0.00	£18.60	£183.60
£170	£42.75	£0.00	£16.60	£186.60
£175	£47.75	£0.00	£14.60	£189.60
£180	£52.75	£0.00	£12.60	£192.60
£185	£57.75	£0.00	£10.60	£195.60

Pension credit if you are a couple (continued)

Your income from all sources	Income above threshold at which savings credit starts	Guarantee credit	Savings credit	Your income including pension credit
£190	£62.75	£0.00	£8.60	£198.60
£195	£67.75	£0.00	£6.60	£201.60
£200	£72.75	£0.00	£4.60	£204.60
£205	£77.75	£0.00	£2.60	£207.60
£210	£82.75	£0.00	£0.60	£210.60
£211.50 [3]	£84.25	£0.00	£0.00	£211.50

[1] Threshold at which savings credit starts (equal to full state basic pension).
[2] Minimum guarantee (and threshold at which savings credit starts to be lost).
[3] Income level at which all savings credit lost.

The state second pension

In April 2002, the government replaced SERPS with a new additional state pension, S2P. This is described in full in Chapter 5, but major changes included:

- higher additional pensions for many people on low earnings (between £4,108 and £11,600 in 2004–5), but still no state pension for people on very low earnings (less than £4,108)
- people caring for children under six or for someone who is elderly or disabled will be treated for pension purposes as if they have earnings (set at £11,600 in 2004–5) and will build up additional pension based on these
- people who are too ill or disabled to work but have been in the work force for at least a tenth of their working life will also be treated as if they have earnings (set at £11,600 in 2004–5) and will build up additional pension based on these.

The government wants as many people as possible to 'contract out' of S2P, which means that they would build up a pension through a private pension arrangement instead (see Chapters 14 and 23). To make sure that people are not discouraged from doing this, the government tops up the pensions of people on low to moderate earnings, even if they are contracted out.

Pension planning and the state system

Central to deciding how much you should save for retirement is your view about what the state might provide. For example, even with the savings credit, the pension credit is still a disincentive to making your own savings for retirement if your income is fairly low and you expect it to remain so. The savings credit may reward you with 60p for every £1 of pension you generate from your own savings but, equally, once your retirement income rises above the minimum guarantee, you lose 40p of savings credit for each £1 of extra retirement income. This is effectively a 40 per cent tax rate, so hardly an incentive to save.

Especially if you are many years from retirement, what elements of the state system can you rely on to be around when you retire? The state basic pension (see Chapter 4) has been fairly stable over the decades, although the rate at which it is increased each year was cut in 1979 (by severing the link to earnings and linking increases instead to price inflation, which is normally lower than earnings inflation). It would be a brave government that further reduced or abolished the state basic pension, so it seems reasonable to plan on the basis that the basic pension will still be there.

The state additional pension (see Chapter 5) has been subject to much more change and it is impossible to rule out further changes in future. But you pay (through National Insurance contributions) to build up a state additional pension so, in effect, you have a deal with the state. This means governments have to be careful how they make changes, so the state additional pension is likely to continue in some form into the future.

The picture is less clear cut regarding the pension credit. The pension credit has been criticised for being overly complicated and, although the government maintains it is affordable, some critics fear it could become too costly for the state to provide in the long run. Because the minimum guarantee rises in line with earnings, whereas the basic state pension rises only in line with prices (which typically rise by less each year than earnings), as the years go by, more and more people will become eligible for pension credit. It is estimated that by 2025 between two-thirds and three-quarters of all pensioners could be eligible for the pension credit and other means-tested benefits. However, it is possible that future governments will continue to support the idea that pensioners should have at least a minimum amount of income to live on. Therefore, you might feel fairly confident planning on the basis that the guarantee credit or, if not that, something similar might still exist when you reach retirement. But it is probably sensible not to bank too heavily on being able to claim the savings credit.

Your own pension arrangements

Occupational pension schemes

Table 3.3 shows how occupational pension schemes have become an increasingly important source of income in recent times.

In general, occupational schemes are the best way in which to save for retirement, largely because your employer must pay some or all of the cost on your behalf. (See Chapter 10 for other advantages.) The fact that your employer is paying the lion's share of the cost, and that any contribution you make is stripped fairly painlessly out of your pay packet before it reaches you, increase your chances of building up a reasonable pension.

A great deal of prominence has been given to cases where occupational schemes have been wound up with too little in the pension fund to pay the promised pensions in full. In the worst cases, some scheme members have lost the bulk of their pension. However, it is important to keep this in perspective:

- only a very small minority of schemes have been affected in this way
- the government is in the process of introducing safeguards to prevent members losing out so badly in future.

Table 3.3: Increasing importance of occupational pensions for people recently retiring

	1981	1990–91	2002–3
Percentage of gross income from each source			
State pensions and benefits	51%	42%	41%
Occupational pensions	17%	23%	27%
Investments (including personal pensions)	14%	20%	11%
Earnings	17%	14%	19%
Other	–	1%	1%

Source: *Social Trends and the Pensioners' Income Series 2002–3*

Saving through an occupational scheme and then losing the bulk of your savings is possible but very unlikely to happen. The likelihood of facing an impoverished old age if you do not save for retirement is not only possible but highly likely.

Stakeholder pension schemes

Not all employers run occupational pension schemes, and if you don't have an employer, then an occupational scheme is simply not an option. In order to fill this gap, the government has introduced stakeholder pension schemes (these are described in Chapter 20).

Employers have to arrange access to a stakeholder scheme through the workplace, unless they already offer an occupational pension scheme or a group personal pension (see below) to which they contribute an amount equal to at least 3 per cent of employees' pay. However, very small employers – those with fewer than five employees – are exempt from this requirement and do not have to offer any pension arrangement for their employees.

Employees do not have to join any pension scheme available through work and can instead make their own pension arrangements, for example, taking out their own stakeholder pension scheme. Employees can also take out stakeholder schemes to top up their pension from an occupational scheme, though currently only if they are not controlling directors of a company and not earning more than £30,000. (Restrictions on the types of pension scheme you can use are due to be removed from April 2006 onwards – see Chapter 9.)

Self-employed people must make their own pension arrangements and can choose stakeholder pension schemes as a way of doing this.

Anyone who is not earning can also pay up to a set amount (£3,600 a year in 2004–5) into a stakeholder scheme. This applies, for example, to carers, people who are off work due to illness or disability, housewives and househusbands, even children.

Stakeholder pensions that you arrange for yourself are simply personal pensions (see below) that meet certain conditions about charges and flexibility to ensure that they offer you a value-for-money deal.

Personal pensions

An alternative to taking out a stakeholder scheme is to choose an ordinary personal pension that does not necessarily meet the stakeholder conditions. In the past personal pensions have built up a poor reputation as being a costly and inflexible way to save for retirement. But the introduction of stakeholder schemes has provided the competitive boost for personal pensions to become more consumer-friendly.

All the same, while a stakeholder scheme will often be the better choice if you are newly starting to save, if you already have a personal pension, you may be better off sticking with it (see Chapter 25).

Personal pensions are open to almost everyone in the same way as stakeholder schemes (see above). So they can be used, for example, by people who are not working, the self-employed and as a way to top up an occupational pension. Employers do not have to offer a personal pension through the workplace, though some do by offering a group personal pension scheme. Although it is called a 'group' scheme, in fact every employee who joins has their own individual personal pension. But your employer may have negotiated special terms, such as lower charges or more flexible contributions, that you would not get if you were not working for that employer.

Other ways in which to save

In order to encourage pension saving, the government offers various tax advantages. On the whole, however, these work to postpone your tax bills from now until after your retirement, rather than saving you tax altogether. (This is explained in Chapters 10 and 19.)

As a result, the other main form of tax-free saving – the Individual Savings Account (ISA) – can be a useful and more flexible alternative to a dedicated pension scheme or plan. See Chapter 32 for more details.

Once your ISA allowance has been used up, you could consider direct investment in, say, unit and investment trusts. There are no particular tax advantages, but these are suitable investments for long-term growth. See Chapter 32.

Where your pension will come from

In summary, if you are in your working years now, you can expect your eventual pension to come from a variety of sources, as shown in Chart 3.1 opposite.

Chart 3.1: Pension sources

First-tier pension	Second-tier pension	Third-tier 'pension'
State basic pension See Chapter 4		
	SERPS pension See Chapter 5	
	State Second Pension See Chapter 5	
	Occupational pension See Chapters 10 to 17	
	Stakeholder pension See Chapter 20	
	Personal pension See Chapters 19 to 25	
		Individual Savings Account (ISA) See Chapter 32
		Unit and investment trusts and similar investments See Chapter 32

Chapter 4

The state basic pension

Despite changes to much of the state pension regime, the basic pension is to remain for the foreseeable future. The government has called it 'a key building block of the pension system'. Over 96 per cent of single pensioners and 99 per cent of pensioner couples receive the basic state pension.

Who qualifies?

Everyone who works and has paid enough National Insurance contributions of the right type is entitled to a state basic pension. If you're not working, you might be given credits towards the pension and, if not, you can pay voluntary contributions towards it.

How much pension?

The basic pension is paid at a flat rate (see Table 4.1). Everyone who has paid enough contributions to qualify for the full pension (see page 41) receives the same amount.

In the 2004–5 tax year, the full basic pension for a single person is £79.60 a week (£4,139 a year).

A married couple can qualify for a higher pension of £127.25 a week (£6,617 a year) based on the husband's National Insurance record. If the wife has reached pension age, her part of the pension is paid directly to her. If the wife is below pension age, the whole pension is paid to the husband and the extra paid on behalf of his wife is reduced if she has earned income of more than £55.65 a week in the tax year 2004–5. ('Earned income' includes any pensions that she receives.)

If both members of a couple qualify for a full pension based on their own contributions, together they will receive twice the single amount: that is, 2 × £79.60 = £159.20 a week (£8,278 a year).

Basic pensions are increased each April, at least in line with price inflation (measured by the yearly change in the Retail Prices Index up to the previous September).

State retirement pensioners also receive a £10 bonus at Christmas time and are entitled to winter fuel payments.

If the basic pension is your only source of income, you can claim pension credit to bring your income up to the minimum guarantee (see Chapter 3).

Couples and the state basic pension

For now, only married women can claim a pension based on their spouse's National Insurance record. However, in future, married men who have reached age 65 will be able to claim a basic pension on their wife's contribution record where the wife reaches state pension age on or after 6 April 2010.

At the time of writing, new laws were currently being debated by Parliament that aim to give same-sex couples who register their relationship as a civil partnership many of the same rights as married couples. This includes the right to claim a basic pension based on their partner's National Insurance record, but only where the partner reaches state pension age on or after 6 April 2010.

Table 4.1: State basic pensions

Tax year (6 April to following 5 April)	Maximum yearly amount of pension		
	Single person	Married couple claiming through husband	Couple each claiming their own pension
1999–2000	£3,471.00	£5,548.40	£6,942.00
2000–1	£3,510.00	£5,610.80	£7,020.00
2001–2	£3,770.00	£6,026.80	£7,540.00
2002–3	£3,926.00	£6,276.40	£7,852.00
2003–4	£4,027.40	£6,437.60	£8,054.80
2004–5	£4,139.20	£6,617.00	£8,278.40

When is the pension paid?

State retirement pensions are payable from the state pension age. Currently, this is 65 for men and 60 for women. But women's pension age is being increased to 65 (see Chart 4.1). Any woman born after 5 March 1955 will not receive a state pension before the age of 65.

Women born between 6 April 1950 and 5 March 1955 are in the transitional period. You can work out your pension age according to the rule in Chart 4.1. Alternatively, Table 4.2 gives some examples. The government website *www.pensionguide.gov.uk* includes a calculator for women that automatically works out their retirement age and date.

CASE HISTORY: Lesley

Lesley was born on 10 December 1951. This means that her birthday falls 20 months and 5 days after 5 April 1950. Therefore she must add 21 months to age 60 in order to find out her state pension age. This comes to 61 years and 9 months. She can start to receive her pension from the beginning of the tax month in which she reaches this age: that is, from 6 September 2013.

Chart 4.1: State pension age

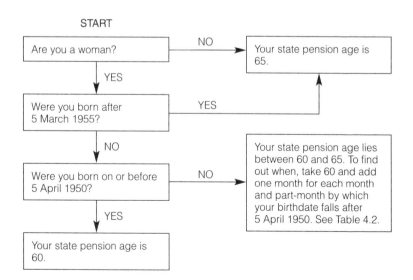

Table 4.2: Examples of pension age for women born between 6 April 1950 and 5 March 1955

Your date of birth	Your state pension age	Date from which you can start to get a state pension
6 April 1950	60 years 1 month	6 May 2010
5 May 1950	60 years 1 month	6 May 2010
6 May 1950	60 years 2 months	6 July 2010
6 October 1950	60 years 7 months	6 May 2011
31 March 1951	61 years	6 March 2012
10 December 1951	61 years 9 months	6 September 2013
15 June 1952	62 years 3 months	6 September 2014
30 November 1952	62 years 8 months	6 July 2015
22 February 1953	62 years 11 months	6 January 2016
1 August 1953	63 years 4 months	6 November 2016
8 January 1954	63 years 10 months	6 November 2017
19 July 1954	64 years 4 months	6 November 2018
25 September 1954	64 years 6 months	6 March 2019
5 March 1955	64 years 11 months	6 January 2020
6 March 1955	65 years	6 March 2020

Source: *Department for Work and Pensions (previously Department of Social Security)*

How you qualify for basic pension

Pay contributions for enough years

To receive the full basic pension, in general you'll have to pay National Insurance contributions for at least 90 per cent of the tax years in your 'working life'. If you pay contributions for less than a quarter of your working life you may not get any basic pension at all.

'Working life' is an official definition which means the tax years from the one in which you reach age 16 to the last complete tax year before you reach state pension age. For men and women born after 5 March 1955, working life lasts 49 years. For women with a pension age of 60, working life is 44 years.

Table 4.3 shows what proportion of the state pension you will receive given the number of years for which you have paid National Insurance contributions.

Table 4.3: How much state pension you will receive

Number of years for which you've made National Insurance contributions	Percentage of the full basic pension for which you qualify	
	Women born on or before 5 April 1950	Women born after 5 March 1955 and all men
9 or less	0	0
10	26	0
11	29	25
12	31	28
13	34	30
14	36	32
15	39	35
16	42	37
17	44	39
18	47	41
19	49	44
20	52	46
21	54	48
22	57	50
23	59	53
24	62	55
25	65	57
26	67	60
27	70	62
28	72	64
29	75	66
30	77	69
31	80	71
32	83	73
33	85	75
34	88	78
35	90	80
36	93	82
37	95	85
38	98	87
39	100	89
40	100	91
41	100	94
42	100	96
43	100	98
44 or more	100	100

If you are a woman caught in the transitional period, your working life will lie between 44 and 49 years. Ask The Pension Service★ – part of the Department for Work and Pensions (DWP) – how many years of contributions you will need.

Pay the right sorts of contribution

For your National Insurance contributions to count towards your pension, they must be the right type (see Table 4.4) and you must basically have paid a whole year's worth: for example, 52 weeks of Class 1 contributions of at least the minimum amount, 52 Class 2 contributions, or 52 mixed contributions.

CASE HISTORY: Sam

Sam's working life will be 49 years long. His wife died when their youngest child was just one and, as a result, he was in low-paid, part-time work for ten years. Although he's back in work now and paying National Insurance contributions, the ten-year gap in his record, on top of another three-year gap when he was at university, means that he will have paid contributions for a maximum of 36 years over his working life. This means that he will be entitled to only 82 per cent of the full-rate basic pension. At 2004–5 amounts, this means that he would get £65.27 a week instead of the full £79.60.

Class 1 contributions
You pay Class 1 National Insurance contributions if you earn more than the primary threshold. The threshold is set by the government each year. In the tax year 2004–5 it is £91 a week (£396 a month or £4,745 a year). As long as your earnings are above this level, you are building up a state basic pension.

In general, you pay contributions at a rate of 11 per cent on your earnings above the primary threshold up to the upper earnings limit (UEL) which is £610 a week in 2004–5 (equivalent to £2,643 a month or £31,720 a year). You also pay contributions at a rate of 1 per cent on all earnings above the UEL.

Table 4.4: Which National Insurance contributions count towards the basic pension

Type of contribution	Description	Do they count?
Class 1, full rate	Paid by employees (and their employers), including company directors, but not paid if you earn less than a set limit.[1]	YES
Class 1, reduced rate	Paid by some married women and widows. (You can choose to switch to the full rate, see Chapter 29.)	NO
Class 2	Paid by self-employed people. Optional if your profits are below a set level. Optional for some married women and widows (see Chapter 29).	YES
Class 3	Voluntary.	YES
Class 4	Paid by self-employed people on profits between set levels.	NO

[1] Employees earning less than this limit, which is £91 a week in 2004–5, also build up entitlement to state basic pension provided they earn at least £79 a week even though they do not have to pay any National Insurance contributions.

Employees who earn too little to pay National Insurance

If you earn less than the primary threshold (£91 a week in 2004–5), you do not pay National Insurance contributions. But the year will still count towards building up your basic state pension provided you earn at least the lower earnings limit (LEL). In 2004–5, the LEL is £79 a week (equivalent to £343 a month or £4,108 a year).

CASE HISTORY: Gill

While the children are in their pre-school years, Gill has been working part-time in her husband Chris's company. In the tax year 2004–5 she earned £85 a week, which is less than the primary threshold (£91 a week). This kept down costs for both Gill and Chris, as there was no National Insurance or income tax to pay on Gill's earnings. But, because her wages are above the lower earnings limit for the year (£79 a week), Gill is still building up a basic state pension. In addition she is also being treated as if she has much higher earnings for the purpose of building up State Second Pension (see Chapter 5). This is a good deal for Gill: she is building up a reasonable state pension at no cost.

Class 2 contributions

If you're self-employed, you build up your basic pension by paying Class 2 National Insurance contributions. These are paid by direct debit or quarterly bill at a flat rate: £2.05 a week in 2004–5.

If your profits are below the 'small earnings exception' (£4,215 in 2004–5) you can choose not to pay Class 2 contributions. In that case, however, you will not be building up a state pension and will lose entitlement also to bereavement benefits for your survivors (see Chapter 6) and incapacity benefit if you are off work sick. At £2.05 a week, Class 2 contributions are such good value that you should think twice about opting not to pay.

In the past, married women could choose not to make Class 2 contributions, whatever their profits. (They were expected instead to rely on their husbands for a pension.) This option was withdrawn from 6 April 1977, but a women who had already made this choice could continue not to pay (see Chapter 29). But in this case, too, a woman would not be building up any basic pension or other benefits.

Since 6 April 1975, if you're a director of your own company you count as an employee (not self-employed) and build up your basic pension by paying Class 1 (not Class 2) contributions.

Contribution credits

If you're not working, in some situations you may be credited with contributions even though you haven't paid them. This applies:

- if you're claiming certain state benefits, such as Jobseeker's Allowance, maternity allowance or incapacity benefit
- to men and women under state pension age who have reached 60 but stopped work. (You do not have to 'sign on' to get the credits)
- for the years in which you have (or had) your sixteenth, seventeenth and eighteenth birthdays if you were still at school and were born after 5 April 1957
- for the years in which you take, or took, part in an approved training course (but not university) if you were born after 5 April 1957.

If you stay at home to care for your children or a sick or elderly relative, you might qualify for Home Responsibilities Protection (HRP). Instead of giving you credits, HRP reduces the number of years' contributions that you need to qualify for a given level of pension. HRP is effective only for complete tax years.

You get HRP automatically if you're not working and are claiming child benefit. In other circumstances you'll need to make a claim.

Class 3 contributions

If you're not paying Class 1 or 2 contributions and you don't qualify for credits or HRP, you will have a gap in your National Insurance record which could prevent a year counting towards your basic pension.

In order to plug any gaps, you can voluntarily pay Class 3 contributions. These are charged at a flat rate: £7.15 in 2004–5. You can go back up to six years to fill in gaps in your contribution record. But you can't pay Class 3 contributions for any periods when you took up the married woman's option to pay National Insurance either at the reduced rate or not at all. See page 279 for further details.

CASE HISTORY: Clare

Clare left school at 18 and went on to university for a three-year course. She is now 25 and earning a good salary working in the City. She has National Insurance credits for the tax years when she reached 16, 17 and 18 and was in school. But the years at university are gaps in her contribution record and could eventually mean that she'll get less basic pension.

Clare can fill this three-year gap by making Class 3 contributions. But she should not delay too long: after this year she will no longer be able to pay contributions for the year in which she reached 19 because it will be more than six years ago. Clare has more time left in which to make good the contributions for the years in which she reached 20 and 21.

State pensions for the over-80s

From the age of 80, all state pensioners qualify for an extra 25p a week (£13 a year).

If you do not qualify for a state basic pension (or the amount that you receive is fairly low), you may be entitled to receive an 'over-80s pension' from the age of 80. This is a non-contributory pension and therefore does not depend on whether you have paid National Insurance. In the tax year 2004–5, the pension is set at £47.65 per person. In practice, you would be likely to get the over-80 pension only if your overall income was relatively low, in which case you would probably be getting an income top-up through the pension credit (see Chapter 3). This means the addition of the over-80 pension would probably be matched by a decrease in your pension credit.

More information

To find out about state pensions, contact The Pension Service★. It can deal with general enquiries, handle claims and supply explanatory leaflets (see Table 4.5).

For more information about National Insurance contributions, contact the Inland Revenue★, which also produces free leaflets (see Table 4.5).

If you are making your own savings for retirement through an occupational scheme or a personal pension, you may get a combined pension statement (see page 103) from that scheme or plan. A combined statement includes a forecast of how much state pension you might get from age 65 based on your actual National Insurance record to date and assuming that you carry on building up state pension between now and state pension age. If you get combined statements from more than one scheme or plan, take care not to double-count your state pension.

If you do not get a combined statement, you can still get a forecast of your possible state pension by completing form BR19 available from The Pension Service★. Allow several weeks for a reply. You might get a forecast without asking because The Pension Service has started to send out forecasts automatically, starting with self-employed people.

Table 4.5: Free leaflets about pensions and National Insurance

Reference	Title	From
CA01	National Insurance for employees	Inland Revenue
CA02	National Insurance for self-employed people with small earnings	Inland Revenue
CA04	National Insurance contributions. Class 2 and Class 3. Direct debit – the easier way to pay	Inland Revenue
CA07	Unpaid and late-paid contributions	Inland Revenue
CA08	Voluntary National Insurance contributions	Inland Revenue
CA12	Training for further employment and your National Insurance record	Inland Revenue
CA13	National Insurance contributions for women with reduced elections	Inland Revenue
CA25	National Insurance contributions for agencies and people working through agencies	Inland Revenue
CA44	National Insurance for company directors	Inland Revenue
CWL2	National Insurance for self-employed people. Class 2 and 4	Inland Revenue
GL23	Social security benefit rates	Department for Work and Pensions
NP46	A guide to state pensions	The Pension Service
PM2	State pension – your guide	The Pension Service
PM6	Pensions for women – your guide	The Pension Service
PM9	State pensions for carers and parents	The Pension Service
PMX1	Update on your state pension options	The Pension Service
BR19L	Understanding your state pension forecast	The Pension Service
CPF3	Combined pension forecasts – technical guide	The Pension Service
CPF5	Your pension statement	The Pension Service/ your pension scheme or plan provider

Chapter 5

State additional pension

The basic pension on its own provides a fairly minimal pension. With the introduction of the State Earnings Related Pension Scheme (SERPS) in 1978, the government made it compulsory for the first time for large numbers of people to contribute towards a second tier pension as well. From April 2002, SERPS was replaced by the state second pension (S2P).

Who qualifies?

SERPS covered most employees – but not those earning less than the lower earnings limit – see Table 5.1. But you did not build up SERPS if you were 'contracted out' – see below. You could not build up SERPS if you were self-employed or not working; for example, because you were at home bringing up children or caring for an elderly relative or you were disabled or too ill yourself to work.

S2P replaced SERPS from April 2002. S2P is not so much a new scheme as a further refinement of SERPS. It addresses some of the drawbacks of SERPS so that under S2P the following people also build up state additional pension:

- people caring for children under the age of six and entitled to child benefit
- other carers looking after someone who is elderly or disabled, if they are entitled to carer's allowance, and
- some people who are unable to work because of illness or disability, provided they are entitled to long-term incapacity benefit or severe disablement allowance and they have been in the workforce for at least one-tenth of their working life.

Under S2P, the self-employed are still excluded from the state additional pension. So too are employees earning less than the lower earnings limit – so for any year you earned less than the amount shown in Table 5.1 you were not building up state additional pension.

If you are a married woman or widow paying Class 1 National Insurance contributions at the reduced rate, you do not build up any state additional pension.

Table 5.1: Lower earnings limit year by year

Year	Lower earnings limit	Year	Lower earnings limit	Year	Lower earnings limit
1978–9	£910	1987–8	£2,028	1996–7	£3,172
1979–80	£1,014	1988–9	£2,132	1997–8	£3,224
1980–1	£1,196	1989–90	£2,236	1998–9	£3,328
1981–2	£1,404	1990–1	£2,392	1999–2000	£3,432
1982–3	£1,534	1991–2	£2,704	2000–1	£3,484
1983–4	£1,690	1992–3	£2,808	2001–2	£3,744
1984–5	£1,768	1993–4	£2,912	2002–3	£3,900
1985–6	£1,846	1994–5	£2,964	2003–4	£4,004
1986–7	£1,976	1995–6	£3,016	2004–5	£4,108

How much pension?

As the name suggests (state *earnings-related* pension scheme), under SERPS the amount of pension you built up depended on your earnings, so that the more you earned the bigger your SERPS pension.

Initially, S2P is still an earnings-related scheme, so that people on high earnings generally build up more pension than people on lower earnings. But people earning at least the lower earnings limit (£4,108 in 2004–5) but less than a 'low earnings threshold' (£11,600 in 2004–5) are treated as if they have earnings at that level and so build up more pension than they otherwise would.

The government has indicated that eventually it may change S2P so that it becomes a flat-rate scheme with everyone in it building up a pension based on the low earnings threshold, but it is not clear when – or even if – this change will go ahead. If it did, it is likely that the pensions already built up by people within, say, 20 years of retirement would not be affected.

The state additional pension you get on reaching state pension age is a combination of SERPS and S2P. The way the schemes work is extremely complicated and it is virtually impossible to do the sums yourself to work out your entitlement. You can get a forecast of your state pension (see *More information* on page 47) and this will include the amount of state additional pension you are expected to get based on your earnings and employment status to date and assumptions about what you are expected to build up in the remaining time until you reach state pension age.

For enthusiasts, an outline of how SERPS and S2P are calculated is included below, starting on page 53.

In the past, higher earners especially have tended to contract out of the state additional pension (see *Contracting out* overleaf). Therefore, although in theory the maximum state additional pension is high (nearly £150 a week in 2004–5 for a high earner), the actual additional pensions received are much more modest. In September 2003, the average amount of additional pension received by recently retired pensioners was £22.46 a week and the average for pensioners (whether

---

Pension tip if you employ family members

If you run your own business and employ, say, your husband or wife, you can arrange their earnings to minimise tax but maximise their state pension. But do bear in mind that the amount you pay must be reasonable given the work they actually do and that they are entitled to receive at least the minimum wage (£4.85 an hour from October 2004).

Tax and National Insurance are due once an employee earns at least the primary threshold, which in 2004–5 is £91 a week (£4,745 a year), so it makes sense to keep their pay below this threshold if you can. However, even though you and the employee pay nothing in contributions and taxes, your employee can still build up state pension if you pay them enough. The employee builds up the state basic pension provided you pay them at least the lower earnings limit of £79 a week in 2004–5 (£4,108 a year). If they earn more than £79 a week, they also build up state additional pension. Moreover, with earnings between £79 and £91 a week, their state additional pension is worked out as if they had earnings of £11,600 a year (equivalent to £223 a week).

---

recently retired or not) who had never been contracted out was just £8.52 a week.

Unlike the state basic pension, there is no way to go back and plug gaps in your state additional pension record. Voluntary (Class 3) National Insurance contributions do not affect your additional pension.

CASE HISTORY: Julia

Julia is employed as a part-time cleaner. Her pay is just below the lower earnings limit (£4,108 in 2004–5), so she does not build up any S2P. If she increased her hours slightly, to bring her pay up to £4,108, she would start to build up S2P. She would be treated as if she had earnings equal to the low earnings threshold (£11,600 in 2004–5), and this would qualify her for £1.18 a week S2P at 2004–5 prices. Over a whole working life, and assuming earnings equal to the lower earnings limit each year, this would build up to a pension payable at age 65 of around £58 a week (at 2004–5 price levels).

Contracting out

You do not build up state additional pension during periods when you are contracted out. 'Contracting out' means that, although you qualify for SERPS or S2P, you are removed from the state additional scheme and instead build up a pension either through an occupational scheme (see Chapter 14), a personal pension (see Chapter 23) or stakeholder scheme (see Chapter 20).

While contracted out, you either pay lower National Insurance on part of your earnings or some of the contributions paid by you and your employer are 'rebated' and paid into your occupational scheme, personal pension or stakeholder scheme.

Usually, you don't have much choice about whether or not you are contracted out if you belong to an occupational scheme – you just accept whichever applies to the whole scheme. But, in other cases, you can choose whether to contract out and making the decision rests on whether the National Insurance rebated is enough to build up a pension by retirement that will be bigger than the state additional pension you give up. This is not an easy decision: the arithmetic is complicated and you are not dealing with certainties. How much state pension you give up depends on your age, sex and earnings; for example, older people stand to lose more state pension than younger people. And you have to make assumptions about how the invested rebates might grow. (More details are given in Chapters 14 and 23.) You may want to take advice from an independent financial adviser★ before deciding whether to contract out or, if you are already contracted-out, before contracting back in. In general, experts in 2004 are very doubtful that contracting out is currently worthwhile even for young people.

How SERPS and S2P are calculated

The state additional pension is worked out over the 'relevant years' of your working life. This means the tax/benefit years from reaching age 16 to the last full year before reaching state pension age if you were born on or after 6 April 1962, or the years from 6 April 1978 to the last year before reaching state pension age if you were born earlier. A tax/benefit year runs from 6 April one year to the following 5 April.

Your SERPS pension

For each relevant year, take your earnings in excess of the lower earnings limit (see Table 5.1) up to the upper earnings limit (see Table 5.2). These are variously called your 'surplus earnings', 'middle band earnings' or 'upper band earnings'. Ignore any earnings in excess of the upper limit.

For any years when you were not working, were self-employed or earned less than the lower earnings limit, your surplus earnings are zero. Earnings for the years from 6 April 2002 onwards (when SERPS was replaced by S2P) are also set to zero.

The surplus earnings for each year are increased in line with earnings inflation up to the last year before you reach state pension age. The government publishes the earnings factors to use.

Find your average revalued surplus earnings by adding together the figures for every relevant year and dividing by the number of relevant years in your working life.

Your SERPS pension is a fraction of the average. For people who reached state pension age before 6 April 2000, the fraction was one-quarter assuming they had been in SERPS for at least 20 years (and

Table 5.2: Upper earnings limit year by year

Year	Upper earnings limit	Year	Upper earnings limit	Year	Upper earnings limit
1978–9	£6,240	1987–8	£15,340	1996–7	£23,660
1979–80	£7,020	1988–9	£15,860	1997–8	£24,180
1980–1	£8,580	1989–90	£16,900	1998–9	£25,220
1981–2	£10,400	1990–1	£18,200	1999–2000	£26,000
1982–3	£11,440	1991–2	£20,280	2000–1	£27,820
1983–4	£12,220	1992–3	£21,060	2001–2	£29,900
1984–5	£13,000	1993–4	£21,840	2002–3	£30,420
1985–6	£13,780	1994–5	£22,360	2003–4	£30,940
1986–7	£14,820	1995–6	£22,880	2004–5	£31,720

there were some other variations in the way SERPS was worked out from the method described above). For people reaching state pension age from April 2037 onwards, the fraction is one-fifth. Between those two dates, the fraction is gradually reduced from a quarter to a fifth. The reduction is made by dividing your SERPS membership into two parts: for the years from 1978–9 to 1987–8, the fraction of one-quarter (25 per cent) is still used; for the years 1988–9 to 2001–2, a different fraction is used, as set out in Table 5.3.

The SERPS pension produced by this calculation is then adjusted for any period during which you were contracted out.

The Example on page 57 shows how the calculation works in practice and how SERPS dovetails with S2P to produce the overall state additional pension.

Table 5.3: SERPS fraction used to work out pension you built up over the years 1988–9 to 2001–2

Year you reach (or reached) state pension age	Relevant percentage
2000–1	24.50%
2001–2	24%
2002–3	23.50%
2003–4	23%
2004–5	22.50%
2005–6	22%
2006–7	21.50%
2007–8	21%
2008–9	20.50%
2009–10 (or later)	20%

Your state second pension

For each relevant year, take your earnings up to the upper earnings limit (see Table 5.2). Ignore any earnings in excess of the upper limit. If in any of those years, you earned at least the lower earnings limit but less than the low earnings threshold (see Table 5.4), set your earnings equal to the low earnings threshold (£11,600 in 2004–5).

Table 5.4: Low earnings threshold and Band 3 threshold year by year

Year	Low earnings threshold	Band 3 threshold*
2002–3	£10,800	£24,600
2003–4	£11,200	£25,600
2004–5	£11,600	£26,600

* The Band 3 threshold is (3 x low earnings threshold) – (2 x lower earnings limit) adjusted for rounding.

For any years when you were caring for a child under six, caring for someone else or unable to work because of illness or disability, set your earnings to the low earnings threshold. For years when you were not working for other reasons, were self-employed or earned less than the lower earnings limit, your earnings are zero. Earnings for the years before 6 April 2002 onwards (when the state scheme was SERPS not S2P) are also set to zero.

Divide your earnings for each year into three bands (see Chart 5.1):

- **Band 1**. From the lower earnings limit up to the low earnings threshold. Earnings below the lower earnings limit are ignored
- **Band 2**. From the low earnings threshold up to the Band 3 threshold – see Table 5.4
- **Band 3**. From the Band 3 threshold to the upper earnings limit.

Next, multiply the earnings in each band by a percentage. The percentages will eventually be 40 per cent for Band 1, 10 per cent for Band 2 and 20 per cent for Band 3. However, there is a transitional period during which the fractions are higher, as shown in Table 5.5. Still looking at each year in turn, add together the results for each band.

You now have an amount for each year. The next step is to increase each amount in line with earnings inflation up to the last full year before you reach state pension age. The government publishes the earnings factors to use.

Table 5.5: S2P Band percentages during the transitional period

Year you reach (or reached) state pension age	Band 1	Band 2	Band 3
2003–4	46.00%	11.50%	23.00%
2004–5	45.00%	11.25%	22.50%
2005–6	44.00%	11.00%	22.00%
2006–7	43.00%	10.75%	21.50%
2007–8	42.00%	10.50%	21.00%
2008–9	41.00%	10.25%	20.50%
2009–10 or later	40.00%	10.00%	20.00%

Chart 5.1: Earnings on which State Second Pension (S2P) is based

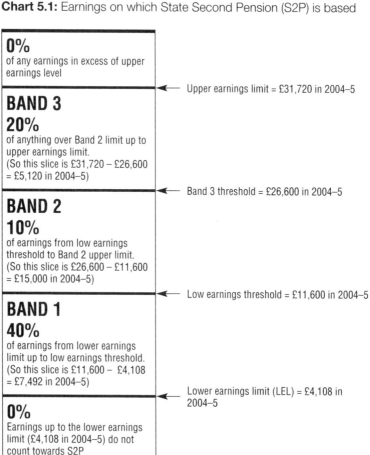

0%
of any earnings in excess of upper earnings level

◄— Upper earnings limit = £31,720 in 2004–5

BAND 3
20%
of anything over Band 2 limit up to upper earnings limit.
(So this slice is £31,720 – £26,600 = £5,120 in 2004–5)

◄— Band 3 threshold = £26,600 in 2004–5

BAND 2
10%
of earnings from low earnings threshold to Band 2 upper limit.
(So this slice is £26,600 – £11,600 = £15,000 in 2004–5)

◄— Low earnings threshold = £11,600 in 2004–5

BAND 1
40%
of earnings from lower earnings limit up to low earnings threshold.
(So this slice is £11,600 – £4,108 = £7,492 in 2004–5)

◄— Lower earnings limit (LEL) = £4,108 in 2004–5

0%
Earnings up to the lower earnings limit (£4,108 in 2004–5) do not count towards S2P

Lastly, add together the revalued amounts for each year and divide by the number of relevant years in your working life. This is the S2P pension you qualify for (before any adjustment for periods you were contracted out).

The Example below shows how the calculation works in practice and how S2P dovetails with SERPS to produce the overall state additional pension.

CASE STUDY: Terry

Terry reaches the state pension age of 65 in May 2005. He has belonged to the state additional pension scheme since it started in 1978. His additional pension is worked out as follows.

Relevant years
Terry has been in the additional scheme from 1978–9 to 2004–5, a total of 27 years.

SERPS pension
Table 5.6 shows how Terry's SERPS pension is worked out. First, his surplus earnings are worked out. These are increased in line with earnings up to state pension age using the factors supplied by the government. Because of changes to SERPS, the earnings are then divided into two groups. For the years 1978–9 to 1987–8, the earnings are summed, divided by the number of relevant years and then a quarter of the total is taken to find the yearly SERPS pension built up over that period. Divide by 52 to find the weekly amount. For the years 1988–9 to 2001–2, the earnings are summed and divided by the relevant years but a lower fraction is taken – in this case, 22 per cent – to find the SERPS built up over that period.

State second pension
Terry was only in the state second pension for a few years so has not had time to build up much S2P. Table 5.7 shows how his S2P is worked out. His surplus earnings are divided into bands and a percentage of each band is taken. The total for the year is revalued in line with earnings, using the factors supplied by the government. The resulting amounts are totalled and divided by 27 to find the S2P built up over the period since 6 April 2002. Dividing by 52 gives the weekly amount.

Table 5.6: Terry's SERPS pension

Tax year	Earnings	Lower earnings limit	Upper earnings limit	Surplus earnings	Earnings factor	Revalued surplus earnings	Average revalued surplus earnings	Fraction	SERPS pension per week
1978–9	£4,000	£910	£6,240	£3,090	545.9	£19,958			
1979–80	£4,800	£1,014	£7,020	£3,786	470.1	£21,584			
1980–1	£6,000	£1,196	£8,580	£4,804	376.3	£22,881	Sum of revalued surplus earnings for years 1978–9 to 1987–8 divided by 27 = £8,851	Applying to years 1978–9 to 1987–8 = 25%	Built up over years 1978–9 to 1987–8 = £42.55
1981–2	£6,400	£1,404	£10,400	£4,996	298.9	£19,929			
1982–3	£7,000	£1,534	£11,440	£5,466	262.3	£19,803			
1983–4	£8,000	£1,690	£12,220	£6,310	236.4	£21,227			
1984–5	£9,500	£1,768	£13,000	£7,732	211.5	£24,085			
1985–6	£12,000	£1,846	£13,780	£10,154	192.2	£29,670			
1986–7	£12,200	£1,976	£14,820	£10,224	168.3	£27,431			
1987–8	£15,000	£2,028	£15,340	£12,972	149.8	£32,404			
1988–9	£16,600	£2,132	£15,860	£13,728	129.8	£31,547			
1989–90	£16,600	£2,236	£16,900	£14,364	107.4	£29,791			
1990–1	£17,300	£2,392	£18,200	£14,908	93.3	£28,817			
1991–2	£19,067	£2,704	£20,280	£16,363	75.6	£28,733			
1992–3	£19,639	£2,808	£21,060	£16,831	64.9	£27,754			
1993–4	£20,228	£2,912	£21,840	£17,316	57	£27,186			
1994–5	£20,835	£2,964	£22,360	£17,871	52.3	£27,217	Sum of revalued surplus earnings for years 1988–9 to 2001–2 divided by 27 = £14,163	Applying to years 1988–9 to 2001–2 = 22%	Built up over the years 1988–9 to 2001–2 = £59.92
1995–6	£21,460	£3,016	£22,880	£18,444	45.9	£26,909			
1996–7	£22,103	£3,172	£23,660	£18,931	41.9	£26,864			
1997–8	£22,767	£3,224	£24,180	£19,543	35.1	£26,402			
1998–9	£23,450	£3,328	£25,220	£20,122	29.2	£25,997			
1999–2000	£24,153	£3,432	£26,000	£20,721	24	£25,694			
2000–1	£24,878	£3,484	£27,820	£21,394	16.6	£24,945			
2001–2	£25,624	£3,744	£29,900	£21,880	12.2	£24,549			

Table 5.7: Terry's state second pension

Tax year	Earnings	Low earnings threshold	Lower earnings limit	Band 3 threshold	Upper earnings limit	Band 1 earnings	Band 2 earnings	Band 3 earnings	44% of Band 1 earnings	11% of Band 2 earnings	22% of Band 3 earnings	Earnings factor	Revalued total from all bands	S2P per week
2002–3	£26,393	£10,800	£3,900	£24,600	£30,420	£6,900	£13,800	£1,793	£3,036	£1,518	£394.39	7.5	£5,320	
2003–4	£27,184	£11,200	£4,004	£25,600	£30,940	£7,196	£14,400	£1,584	£3,166	£1,584	£348.58	3.8	£5,293	Average of revalued totals for years from 2002–3 to 2004–5 divided by 27 and converted to weekly amount = £11.30
2004–5	£28,000	£11,600	£4,108	£26,600	£31,720	£7,492	£15,000	£1,400	£3,296	£1,650	£308.00	0	£5,254	

59

Total state additional pension

The total additional pension that Terry has built up over his 27 years in the scheme is £42.55 + £59.92 + £11.30 = £113.77 a week. In practice, someone with earnings as high as Terry's is likely to have been contracted out for at least some of the years since 1978, so would receive less state additional pension but would instead also have a private pension, e.g. an occupational scheme.

State graduated pension

This was an earlier state earnings-related pension scheme, which ran from 6 April 1961 to 5 April 1975. If you belonged to the scheme, the National Insurance that you paid was related to your earnings. The total that you paid is divided into units: if you're a woman, every £9 paid counts as one unit; if you're a man, every £7.50 paid counts as one unit. (The difference reflected the higher cost of women's pensions, due to their earlier retirement date and higher life expectancy.)

How much graduated pension you receive depends on the number of units that you have. In 2004–5, each unit is worth 9.63 pence a week. The biggest graduated pension that a man can have is £8.27 a week (£430 a year). The biggest graduated pension that a woman can have is £6.92 a week (£360 a year).

In practice, you might receive less than this if you have been 'contracted out'. This means that the employer's pension scheme that you belonged to at the time will pay you a broadly equivalent pension. Graduated pensions are paid alongside your basic state pension and are increased each year in line with inflation in the same way (see page 39).

More information

If you are making your own savings for retirement through an occupational scheme or a personal pension, you may get a combined pension statement (see page 103) from that scheme or plan. A combined statement includes a forecast of how much state pension you might get from age 65, including any state additional pension based on your earnings and employment status to date and assuming that you carry on building up additional pension in the same way between now and state pension age. If you get combined statements from more than one scheme or plan, take care not to double-count your state pension.

If you do not get a combined statement, you can still get a forecast of your possible state pension by completing form BR19 available from The Pension Service★. Allow several weeks for a reply. You might get a forecast without asking because The Pension Service has started to send out forecasts automatically.

Table 5.8: Free leaflets with information about the state additional pension

Reference	Title	From
NP46	A guide to state pensions	The Pension Service
PM2	State pension – your guide	The Pension Service
PM7	Contracted-out pensions – your guide	The Pension Service
PM9	State pensions for carers and parents	The Pension Service
PMX1	Update on your state pension options	The Pension Service
BR19L	Understanding your state pension forecast	The Pension Service
CPF3	Combined pension forecasts – technical guide	The Pension Service
CPF5	Your pension statement	The Pension Service/ your pension scheme or plan provider

Chapter 6

Other benefits from the state system

It is common to think of an employer's pension scheme (and other private pension arrangements) as providing a package of benefits rather than just a retirement pension. Similarly, the state contributory scheme 'buys' you more than just a retirement pension.

State benefits are also payable in the event of death or illness. However, these benefits are limited, and to ensure adequate protection you will usually need to make your own private provision as well. The rules for claiming these benefits are complex, and only an outline of the main entitlements is given here.

Benefits payable in the event of death

Death before a widow/er reaches state pension age

Benefits are available to both widows and widowers. For your surviving spouse to qualify, you must have made the appropriate National Insurance contributions (see Chart 6.1). Your widow or widower may be eligible for the following benefits:

- **bereavement payment** A tax-free lump sum of £2,000. Your widow or widower must be under the age of 60 or, if over 60, you must not have been receiving (or eligible to receive) the state basic retirement pension
- **widowed parent's allowance** A regular taxable income set at the same level as the state basic pension (£79.60 a week in 2004–5) plus half (or sometimes more) of any state additional pension that you were entitled to (see page 66). The payment continues until the youngest child ceases to be dependent or until the widow or widower remarries or starts to live with someone as if they were

married. Since April 2003, child supplements previously included in the allowance are replaced by child tax credit (see page 69).

• **bereavement allowance** A regular taxable income payable to widows and widowers over the age of 45 and without dependent children. This income is payable for 52 weeks only. The amount that your widow or widower receives depends on her or his age at the time of your death – see Table 6.1. The payments continue until either 52 weeks are up, state pension age is reached or the recipient remarries or starts to live with someone as if they were married. People aged 55 or over when the new benefits started who are widowed within the first five years of the new system may receive extra financial help when the bereavement allowance stops if they are then claiming means-tested benefits.

Table 6.1: Amount of bereavement allowance in 2004–5

Age of widow/er at time of spouse's death	Weekly amount
45	£23.88
46	£29.45
47	£35.02
48	£40.60
49	£46.17
50	£51.74
51	£57.31
52	£62.88
53	£68.46
54	£74.03
55 or over	£79.60

Death after a widow/er reaches state pension age

Where death occurs after you have both retired, state help is given through the state pension system.

If your widow/er gets less than the full-rate basic pension based on their own contributions, they can claim a combined pension using your contribution record too. The maximum basic pension that they can receive is the full rate that a single person can receive, i.e. £79.60 a week in 2004–5. They can also inherit half (or sometimes more) of any additional state pension to which you were entitled – see below.

Chart 6.1: Help from the state for widows and widowers on death before retirement

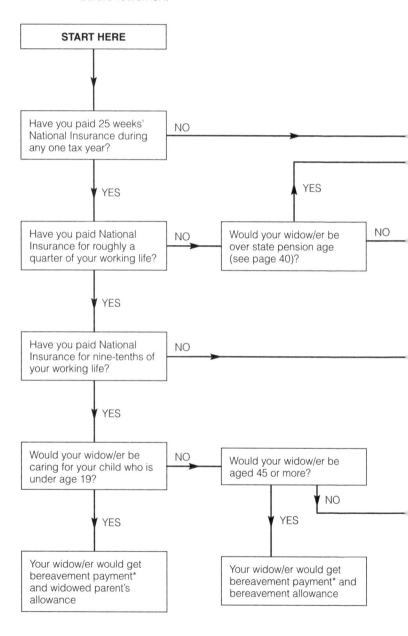

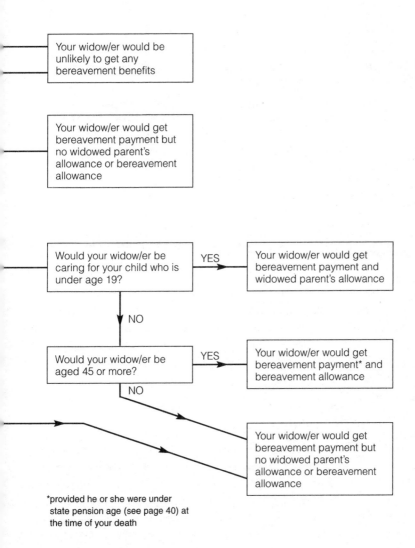

Your widow/er would be unlikely to get any bereavement benefits

Your widow/er would get bereavement payment but no widowed parent's allowance or bereavement allowance

Would your widow/er be caring for your child who is under age 19?

YES → Your widow/er would get bereavement payment and widowed parent's allowance

NO

Would your widow/er be aged 45 or more?

YES → Your widow/er would get bereavement payment* and bereavement allowance

NO

Your widow/er would get bereavement payment but no widowed parent's allowance or bereavement allowance

*provided he or she were under state pension age (see page 40) at the time of your death

Inherited additional pension payable with widowed parent's allowance or where death occurs after retirement

In the event of death before 6 October 2002, your husband or wife could inherit your whole SERPS pension. But, if you die on or after that date, the amount of SERPS pension they can inherit depends on the date you reached (or would have reached) state pension age, as shown in Table 6.2.

Table 6.2: Amount of your SERPS pension which your widow or widower can inherit

Date you reached (or would have reached) state pension age	Proportion of SERPS pension your widow or widower can inherit [1]
5 October 2002 or earlier	up to 100%
6 October 2002 to 5 October 2004	up to 90%
6 October 2004 to 5 October 2006	up to 80%
6 October 2006 to 5 October 2008	up to 70%
6 October 2008 to 5 October 2010	up to 60%
6 October 2010 or later	up to 50%

[1] When added to any SERPS pension they have built up in their own right, the total must not exceed the maximum SERPS pension a person could have In 2004–5, this maximum is £140.44 a week.

Whenever death occurs, your widow or widower can only ever inherit half of any S2P you have built up. When added to S2P they have built up in their own right, the total must not exceed the maximum S2P a person could have. In 2004–5, this maximum would be around £9 a week where the deceased had been in the state additional scheme since 1978.

Unmarried couples

Bereavement benefits and the special rules for widow/ers widowed after retirement apply only to married couples living together. Assuming a bill before Parliament at the time of writing becomes law, registered same-sex couples will from a date yet to be announced become entitled to the same bereavement benefits as married couples. Bereavement benefits do not apply to unmarried or unregistered couples. However, such couples may be able to claim other state benefits (see opposite).

Other state benefits

Anyone left looking after a child can claim child benefit, usually until the child reaches 19. Child benefit is not means-tested and is paid at flat rates of £16.50 a week for the eldest or only child and £11.05 for each subsequent child in 2004–5. A single parent who cannot work because of their caring responsibilities may be able to claim income support if their income and savings are low. A parent may also be eligible for child tax credit (CTC) and, if on a low income, might qualify for working tax credit (WTC) which includes an element payable towards child care.

A surviving partner who is retired might qualify for a minimum income guarantee through pension credit (see page 27).

A surviving partner under pension age and without children would normally be expected to find work and support themselves. If on getting work, their income was low, they might be able to claim WTC.

In all the above cases, if income is low, they might also get housing benefit and council tax benefit.

Benefits payable in the event of early retirement

Voluntary early retirement

You can't receive a state retirement pension before reaching state pension age. So, if you choose to retire early, you must plan to manage without your state pension until you reach the age of 65, 60 or whichever pension age applies to you (see page 40).

You'll also need to consider whether to continue paying National Insurance voluntarily if you retire before age 60 (see page 279). Unless you have already paid enough contributions for the full basic pension, stopping your contributions will mean a lower state pension when it starts.

Early retirement due to ill-health

Even if you retire early because of ill-health you can't start your state retirement pension before state pension age. But you might qualify for other state or statutory benefits.

The main contributory benefit that you may receive if you are off work for a long time because of illness or disability is long-term incapacity benefit. This is a regular taxable income, payable, in most cases, from the fifty-third week of illness (short-term incapacity benefit or statutory sick pay is payable during the first year of illness). Long-term incapacity benefit comprises the basic benefit, increase for an adult dependant and an age-related addition (see Table 6.3). There is no increase for dependent children but you might instead be able to claim child tax credit (see opposite).

In order to qualify for long-term incapacity benefit, you must already, at the twenty-eighth week of illness, have passed a 'personal capability assessment'. You will need to be found largely unable to do any work in order to qualify for incapacity benefit. But there is a more positive side to the test, too, with an attempt to define your skills with a view to helping you to find suitable work if you want it.

In addition, you must also meet two National Insurance contribution tests. These are:

- that you have actually paid (and not just been credited with) Class 1 National Insurance contributions on earnings of at least 25 times the lower earnings limit (LEL) or the equivalent Class 2 contributions in one of the last three tax years before the day you start to claim. In this way, incapacity benefit is restricted to people who have recently worked
- that you must have been paid or credited with Class 1 or 2 contributions for substantially the whole of the two tax years before the benefit year when you start to claim. (A benefit year roughly coincides with a calendar year.)

Table 6.3: Long-term incapacity benefit in 2004–5

		Weekly amount	Yearly amount
Basic benefit		£74.15	£3,856
Age-related addition	Higher rate (under age 35 at start of claim)	£15.55	£809
	Lower rate (aged 35–44 at start of claim)	£7.80	£406
Extra for dependent adult (for adult looking after children or where husband or wife is aged 60 or over, provided that their earned income is no more than £55.65 a week)		£44.35	£2,306

The amount of incapacity benefit that you receive is reduced by 50p for every £1 of pension that you get from a private arrangement (for example, an employer's pension scheme, personal pension or income protection insurance) in excess of a set limit. This limit is £85 a week in 2004–5.

CASE STUDY: Rick

Rick has severe back problems which have kept him off work for the last year. He qualifies for £74.15 a week incapacity benefit, but this is reduced because he also has income protection insurance which is paying him £130 a week. This is £45 more than the £85 threshold at which benefit starts to be lost. His incapacity benefit is reduced by 50p for every £1 of the excess, in other words 0.50 × £45 = £22.50. Therefore he gets incapacity benefit of £74.15 – £22.50 = £51.65 a week. His total income is £130 + £51.65 = £181.65.

Child and working tax credit

If you have children, you may be eligible for both child tax credit (CTC) and working tax credit (WTC) or just CTC. In either case, the benefits are not just restricted to low income households. You can qualify for at least some CTC even if your household income is as high as £58,175 in 2004–5 (or £66,350 if you have a child under age one).

If you have no children, you may be able to claim WTC if you work but your income is low, you can't work because of disability or you are aged 50 or more and have recently started work after a period claiming certain state benefits.

WTC and CTC are integrated and you make a single claim for both benefits. The amount you get depends on how many elements – see Table 6.4 – for which you qualify and your income worked out in broadly the same way as for tax purposes. You add together the relevant elements and then, for every £1 by which your income exceeds a first threshold (£5,060 in 2004–5), your WTC and the individual element(s) of CTC are reduced by 37p. WTC is reduced first with the childcare element last, then the CTC. If you qualify only for CTC, the threshold at which you start to lose the individual elements of CTC is higher (£13,480 in 2004–5).

Any household with children may qualify for the family element of CTC. But this is reduced when the household's income reaches a second threshold (£50,000 in 2004–5). You lose £1 of credit for every £15 of income over the threshold.

Table 6.4: Tax credits in 2004–5

Element	Amount
Working tax credit	
Basic (applies to all claimants)	£1,570
Lone parent or couple	£1,545
Working 30 hours per week	£640
Disabled worker	£2,100
Severe disability	£890
50-plus working 16–29 hours per week	£1,075
50-plus working 30+ hours per week	£1,610
Childcare: 70% of eligible costs which are up to £135 a week for one child and £200 a week for two or more	Maximum £7,280
Child tax credit	
Individual element per child (increased if child disabled or severely disabled)	£1,445
Family element	£545
Family element if you have a child under age one	£1,090

CASE STUDY: Shibani

Shibani's husband died in August 2004 leaving her to raise their four-year-old daughter, Usha, on her own. Shibani works and earns £350 a week (£18,200 a year) but has to pay £100 a week (£5,200 a year) for childcare. In 2004–5, she is eligible to claim tax credits of just over £4,500 worked out as follows:

Working tax credit

Basic element	£1,570
Lone parent or couple	£1,545
Working 30 hours per week	£640
Childcare: 70% of eligible costs (i.e. £70 a week)	£3,640

Child tax credit

Individual element per child	£1,445
Family element	£545
Total credits before adjustment	£9,385
Shibani's income	£18,200
First threshold	£ 5,060
Excess of income over threshold	£13,140
Reduction in tax credits at 37p per £1 excess	£ 4,861
Shibani's tax credits after adjustment	**£ 4,524**

More information

You can find out about the state benefits payable when someone dies or if you are unable to work because of illness from your local Jobcentre Plus★ if you are under state pension age or The Pension Service★ if you are older. The Department for Work and Pensions (DWP)★ and Inland Revenue★ produce a variety of free leaflets – the main ones are listed in Table 6.5.

Table 6.5: Free leaflets about benefits payable in the event of death or illness

Reference	Title	From
NP45	A guide to bereavement benefits	Department for Work and Pensions
BP1	For help and guidance when someone dies	Department for Work and Pensions
GL14	Widowed?	Department for Work and Pensions
SERPSSL1	Important information for married people – inheritance of SERPS	Department for Work and Pensions
GL16	Help with your rent	Department for Work and Pensions

GL17	Help with your council tax	Department for Work and Pensions
RR2	A guide to housing benefit and council tax benefit	Department for Work and Pensions
IS20	A guide to Income Support	Department for Work and Pensions
IB1	A guide to incapacity benefit	Department for Work and Pensions
SD1	Sick or disabled?	Department for Work and Pensions
GL23	Social security benefit rates	Department for Work and Pensions
CA09	National Insurance contributions for widows and widowers	Inland Revenue
CH2 (form) and CH2 (notes)	Claiming Child Benefit	Inland Revenue
WTC2	Child tax credit and working tax credit – a guide	Inland Revenue

Chapter 7

How safe is your state pension?

The government is extremely unlikely to go bust and so be unable to pay the pensions that it owes. In that sense, the pensions that you build up within the state system are very secure.

However, retirement planning means taking decisions now that will be a long time bearing fruit. It is therefore extremely important that you should be able to plan with certainty. This is where the state, unfortunately, has a habit of letting you down. The state pension system has been changed numerous times in recent years, and many of the changes have meant that you'll get less pension when you eventually retire.

The chances of your being affected by changes to the state system should reduce the closer you get to state pension age. In general, changes have been introduced gradually, and people close to retirement are sometimes excluded from them. But if you are now relatively young you should be aware that what the state promises today could be very different by the time you are a pensioner.

The only thing that you can do to protect yourself against changes to the state system is to save a bit extra privately in order to cushion yourself against any cutbacks.

State cutbacks

These are the main ways in which retirement benefits for future state pensioners (and sometimes current pensioners) have been cut back over the last 25 years.

Breaking the link with earnings

When the Conservative Party came to power in 1979, state pensions were being increased each year in line with the better of earnings and price inflation. The Conservatives cut the link with earnings (which tend to increase faster than prices) in order to save the state money. As a result, the state basic pension for a single person has fallen from over a quarter of average male earnings in 1979 to about one-seventh today.

Cutting state additional pensions

The State Earnings Related Pension Scheme (SERPS) was introduced by a Labour government, but with all-party backing. This cross-party support should have ensured that the scheme survived in the long term. But by 1988 the (by then Conservative) government was looking for cost savings and cut back SERPS benefits. The cuts were phased in over a long period, but meant that the maximum SERPS pension would eventually be just one-fifth of earnings between the lower earnings level (LEL) and upper earnings level (UEL) instead of the original one-quarter. In addition, SERPS would be based on average lifetime earnings instead of the best 20 years' earnings, as had originally been intended.

From 2002 SERPS has been replaced by a new state pension, S2P. This undoubtedly provides much better pensions for many people on low earnings and gives state additional pensions for the first time to some groups who are unable to work. However, S2P may be switched from being earnings-related to a flat-rate scheme. This was originally mooted to happen from 2006 but has not been mentioned lately, so it is now unclear when or even if this change will go ahead. If it did, it would result in high earners and some moderate earners getting less pension than they would have had under SERPS.

Changing the way that you contract out

Contracting out means giving up part or all of the additional pension and receiving a pension from an employer's pension scheme or personal pension instead. Originally, an employer's pension would have been broadly equivalent, but any difference didn't matter because your SERPS pension plus contracted-out pensions would together always have equalled the full SERPS that you would have got had you never contracted out. In 1988 new ways of contracting out were introduced, and the direct link to SERPS was broken. Further changes were introduced from April 1997. The upshot was that you might be better off contracting out of SERPS, but also run the risk of ending up with a lower pension. (See Chapters 14 and 23.)

With the introduction of S2P, the contracting-out terms are being rejigged once again. But, this time, the changes at least favour employees on low to moderate earnings, because the government will ensure that they do not receive less pension by contracting out than they would have had through S2P. Higher earners are not protected in this way.

Cutting women's pension rights

Women born after 5 April 1950 have to wait longer than women born on or before that date to start their state pension. Equalising the state pension ages for men and women seems a fair change to make, but it also saves the government money.

Reduced protection against inflation

Before April 1997 SERPS pensions and contracted-out pensions were together largely increased in line with inflation each year, once they started to be paid. From April 1997 onwards contracted-out pensions must be inflation-proofed only up to a maximum of 5 per cent a year and the maximum is due to be cut again (probably from 2005) to just 2.5 per cent for salary-related occupational schemes and abolished altogether for money purchase schemes and plans. You bear the risk of the pensions falling well behind if inflation returns to the high levels seen in the 1970s and 1980s.

On the plus side . . .

The Labour government in power since 1997 has taken steps to improve the incomes of today's pensioners through, for example, above-inflation increases to the basic pension, the introduction of a minimum income for all pensioners and the savings element of the pension credit. If the pension credit survives into the long term, it could ensure you have at least a minimum living pension, but at this stage the life expectancy of the scheme is anyone's guess. You would be taking a big gamble if you limited your own savings now on the basis of what the state safety net might provide many decades in the future.

Chapter 8

The pension gap

In Chapters 1 and 2 we looked at the amount of income that you expect to need to support a comfortable retirement (see Calculator in Chapter 2).

As the subsequent chapters have shown, some of that income will probably come from the state pension system. In order to estimate how much this may be, you should check a combined pension statement (see page 103) or obtain a retirement forecast from The Pension Service★ (see page 47). Having done this, you can subtract your expected state pension from your desired income.

What remains is the amount of pension that you will need to build up through private pension arrangements: in other words, occupational schemes, stakeholder schemes and personal pension plans. This is the pension gap.

Chapters 10 to 27 look in detail at how to plug your pension gap using pension schemes and plans. Your pension gap is expressed in today's money. Since April 2003, statements from occupational schemes, personal pensions and stakeholder schemes have to include a forecast of the pension you might get at retirement also in today's money. This makes it easy for you to get an idea of whether you are on track to meet your pension target or whether you need to save extra. Chapters 28 to 32 consider your options if you do need to boost your savings.

Bear in mind that a forecast is just an indication of what might happen based on various assumptions. In practice, the future might turn out to be very different so it is important to check your progress often and, if you can afford it, to save a bit extra just in case the future does not pan out quite as well as you had hoped.

Table 8.1: Pension-gap calculator

		Example	Your figures
Your desired yearly retirement income in today's money (see Chapters 1 and 2)	A	£28,000	
The amount of pension that you can expect from the state (see Chapters 4 and 5)	B	£4,576	
Your pension gap in today's money	C	£24,000	

CASE HISTORY: Jules

Jules currently earns roughly £40,000 a year and hopes to retire in 30 years' time on a pension of, say, £28,000.

Jules expects to get the full state basic pension, currently £4,139 a year. His retirement forecast from The Pension Service also shows that he should also get a small additional state pension.

Jules completes the calculation in Table 8.1 and finds that his pension gap is £28,000 − £4,576 = £23,424. The calculations are broad, and he should err on the side of caution, so he rounds this figure up to £24,000.

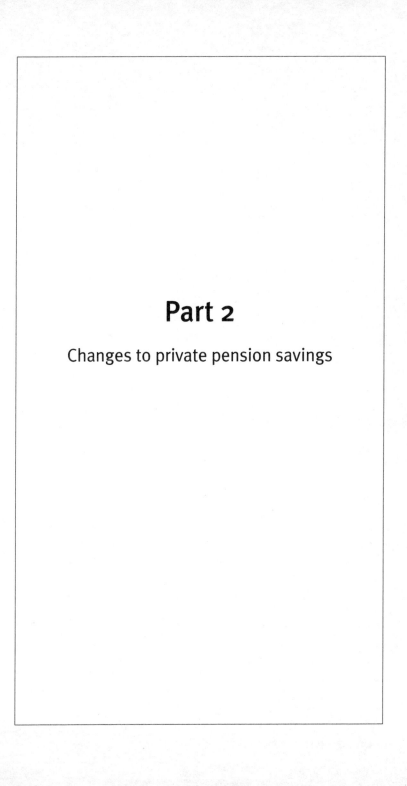

Part 2

Changes to private pension savings

Chapter 9

Important changes from 2006

Chapters 10 to 31 of this book describe various ways you can currently save for retirement using pension schemes and plans that have tax advantages designed to encourage you to save. There are so many chapters because there are many different types of scheme and plan and each comes with its own rules about how much you can pay in and the benefits you can take out.

The various limits on contributions and benefits are designed to keep a lid on the cost to the state of the tax breaks. From time to time, they have been changed, though generally the government is careful to ensure that any change does not reduce benefits that have already been built up in the past and applies only to benefits being built up in future. As a result, there is layer upon layer of rules that have over the years become more and more complicated. The system has become increasingly expensive for employers and pension providers to administer and too complicated for most savers to understand.

This is all due to change from 6 April 2006. The varying tax regimes applying to different types of pension scheme and plan are being swept away and replaced by a single, much simpler system as outlined below.

The description below uses some terms with which you may be unfamiliar – such as 'defined contribution', 'defined benefit', 'annuity' and 'income drawdown'. They are only briefly defined in this chapter and you will find more detail in Chapters 10 to 31.

The lifetime allowance

Under the new system, there will be a single lifetime limit on the amount of savings you can build up through pension schemes and plans that enjoy tax breaks. The lifetime allowance will start at £1.5 million in 2006–7 and be increased each year. The increases will be set for five years at a time – see Table 9.1 for the first five years – and aim broadly to raise the lifetime limit in line with price inflation.

The lifetime allowance applies to your combined savings in all types of pension scheme and plan – for example, occupational schemes, personal pensions, retirement annuity contracts, stakeholder schemes, additional voluntary contribution schemes and so on. There are broadly two types of pension scheme or plan:

- **defined contribution** With these, money goes in, is invested and the resulting fund is used to buy a pension. To see how your savings compare to the lifetime allowance, you simply take the size of the pension fund at retirement. So, if your fund at retirement is £120,000, it uses up £120,000 of your lifetime allowance

- **defined benefit** In these schemes, you are promised a pension of a certain amount usually worked out on the basis of your pay shortly before retirement and the length of time you have been in the scheme. To measure these benefits against the lifetime limit, your pension is first converted into a notional lump sum (the amount of money it is reckoned would be needed to buy a pension of that size). The government sets out the factor to be used to make the conversion and has said it will be 20. For example, if your pension will be £20,000 a year, this is deemed to be equivalent to a lump sum of 20 × £20,000 = £400,000 and so uses up £400,000 of your lifetime allowance.

If you have already started taking some pension before 6 April 2006, you will be treated as having used up a percentage of your lifetime allowance, so reducing the amount available for further pension savings. For this purpose, the pension you have already started will be multiplied by a factor of 25 to find the amount of lifetime allowance used up. For example, if you are already receiving £6,000 a year pension, the amount of lifetime allowance used up will be deemed to be 25 × £6,000 = £150,000, leaving you £1.35 million of unused allowance in 2006–7 or 90 per cent of unused allowance at future rates.

There are special arrangements to increase the lifetime allowance if, at 6 April 2006:

- your pension savings already exceed the lifetime allowance. The lifetime allowance is increased in line with the excess. This is called 'primary protection'

Table 9.1: The lifetime allowance

If you retire in the tax year:	The lifetime allowance is:
	£ million
2006–7	1.50
2007–8	1.60
2008–9	1.65
2009–10	1.75
2010–11	1.80

- you are no longer paying into any scheme or plan but have savings built up that you have yet to take as pension. Provided you do not resume actively contributing to any scheme or plan, your savings will be exempt from the lifetime allowance. This is called 'enhanced protection'.

If you want to take advantage of either primary protection or enhanced protection, you will need to register this intention with the Inland Revenue.

The annual allowance

In addition, there will be an annual allowance starting at £215,000 in 2006–7. This is the amount by which your pension savings may increase each year whether through contributions paid in or additions to your promised benefits. An addition to the promised benefits must be converted to a notional lump sum before it can be compared with the annual allowance. The government has said to do this, the benefit should be multiplied by a factor of 10. So, if your promised pension increases by £500, this is equivalent to a lump sum of 10 × £500 = £5,000, using up £5,000 of your annual allowance.

Again, the limit will be increased each year and Table 9.2 shows the amounts for the first five years.

The annual allowance will not apply in the year you start your pension (or you die). This gives scope for extra-large, last-minute pension enhancements (for example, as part of a redundancy or ill-health package).

Table 9.2: The annual allowance

Tax year	Annual allowance
2006–7	£215,000
2007–8	£225,000
2008–9	£235,000
2009–10	£245,000
2010–11	£255,000

Breaking the lifetime or annual limits

If at retirement the value of your pension fund exceeds the lifetime allowance, there will be a special income tax charge on the excess of either 55 per cent, if you take the excess out of the fund as a lump sum, or 25 per cent if you leave it in the fund (to be taken as pension, which is taxable as income).

If the increase in the value of your savings any year exceeds the annual allowance, the excess is taxed at 40 per cent.

Contribution and benefit limits

All the present contribution and benefit limits will be swept away. The only restrictions will be:

- **contributions** The maximum you can pay in each year is either an amount equal to your taxable earnings or £3,600, whichever is greater
- **tax-free lump sum** At retirement, you can take up to one-quarter of the value of your total pension fund as a tax-free lump sum.

On death before retirement, in general your savings can be paid out to your survivors either as income or as a lump sum. Income will be taxed as such in the hands of the recipient in the normal way. A lump sum up to the value of your lifetime limit will be tax-free, but any excess will be subject to tax at 55 per cent.

If you leave a scheme before two years' membership, you can take a refund of contributions (though you must be offered the choice instead of a transfer value to pay into another pension scheme or plan). A refund of contributions will be paid after deduction of tax at 20 per cent on the first £10,800 and 40 per cent on any excess.

Tax relief

Contributions will continue to qualify for tax relief in the same way as now. So relief will either be given:

- **at source** This will be the case if you are paying into, say, a personal pension, stakeholder scheme or free-standing additional voluntary contribution scheme. You deduct an amount equal to tax relief at the basic rate before handing your contribution to the pension provider. The provider claims the relief from the Inland Revenue and adds it to your pension fund. If you are entitled to higher-rate tax relief, you claim this from your tax office – for example, through your annual tax return
- **through PAYE** This applies if you are paying into an occupational pension scheme. Your employer deducts the contributions from your pay before working out your tax bill thus automatically giving you tax relief up to your highest rate of tax.

Pension funds will continue to grow largely tax-free – in other words, with dividends and similar income being taxed at 10 per cent, but other income and gains building up tax-free.

You will be able to take up to a quarter of the value of your pension savings at retirement as a tax-free lump sum. This will apply even to savings that result from contracting-out of the state additional scheme which, at present, often cannot be taken as a lump sum.

When you can start your pension

Except in the case of ill-health, you must start your pension between a minimum age (currently 50 but due to rise to 55 by 2010) and age 75. It will be up to schemes how they implement the increase in the minimum age to 55. Special rules will protect the right of people in certain occupations to retire earlier provided they had the right already on 10 December 2003, but the lifetime limit will be reduced where it is to be applied at an earlier age. The reduction will be 2.5 per cent of the limit for every year in advance of age 55. Any unused part of the lifetime allowance can be carried forward to set against future pension savings.

Taking your pension

As now, you will not necessarily have to convert all your savings (net of any amount taken as a lump sum) into pension in one go – you can arrange a staggered start so that, for example, you periodically increase your pension income as you gradually wind down from work.

For each tranche of pension you start before age 75, you may have a range of options (but depending on the rules of your individual scheme). You may be able to:

- have a pension paid direct from your occupational scheme
- use your pension fund to buy an annuity to provide an income for the rest of your life
- use part of your fund to buy a limited period annuity lasting just five years leaving the rest of the fund invested, or
- opt for income drawdown which lets you draw an income direct from your pension fund while leaving the rest invested. Under the new rules, the minimum income will in fact be zero, so you could take the tax-free lump sum but put off drawing an income for a while. The maximum income will be 120 per cent of a standard annuity rate to be published by the Financial Services Authority★. On death, the remaining pension fund can be used to provide pensions for your dependants or paid to your survivors as a lump sum but is then subject to a tax charge of 35 per cent.

At age 75, you must opt for one of the following:

- have a pension paid direct from your occupational scheme
- use your pension fund to buy an annuity to provide an income for the rest of your life, or
- opt for an alternatively secured pension (ASP). This is basically income drawdown but with the maximum income restricted to just 70 per cent of the annuity rate for a 75-year-old (even though as time goes on you will be older than 75). The minimum income will be zero. On death, the remaining fund can be used to provide dependants' pensions or, if there are no dependants, left to charity or absorbed into the scheme to help pay other people's pensions and you can if you choose nominate the person (or people) whose pensions you want enhanced.

What do the proposals mean for you?

For most people – initially at least – the new regime will be a welcome simplification. The vast majority retire with savings well below the

£1.5 million lifetime allowance and savings growth easily within the proposed annual allowance. Over time, this may change because the allowances seem set to be increased in line with price inflation, whereas what you pay into your savings and, in many cases, what you get out tend to increase in line with earnings. Typically, earnings increase faster than prices, so eventually the lifetime and annual allowances might not look so generous but this will take a relatively long time to happen.

However, for some people – the Inland Revenue estimates around 5,000 – in particular, high-earning executives, the allowances already look very tight and the new regime may mean they lose out. If this applies to you, you need to look carefully at the options to register for either primary protection or enhanced protection (see page 82) and it may be worth you and/or your employer paying as large amounts as possible into your pension scheme before the new regime starts in April 2006. You might also want to negotiate with your employer over replacing pension benefits in future with other benefits or extra pay. This is a complex area, so get advice from an independent financial adviser★ specialising in pensions or a consulting actuary★.

Part 3

Pensions through your job

Chapter 10

A pension through your job

Changes on the way
This chapter and the other chapters in Part 3 describe occupational pensions under the rules which apply in 2004. Major changes to the rules are due to come into effect from 6 April 2006 – see Chapter 9 for an outline of the new regime.

If you're an employee, you'll often be eligible to join an occupational pension scheme run by your employer. In nearly all cases this will be the best way to save for your retirement, because:

- by law, your employer must pay a substantial part of the cost of providing your pension. Some schemes are 'non-contributory', in which case the employer pays *all* the cost
- your employer often pays the administration costs of running the scheme separately, instead of these coming out of the money intended for pensions

Warning
Some employers offer you the chance to join a group personal pension scheme (GPPS) or to take out a personal stakeholder scheme organised through your workplace. These are not the same as an occupational pension scheme (sometimes called a superannuation scheme). GPPSs and most stakeholder schemes are types of personal pension plan and do not benefit from the advantages listed above. For more details, see Chapters 13 and 20.

- the scheme usually provides a package of benefits, not just a retirement pension. Table 10.1 lists the benefits a typical scheme might provide
- some schemes (called final salary schemes, see Chapter 11) provide a pension and other benefits that are worked out as a certain proportion of your earnings. This means that you can plan for retirement with a fair degree of certainty.

These advantages are very hard to beat. Trying to provide the same benefits completely out of your own pocket would be very costly. You should think twice before deciding not to join your employer's pension scheme.

Although there has been a lot in the news about pension schemes being 'in deficit' and some schemes closing with members losing some or even all of their pensions, it is important to keep these problems in perspective:

- the schemes affected are 'final salary schemes' – see Chapter 11. The problems arise because these schemes are designed to protect you as far as possible from the ups and downs of the stock market. Other

Table 10.1: Benefits from a typical employer's pension scheme

Retirement benefits	Pension at retirement Tax-free lump sum at retirement
Early retirement benefits	Reduced pension if you choose to retire early
Protection if you become ill or disabled	Pension if you have to retire early due to ill-health
Protection for dependants	Pension for your widow/er if you die before retirement Pension for your widow/er if you die after retirement Pension for other dependants (e.g., unmarried partner and children) if you die Lump-sum life insurance paid to your dependants if you die before retirement
Protection against rising prices	Increases to pensions once they start to be paid (but not necessarily full protection against inflation)

types of pension scheme are not affected but only because they do not offer any protection of this sort. Most people in other types of pension scheme will have been more badly affected by the 2000–3 stock market crash than those in the average final salary scheme

- although many private sector final salary schemes are closing to new members and some are no longer allowing existing members to build up further benefits, most seem likely to honour their promises to pay pensions built up so far
- many people who belong to final salary schemes work in the public sector. The government is very unlikely to fail to pay the promised pensions from these schemes because it can always fall back on taxes to foot the bill
- the risk of losing the pension you have built up in a final salary scheme looks small compared with the near certainty of being poor in your old age if you fail to save for retirement.

See Chapter 17 for information about how you might be protected when you save through an occupational pension scheme.

Tax advantages

In common with other types of pension scheme and plan, there are special tax advantages if you save for retirement through an occupational pension scheme, as follows:

- you receive tax relief on the amount that you pay into the scheme
- what your employer pays into the scheme on your behalf counts as a tax-free benefit
- capital gains on the invested contributions build up tax-free. Some of the income also builds up tax-free, but not income from shares, unit trusts and similar investments
- at retirement, part of the pension fund can be taken as a lump sum which is tax-free. The rest must be taken as taxable pension.

The part of your pension savings which provides the tax-free lump sum is completely free of tax.

The remainder of your pension savings have the advantage not of tax freedom but of tax deferment. You receive tax relief now, but, when you start to withdraw your savings as pension, tax may be due. However, people aged 65 and over receive more generous tax allowances than younger people (see Chapter 34) and you may well pay tax at a lower rate in retirement than you do now, so even tax deferment is likely to save you tax.

CASE HISTORY: Max

Max pays £2,000 a year into his employer's pension scheme. He gets tax relief on this at the highest rate of tax, 40 per cent. The relief comes to £800, so the net cost to him of saving this amount is only £1,200.

Max's employer pays into the scheme too and, at retirement, Max qualifies for a tax-free lump sum of £60,000 and pension of £18,000 a year. Once he retires, Max is a basic-rate taxpayer. In 2004–5 the basic rate is 22 per cent.

Max has benefited from 40 per cent tax relief on his savings, which is only partially recouped through the much lower tax rate on his pension.

Who qualifies?

An occupational scheme may be open to all employees, or restricted to employees in a particular group – for example, there might be one scheme for works staff and another for management. But a scheme is not allowed to discriminate between the people who can and cannot belong on the grounds of sex, sexual orientation or disability. This ban includes indirect discrimination – for example, if a firm employs both full-time and part-time workers and there is a higher proportion of women amongst the part-timers, the firm could not normally exclude part-timers from membership of its pension scheme, as this would amount to indirect sex discrimination against the female workers.

If your employer runs a scheme for which you are eligible, you don't have to join it; and, if you're already a member, you can leave the scheme. But there may be restrictions on joining or rejoining the scheme later on, for example it might not accept employees over a certain age, or it might not be open to employees who were previously members but had chosen to leave.

Not all employers have an occupational pension scheme. You might be offered another type of pension arrangement through work – a GPPS or a personal stakeholder scheme – and you will have to weigh up whether this is worth joining. If you don't belong to any type of pension scheme or plan through work, you'll need to make your own pension arrangements (see Part 4).

How much pension?

How much pension you'll get from an occupational pension scheme depends, in part, on what type of scheme it is. There are two main types:

- **defined benefit schemes (the most common being final salary schemes)** These promise you a given level of pension and other benefits in relation to your salary. See Chapter 11 for details
- **money purchase schemes (also known as defined contribution schemes)** With these, in effect, you build up your own savings pot, which is used to buy a pension. See Chapter 12 for details.

Some employers run 'hybrid schemes', which operate both the final salary and money purchase systems, for example paying you whichever pension works out to be the most.

The maximum pension and other benefits

Whichever type of pension scheme your employer offers, the government limits the maximum pension and other benefits that you can receive. Standard benefits from most schemes are well within these limits.

Inland Revenue limits

Occupational pension schemes benefit from significant tax advantages, and so the Inland Revenue puts some limits on the amount of pension, and other benefits, that such schemes can provide. The main limits are set out in Table 10.2. They are set in relation to final salary, and, in all but a few cases, these overall limits apply even to schemes that don't work out benefits in terms of final salary – in other words, the limits apply to money purchase schemes, flat-rate schemes, salary grade schemes and so on, as well as final salary schemes (see Chapters 11 and 12). 'Final salary' for the purpose of these overall limits is defined in the tax legislation and is usually:

Table 10.2: Main tax limits on your pension from an employer's scheme

Description of scheme to which you currently belong [1]	Limit on your pension [2] at retirement [3]	Limit on your lump sum at retirement [3]
'Post-1989 regime'		
a) Scheme set up on or after 14 March 1989, or b) Scheme set up before 14 March 1989 but you joined on or after 1 June 1989, or c) Scheme set up before 14 March 1989 which you joined on or after 17 March 1987 but before 1 June 1989, if you elect to be treated under the 'post-1989 regime'	⅔ of final salary up to a maximum of £68,000[4]	1½ times final salary up to a maximum of £153,000[4]
'1987–9 regime'		
Scheme set up before 14 March 1989 which you joined on or after 17 March 1987 and before 1 June 1989 (unless you opted to be treated under the 'post-1989 regime' – see above)	⅔ of final salary	1½ final salary up to a maximum of £150,000
'Pre-1987 regime'		
Scheme you joined before 17 March 1987	⅔ of final salary	1½ times final salary

[1] As well as the three categories of scheme listed here, it is possible for you to have joined a scheme after 1987 or 1989 but for pre-1987 or pre-1989 rules to apply: for example, where your employer's business has been restructured or merged with another business, or where you changed from one of your employer pension schemes to another due to promotion.

[2] This is the limit which applies if all your benefits from the scheme are taken as pension. If part is taken as a lump sum (or certain other benefits), the maximum you can take as pension is reduced to less than the amounts shown in this column.

[3] Under the '1987–9 regime' and 'pre-1987 regime', these maximum limits apply at the normal retirement date for the scheme. Under the 'post-1989 regime', the limits apply at any age within the range 50 to 75.

[4] This is the limit for the 2004–5 tax year. The limit is based on an 'earnings cap' which puts a ceiling on the amount of final salary that can be used in the calculation. The earnings cap is usually increased each year in line with the Retail Prices Index and is set at £102,000 for 2004–5.

- your earnings in any one year out of the last five years before retirement
- the yearly average of your earnings during a three-year period ending any time within the last ten years before retirement. This is the more commonly used limit, and the one which must usually be used if you're a director of your own company (see Chapter 27).

Remember that these are Inland Revenue definitions – your employer scheme may use less generous definitions.

If your employer scheme is unusually generous, or if the Inland Revenue definition of final salary results in your pension benefits being limited to less than the available investment fund could 'buy', the earnings used to calculate final salary can be increased, up to retirement, in line with the relevant change in the Retail Prices Index. This process, dynamisation, effectively raises the Inland Revenue limits on all your benefits.

Normally, the maximum pension and other benefits build up over a period of 40 years: pension builds up at a rate of one-sixtieth of final salary for each year you're with the employer; the maximum lump sum builds up at a rate of three-eightieths of final salary for each year. If you can't build up your pension over such a long period as 40 years, the rules allow for a faster build-up of pension. The rules are complicated and, along with the other limits set out above, will cease to apply once the new, simplified regime starts in April 2006. If you are due to retire before then and think they might help you, see Inland Revenue manual IR12 *Practice notes on the approval of occupational pension schemes* which is available on the Inland Revenue★ website (or your local tax office might have a reference copy you can consult).

When is your occupational pension paid?

Your occupational scheme sets a normal pension age at which you will usually start to receive your pension. Once, it was common for schemes to set a lower pension age for women than for men, and the most favoured option was to choose the same ages as are currently used for the state pension – i.e. 60 for women and 65 for men. However, the majority of schemes now have the same pension age for men and women. The most popular age is 65, though a sizeable minority have equalised at age 60.

The tax rules prevent the maximum possible pensions being paid at very early ages. Under the 'pre-1987 regime' and the '1987–9 regime', the maximum pension can't usually be paid before age 60 (men) and 55 (women). For the 'post-1989 regime', the lowest age at which full pensions can be paid is 50. There are exceptions: for example, people in certain professions – such as divers or professional footballers – can retire earlier with a full pension. Special rules apply if you have to retire early due to ill-health (see Chapter 15).

In most cases, you must give up your job in order to start taking a pension from an occupational scheme. It may be possible to give up your job but continue to provide services to your former employer as a self-employed consultant. However, you must normally satisfy the Inland Revenue that your work status really has changed – if it thinks you are still really employed by the company, it may remove the tax relief from any tax-free lump sum you have drawn from the pension scheme, so you could face a hefty tax bill.

These rules are due to be swept away – possibly from 2005 or maybe 2006 – to allow you much greater flexibility, so that in future you will be able to start your pension from an employer's scheme while still working for that employer. This opens up the possibility of, say, drawing a partial pension while easing back to part-time work.

Pension increases

The tax rules put a limit on the amount by which your pension can be increased once it starts to be paid. Assuming your starting pension is the maximum possible allowed under the Inland Revenue rules (see Table 10.2), the maximum increase is the amount needed to keep pace with price inflation as measured by changes in the Retail Prices Index. If your starting pension is less than the Inland Revenue maximum – as it often will be – you can have bigger increases, provided the pension never exceeds what the inflation-increased maximum would be.

For most people, maximum increases are not the concern. The important issue is: what is the minimum protection against rising prices which you can expect? If you are contracted out of the state additional pension, there are special rules concerning pension increases (see Chapter 14). For non-contracted-out pensions, the rules are as follows.

For pensions built up from 6 April 1997 onwards, limited price indexation (LPI) applies. This means that, each year, your pension must be increased in line with inflation up to a maximum of 5 per cent a year. However, the maximum is due to be reduced to just 2.5 per cent for salary-related pensions built up from a date yet to be announced – but probably April 2005 – and abolished altogether for money-purchase schemes.

A limited version of LPI applies to some pensions built up before April 1997. Particularly during the 1980s, good investment returns meant that many defined benefit schemes built up surplus funds – i.e. the scheme had more assets than needed to meet its liabilities to pay pensions and other benefits. Tax rules were altered to force schemes to run down their surpluses (which were seen to be an unnecessary cost to the government in terms of tax relief) and there were several options open to schemes: benefits could be improved, contributions paid by employers and/or employees could be reduced or waived altogether for a time (a 'contribution holiday'), or the surplus could be paid to the employer. The last option is particularly controversial. Employers argue that they foot the bill – whatever it is – for the defined benefits from final salary and similar schemes. If investment returns are poor, employers have to cough up extra to ensure that pension funding stays on track to meet the promised benefits. Therefore, they argue, if investment returns are good, they should be able to claw back the surplus funds in the scheme. Opponents argue that, once the money is in the pension fund, it is being held on trust for the pensioners and other beneficiaries, and that the employer has no right to have it back. A compromise was struck and, from 17 August 1990 onwards, if an employer is to receive a payment of surplus out of a pension fund, it can go ahead only if the scheme has first ensured that pensions from the scheme (whenever they were built up) will be increased by inflation up to the LPI limit once they start to be paid.

For other non-contracted-out pensions built up before 6 April 1997, there is no legal requirement for pensions to be increased once they start to be paid. Whether or not they are depends on the individual scheme. Public-sector schemes guarantee to increase pensions in line with inflation, however high it turns out to be. A few private-sector schemes offer this guarantee as well. Many schemes already guarantee LPI increases for the whole of their pensions, sometimes paying more on a discretionary basis. Some schemes make no guarantees at all, paying only discretionary increases based each year on what the employer feels can be afforded.

What do you pay?

Some employer schemes are *non-contributory*. This means that your employer pays the whole cost of the scheme, and you contribute nothing. The majority of schemes, however, are *contributory*, which means that you pay part of the cost, and your employer pays part. Usually, you pay a given proportion of your salary into the scheme, commonly around 5 per cent.

With money purchase schemes, your employer will also pay a specified amount or percentage of your salary. But with final salary schemes (and other defined benefit schemes – see Chapter 11), the employer will provide however much is needed to make up the balance of the cost of providing the pensions and other benefits.

Both you and your employer get tax relief on contributions to an employer scheme. Tax relief on your contributions is given by deducting them from your pay before your tax bill is worked out, and you get relief up to your highest rate of tax.

CASE HISTORY: Sarah

Sarah earns £16,000 a year working in a stockbroker's library and is a member of the pension scheme. The firm pays most of the cost of the scheme, but Sarah contributes 3 per cent of her pay, which comes to £480 a year. However, the cost to Sarah is less than this, because she gets tax relief on the contributions. As she pays tax at the basic rate of 22 per cent on at least £480 of her income, the after-tax-relief cost of the contributions is only £374.40 (i.e. £480 × [1 – 0.22] = £374.40).

The Inland Revenue limits the amount you can contribute to an employer scheme. The limit is 15 per cent of your earnings. If you are covered by the 'pre-1987 regime' or the '1987–9 regime', there's no other limit on the amount you can contribute. But, if the 'post-1989 regime' applies to you, there's also an overall cash limit on the amount which can qualify for tax relief. The limit for the 2004–5 tax year is £15,300. The cash limit is usually increased each year in line with inflation as measured by the Retail Prices Index. There's no Inland Revenue limit on the amount your employer can pay into a scheme as such, though there are rules to prevent him or her paying in more than is needed to provide the maximum possible benefits.

Top-up schemes

In general, very few employer schemes will promise or provide benefits that are anywhere near the maximum limits laid down by the Inland Revenue. However, the earnings cap that applies under the 'post-1989 regime', setting an overall cash limit on the size of pension and lump sum you can get, can be an unwelcome restriction on the pension benefits that a scheme can offer if you are a high earner.

In order to address this problem, at the time the earnings cap was introduced the government also allowed for the establishment of top-up schemes which can be used to provide a pension (and other benefits) over and above the amounts allowed by the Inland Revenue limits. The drawback is that top-up schemes don't benefit from the special tax advantages which normally apply to pension schemes – but, on the plus side, top-up schemes can be very flexible, because you don't have to take the bulk of the pay-out as pension. There are two broad types of top-up scheme:

- **unfunded schemes** With these, your employer simply pays you benefits at the time you reach retirement. You are liable for income tax on the benefits (even if they are paid as a lump sum)
- **funded schemes** (also called Funded Unapproved Retirement Benefit Schemes or FURBS). Your employer pays contributions which build up a fund to provide the eventual benefits. At the time the contributions are made, they count as fringe benefits on which you're liable for income tax. Usually, the fund is arranged as a trust, and income and gains from the trust will generally be taxed only at the basic rate, even if your own tax rate is higher than this. (The government closed a loophole by which FURBS could be invested tax-free by using an offshore fund.) There is no tax to pay on the benefits when they are paid out.

From your point of view, a funded scheme offers better security because you know the money is being built up to pay the benefits. With an unfunded scheme, you could lose your top-up benefits if your employer went bust.

More information

If your employer runs a pension scheme which you are eligible to join, you must be given some information about it automatically; other information should be supplied on request. Table 10.4 summarises the main information available.

The explanatory booklet sets out the basic information about the scheme – for example, what type of scheme it is, who contributes and how much, what benefits are paid at retirement, on early retirement and in the event of death. It will also give details of the person to

Table 10.3: Information about your pension scheme

Type of information	When it is given out	Nature of disclosure
Explanatory booklet	Within 2 months of the start of your employment if you are eligible to join	Required by law
	Within 13 weeks of joining the scheme	Required by law
Summary trustees' report and scheme accounts	Annually	Good practice but not required
Full trustees' report and scheme accounts	Copy of the current version on request; previous four years open to inspection on request	Required by law
Annual benefit statement	Annually	Required by law if it is a money purchase scheme Other schemes – good practice and due to become compulsory some time after spring 2005
Options on leaving the scheme and statement of transfer value of your pension rights	Within 3 months of a request (provided information has not already been given within last 12 months) and when your membership of the scheme ends	Required by law
Announcement of changes to the scheme	If practicable before the change is made, but, in any case, within one month after the change	Required by law

contact if you need further information. Do read the booklet and store it safely for later reference.

The benefit statement is a projection of the pension and other benefits which you and your dependants stand to receive from the scheme. Although at present not compulsory for all schemes, good schemes will provide a statement every year and, just like a bank or building society statement, it is very useful in helping you to keep track of how your savings are building up. Since April 2003, all forecasts from money purchase schemes must show the pension you might get at retirement expressed in today's money. (Previously, this figure was often shown in future money – a telephone number figure that looked wildly generous but in fact might be worth very little once inflation over the intervening years was taken into account.) Forecasts from final salary schemes are generally in today's money anyway. A forecast in today's money makes it much easier for you to plan the amount you save. If the projected pension looks to be falling short of the retirement income you expect to need, consider increasing your savings: for example, by making additional voluntary contributions (see Chapter 30). Similarly, if the life cover and dependants' pensions would not be enough for your family to live on, consider taking out extra life cover.

'Combined benefit statements' are gradually being introduced (and the government is giving itself powers to make their provision compulsory if need be). These use information from the Department for Work and Pensions about your state pension entitlement to show the pension you can expect from the state as well as your expected occupational pension. If you receive a combined benefit statement, you will not need to get a Retirement Pension Forecast (see page 47) in order to check your likely state pension. However, check carefully whether the document you receive really is a combined benefit statement. Many ordinary benefit statements include an indication of your possible state pension, but using the standard basic pension for a single person rather than a figure which is personal to you and based on your National Insurance record. A combined statement might look something like Figure 10.1.

Many schemes automatically send you a summary of the annual report and accounts. This is usually in an easy-to-read form, and there is a standard way in which schemes are now recommended to present this information. Expect to see a fund account showing how the value of the scheme's assets has changed over the year, as a result of

Figure 10.1: Example of a combined benefit statement

Your combined pension statement

Total state retirement pension you have earned up to 5 April 2004	£303 a month
When you reach state pension age (65), the DWP expect your total state retirement pension to be	£450 a month
If you stay in the Good2U plc Pension Scheme until you reach 65 (the normal retirement date for the scheme), your pension is forecast to be	£1,600 a month
Your combined pension from Good2U plc Pension Scheme and the State when you are 65 is forecast to be	£2,050 a month

Important information about your state pension statement
All amounts are shown at today's prices

State retirement pension includes basic state pension and any State Second Pension, SERPS and graduated retirement benefit.

Your state retirement pension is based only on your own National Insurance contributions and assumes you will continue to pay or be credited with full-rate contributions.

The amount of state retirement pension shown here is what you could get. The amount you get when you actually retire may be different because of changes in your circumstances or changes in the law.

If you receive more than one combined pension statement a year, please remember that you should only count once the state retirement pension amount shown on each statement.

If you would like more information about your state retirement pension please ask for a leaflet.

contributions and investment returns being added and payment of benefits being deducted. There will also be a 'net asset statement' showing how the pension fund is invested in various broad categories of assets, such as UK shares, fixed-interest stocks, property, overseas investments and so on.

The simplified report and accounts are not legally required, but you must have access to the full report and accounts if you want to see them. You also have the right to see the actuary's valuation of the scheme, which is usually made every three years. The actuary uses various assumptions to estimate whether the scheme assets are adequate to pay the pensions and other benefits as they fall due – this is a valuation on an 'on-going basis'. He or she also assesses whether the assets would be enough to pay all the benefits due to members if the scheme had to be wound up today (see Chapter 17) – a valuation on a 'discontinuance basis'.

Similarly, you have the right to inspect the scheme trust deed and rules. These are usually very technical documents that you would consult if you needed to check very precisely how some aspect of the scheme operated. If you want copies of these documents, a 'reasonable' charge can be made. You do not have the right to inspect minutes of trustees' meetings at which the trustees made decisions about individual cases – for example, which dependants should receive any lump sum or pensions in the event of a member's death.

Your main source of additional information about your employer pension scheme is the scheme officials or your Human Resources (personnel) department at work. The scheme officials are usually the pensions administrator and the trustees of the scheme. They are also the people you should go to initially if you have a problem. For more about what to do if you face problems concerning your employer pension scheme, see Chapter 35.

Table 10.4 lists some useful leaflets about employer pension schemes.

Table 10.4: Information about employer pension schemes

Name of booklet/leaflet	Published by
FSA guide to saving for retirement – starting to save	Financial Services Authority
FSA guide to saving for retirement – reviewing your plans	Financial Services Authority
FSA guide to the risks of opting out of your employer's pension scheme	Financial Services Authority
Understanding your yearly pension statement	Financial Services Authority
PM3 Occupational pensions – your guide	Department for Work and Pensions

Chapter 11

Salary-related schemes

Final salary schemes (also called 'defined benefit' schemes) are quite unlike most other types of saving and investment. You are promised (but not guaranteed) a certain level of pension (and other benefits) in relation to your earnings, which is independent of the amount that you pay into the scheme.

The advantage of this type of scheme is that you can plan ahead with some certainty. Your earnings are likely to keep abreast of inflation, so the pension that you are building up automatically does so too. This makes tracking whether you'll have enough to live on in retirement a relatively simple matter.

Final salary schemes work best when:

- you remain with the same employer for a long time, or
- you work in the public sector, where special arrangements often ensure continuity in your pension savings if you change jobs (see Chapter 16).

If you are not in the public sector, such schemes are not quite so good when you change jobs frequently or have a broken career (for example, because you took time off to raise a family), but the disadvantages which job-movers used to suffer were substantially reduced by changes in the law during the mid-1980s. For the majority of people, whether they change jobs frequently or not, an occupational pension scheme (if available) is now likely to be the best way to save for retirement.

The pension promise

In a contributory scheme, you'll be required to pay something towards the cost of meeting the pension promise: typically, you may pay in perhaps 5 per cent of your salary. Your employer pays the balance of the cost, which will vary from year to year but may be around, say, 10 per cent of salaries on average. When the invested contributions are growing well, your employer may not need to pay in quite so much, but if investments perform badly, your employer will probably have to pay in substantially more to ensure that the promised pensions can still be paid as they fall due. In a non-contributory scheme, your employer pays the full cost of providing the promised pensions.

A key point about final salary schemes is that they are a relatively low-risk way for you to save for retirement: in general, you will receive the promised pension however well or badly the invested contributions perform. Your employer, rather than you, bears the investment risk.

From the employer's point of view, final salary schemes are relatively high risk. The employer is committed to paying in whatever it takes to ensure that the pension promises are kept. This potentially open-ended commitment is more than the average small employer can take on, so final salary schemes are invariably offered only by larger employers.

Even many larger employers are finding the open-ended cost of final salary schemes, together with the complex red tape which applies to these schemes, too much to bear. Surveys by the National Association of Pension Funds (NAPF) suggest that possibly over half (55 per cent) of final salary schemes have closed to new members over the last three years. Some have also stopped existing members building up any further benefits. Most employers are required by law to offer some type of pension arrangement through the workplace and the 2003 NAPF survey found that the most common substitute for the final salary scheme is a money purchase scheme (favoured by 45 per cent of employers who had closed their final salary scheme), followed by a

---

CASE HISTORY: Jo

Jo has worked for Happy Holdings plc for ten years and expects to stay there until she retires in 13 years' time. She belongs to the pension scheme (a final salary scheme) and works out that she is on track to retire with a pension equal to half her salary. Assuming that she will earn at least the same as she does now, Jo is confident that this will provide her with enough retirement income when added to her state pension.

---

stakeholder scheme (23 per cent) and group personal pension (13 per cent). However, 8 per cent had stuck with the defined benefit principle and opted for a career average scheme (see page 112).

Table 11.1: The pros and cons of an employer's final salary scheme

Pros	Cons
Tax advantages	Can be difficult to understand
Employer pays some or all of cost	You might lose out when changing jobs
Employer may pay running costs separately	Scheme might close if employer finds it too costly or risky
Predictable pension and other benefits	In worst scenario, scheme might wind
Pension keeps pace with inflation during the period in which it is building up	up – see Chapter 17
No investment risk	

Your pension at retirement

The pension you'll receive is worked out according to a formula and is based on:

- **your final salary** This is the amount that you are earning at or near retirement. The precise definition of final salary varies from scheme to scheme (see page 110)
- **years of membership** In other words, the number of years during which you've been a member of the scheme. In line with the government limits (see Chapter 10), the maximum pension usually builds up over 40 years
- **the accrual rate** This is a fraction of the earnings which you get as pension for each year of membership. Commonly, it is one-sixtieth or one-eightieth.

Table 11.2 shows how your pension might build up in a one-sixtieth scheme.

Your pension if you leave before retirement

Provided that you have belonged to the pension scheme for at least two years, if you leave (for example, because you change jobs) you are still entitled to receive a pension from that scheme when you reach retirement.

CASE HISTORY: Harry

Harry belongs to a final salary scheme that promises a pension of one-eightieth of final salary for each year of membership. Harry will have been in the scheme for 12 years when he retires and expects his salary then to be about £27,000 a year. He can expect a pension of:

£27,000 × 12 × $\frac{1}{80}$ = £4,050 a year.

The pension that you'll get is still based on the number of years that you were in the scheme and the normal accrual rate. But, instead of the pension being based on your salary at retirement, it is now based on your final salary at or near the time when you left the scheme.

At one time, this pension (called your 'preserved pension') would have been frozen at that amount. But preserved pensions built up from 1 January 1985 onwards (assuming that you left the scheme on or after 1 January 1986) must be increased in line with inflation up to a maximum of 5 per cent a year between the time that you left the scheme and the time that you retire (due to be reduced to 2.5 per cent

Table 11.2: Example of pension building up in a final salary scheme

Number of years that you have been a member of the scheme	The pension that you have built up assuming that the scheme pays one-sixtieth of final salary for each year of membership and that you earn:			
	£15,000	£25,000	£35,000	£45,000
1	£250	£417	£583	£750
5	£1,250	£2,083	£2,916	£3,750
10	£2,500	£4,167	£5,833	£7,500
15	£3,750	£6,250	£8,750	£11,250
20	£5,000	£8,333	£11,667	£15,000
25	£6,250	£10,416	£14,583	£18,750
30	£7,500	£12,500	£17,500	£22,500
35	£8,750	£14,583	£20,417	£26,250
40	£10,000	£16,667	£23,333	£30,000

a year probably from 2005). Even so, in terms of pension, you'll tend to lose out as compared with staying in the scheme until retirement because:

- if you'd stayed, your pension would have kept pace with your earnings rather than prices. Earnings generally increase at a faster rate than prices. Your own earnings might have increased even more rapidly, perhaps because of promotion
- if inflation averages more than 2.5 per cent a year between the time that you left and the time that you retire, the buying power of the preserved pension will be eroded.

In general, the effect on your pension rights will not be a major factor in your decision about whether to stay in your current job or leave. However, you should be aware of the impact that leaving has on your pension and should check that your new employer will provide a reasonable replacement pension, or that your new salary is high enough to compensate for your lost pension rights.

As an alternative to receiving a preserved pension from a former employer's scheme on retirement, you can transfer your pension rights to another pension arrangement (see Chapter 16).

What is final salary?

Your final salary is defined in the rules of your scheme. It can have a variety of meanings: for example, your average pay over the last three years, the average of the best three years' pay out of the last ten, or earnings on a specified date.

Not all of your earnings will necessarily be included in the calculation. What counts are your 'pensionable earnings'. These might mean just your basic salary, or they could include overtime pay, bonuses and commission and other payments, too. Some schemes reduce pensionable earnings to take account of the basic pension that you will get from the state.

The pensionable earnings used in the pension formula for your scheme will also be used to set your contributions to the scheme, if it is a contributory one.

CASE HISTORY: Jonathan

Jonathan belongs to a pension scheme which aims to provide a maximum pension of two-thirds of final salary after 40 years. It expects part of that two-thirds pension to be provided by the state basic pension. The scheme's definition of pensionable earnings is therefore basic salary in excess of £3,900 (a slice roughly equal to the current level of state basic pension). The slice is increased each year roughly in line with increases in the state pension. In Jonathan's case, his pensionable earnings are his salary of £18,000 – £3,900 = £14,100 a year. This is the amount used in the pension formula and also to work out his 5 per cent contribution to the scheme. Currently, his monthly contribution is (5% × £14,100) ÷ 12 = £58.75.

Tax-free lump sum

So far we have looked at the pension that you may get from a final salary scheme without taking into account the tax-free lump sum that you can take at retirement.

Most schemes work to the Inland Revenue maximum (see Chapter 10), allowing you in most cases to build up a lump sum of three-eighticths of your final salary for each year of membership. This gives an overall maximum lump sum of $1\frac{1}{2}$ times final salary after 40 years.

CASE HISTORY: Andrew

Andrew retires on a final salary of £36,000. He has belonged to his employer's pension scheme (a one-sixtieth scheme) for 40 years and has built up the maximum possible pension: 40 × ¹⁄₆₀ × £36,000 = £24,000.

Andrew decides to swap part of this pension for a tax-free lump sum of 1½ times his final salary. This comes to 1½ × £36,000 = £54,000.

According to the rules of his scheme, his pension is reduced by £1 for every £12 of the lump sum. In total, his pension is reduced by £54,000 ÷ 12 = £4,500 to £19,500. This is £19,500 ÷ £36,000 = 54% of his final salary.

In some schemes the lump sum is optional. If you decide to take it (and most people do, for very good reasons, see Chapter 33), the amount of pension that you receive is reduced. For example, your pension is typically reduced by £1 for every £12 that you take in cash. As a rough guide, if you are entitled to the maximum pension of two-thirds of your final salary and you opt to take the maximum lump sum of 1½ times your final salary, your pension will be reduced to about half your final salary.

In other schemes the lump sum is automatically part of the benefits package, and the pension has already been calculated on the basis that some of the pension fund will be earmarked to provide lump sums. In such schemes the pension will often accrue at a rate of one-eightieth for each year of membership. This is because a one-eightieth pension (maximum pension of half the final salary after 40 years) plus a maximum lump sum (of 1½ times the final salary) is about the same as a one-sixtieth pension before the deduction for any lump sum.

Other types of defined benefit scheme

Final salary schemes are the most common defined benefit pension scheme run by employers, but they are not the only type.

In the past you could also find flat-rate schemes, for example, which paid a given cash amount of pension for each year of membership. The high inflation rates experienced during the 1970s and 1980s severely eroded the value of these pensions, which are now obsolete.

However, 'career average salary schemes' are still in use and making a comeback. They are particularly good if your earnings peak before the end of your career. The scheme is similar to a final salary scheme in most respects, with your pension being worked out according to a formula. But, instead of using final salary in the formula, a career average salary scheme uses the average of your earnings throughout the whole time that you were a member of the scheme.

Of course, inflation erodes the value of salary earned in the earlier years of membership, so a pension based in part on the actual earnings of years ago is likely to be fairly trivial. A good career average scheme will therefore revalue earnings from earlier years in line with either earnings or price inflation. For many people, their best earning years tend to be towards the latter part of their career when they are experiencing the greatest seniority and experience. Therefore, a career

CASE HISTORY: Ruby

Ruby has worked for her current firm for 15 years and has been a member of its non-contributory pension scheme for the whole of that period. She is now 52 and has just been head-hunted by another company. In all probability, she could stay with her current firm until retirement, continuing to make a successful name for herself. But she likes the idea of a new challenge and decides to leave.

Table 11.3 shows the impact of her decision on her pension from the old firm. Ruby should make sure that the new firm offers a high enough salary and/or has a good enough pension scheme to ensure that the pension that she builds up with the new company is at least as good as the pension she is missing out on by leaving her old firm.

Table 11.3: Ruby's retirement pension

	Ruby's pension from the old firm	
	Position had Ruby stayed with the old firm until retirement	Position given that Ruby leaves the old firm
Ruby's final salary, assuming that it increases by 5 per cent a year on average	£80,000	£54,000
Number of years in the scheme	23	15
Accrual rate	$\frac{1}{60}$	$\frac{1}{60}$
Pension on leaving	£30,667	£13,500
Increase in pension between leaving and retirement, assuming inflation averages 2.5 per cent a year	N/a	£2,948
Pension payable at retirement	£30,667	£16,448

average scheme will tend to produce a lower pension than a final salary scheme. This is precisely why employers are showing renewed interest in career average schemes. The tendency towards lower pensions helps to contain the cost of offering a pension scheme.

More information

In order to find out what pension you can expect from your employer's pension scheme, check your most recent benefit statement or ask for a new one. Figure 11.1 shows the sorts of figure that you might see on the benefit statement for a final salary scheme. You might get a combined pension statement (see page 103), in which case the statement will show your possible state pension based on your actual National Insurance record, rather than just showing the standard basic pension rate.

Figure 11.1: Example of a benefit statement for a final salary scheme

Date of birth:	22/8/1964
Normal retirement date:	31/8/2029
Pensionable service:	34 years 6 months
Pensionable salary:	£12,154
Final pensionable salary:	£12,154

At your normal retirement date you will receive a pension of about 43.25 per cent of your final pensionable salary, part of which may be taken as a tax-free cash sum. Because your pension is based on final pensionable salary, it will grow in line with your earnings.

Pension based on current final pensionable salary:	£5,256.61 a year

In addition to your scheme pension, you may receive a state basic pension. You should check your entitlement with the DWP.

The state basic pension for a single person is currently:	£3,926.00 a year

Chapter 12

Money purchase schemes

Money purchase pension schemes are much like any other form of saving and investment. Money is paid in, it grows and the proceeds are eventually withdrawn, in this case to provide a pension.

The main advantage of this type of scheme is its simplicity and portability. It is very easy to understand how it works and to check the state of your 'pension account'. And it's pretty straightforward to transfer your accumulated savings from one scheme to another (see Chapter 16).

No promises

However, it is much more difficult to plan for retirement using this type of scheme. There is no inherent tendency for the pension which is building up to keep pace with inflation, and, because so many unpredictable factors are involved, it's very hard to estimate the level of pension that you will eventually receive.

One of the most important factors influencing your pension is how well the invested contributions grow. Other things being equal, if investments perform well you'll get a big pension; if they perform badly you'll get a small pension. Similarly, your pension will depend on the rate at which you can convert your pension fund into pension, and this will depend on investment conditions at the time when you retire. In other words, you bear the full investment risk.

From the employer's point of view, money purchase schemes are reassuringly predictable. The employer must pay into the scheme, but at a pre-set rate which need not change at all from year to year. So the cost of the scheme is known and can't surge unexpectedly. For this reason, money purchase schemes are particularly popular with smaller employers who cannot easily cope with the shock of rising expenses. Many larger employers who want to contain the cost of their pension schemes have switched to money purchase schemes in recent years (see page 107). A few, wishing to contain cost but still provide employees with some protection from investment risk, instead offer cash balance schemes (see page 122).

Table 12.1: The pros and cons of an employer's money purchase scheme

Pros	Cons
Tax advantages	Unpredictable pension and other benefits
Employer pays some or all of the cost	Employers tend to pay less of the cost than with a final salary scheme
Employer may pay running costs separately	No tendency for pension to keep pace with inflation during period in
Simple	which it is building up
Easy to transfer if you change jobs	You bear the investment risk

CASE HISTORY: Harry and Bob

Harry and Bob became friends at work. They both belonged to their employer's pension scheme (a money purchase scheme) and had been paying into it for the same number of years when they retired.

Harry is the older of the two, and retired in December 2000 on a pension of £6,600 a year. Bob retired in January 2002. Between December 2000 and January 2002, the stock market fell by nearly 20 per cent. On top of that, annuity rates (which tell you the amount of pension you can buy with a pension fund) fell by about 4 per cent. As a result, despite having paid in broadly the same amount in contributions, Bob's pension was only £5,121 a year.

Bob lost out by £1,479 a year simply because of the investment conditions at the time he retired.

Your pension on retirement

The pension that you'll receive depends on the following factors:

- the amount paid into the scheme on your behalf by your employer. This will often be a fixed percentage of your salary: for example, 5 or 6 per cent. But in some schemes the percentage varies with, say, your age and/or length of service
- if it is a contributory scheme, the amount paid into the scheme by you (often a fixed percentage of salary): for example, 5 per cent
- charges deducted from the scheme. Some employers pay the administration costs separately
- how well the invested contributions grow
- the rate, called the 'annuity rate', at which the pension fund can be converted into pension. The annuity rate at the time you retire sets the general level of income that you will receive throughout your retirement (See Chapter 33).

Chart 12.1 shows how stock market growth and annuity rates have varied over the past decade.

A major problem for money purchase schemes has been the persistent decline in the annuity rate in recent years. As an indication, using level annuity rates: at the start of the 1990s a man retiring at the age of 65 could receive over £1,500 of pension for each £10,000 in his pension fund; by June 2004 he could get just £742, a fall of over half.

CASE HISTORY: Hannah

Hannah pays 3 per cent of her earnings into her company's money purchase scheme. Her employer adds another 10 per cent of her earnings.

Hannah's pay, and therefore her contributions, too, have grown by an average 2 per cent a year during the 17 years that she has been in the scheme. By the time of her retirement at the age of 65, Hannah is earning £36,000 a year, and her pension fund has grown to £106,037. The annuity rate is £681 for each £10,000 in the fund, so Hannah's pension will be £681 ÷ £10,000 × £106,037 = £7,221 a year. This pension will not increase so its buying power will tend to decline over the years as prices rise.

Chart 12.1: Stock-market performance and annuity rates

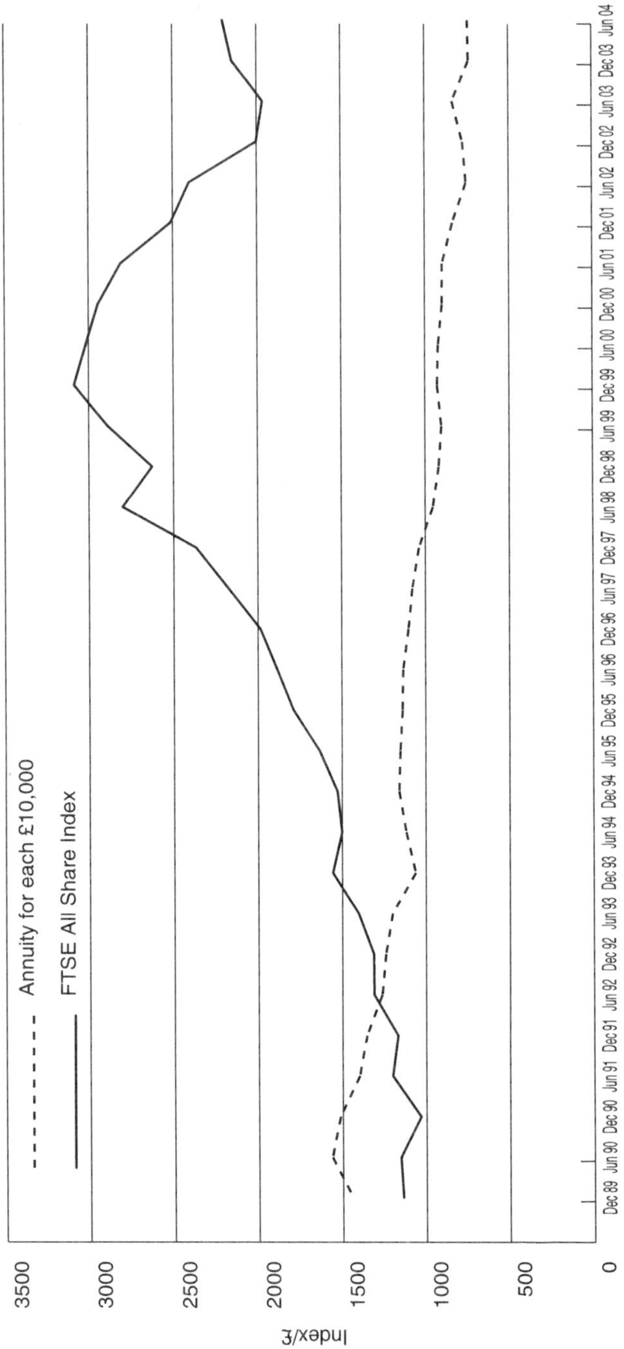

Your pension if you leave before retirement

Provided that you have belonged to the pension scheme for at least two years, if you leave (for example, because you change jobs) you are still entitled to receive a pension from the scheme when you reach retirement age. This is called a 'preserved pension'.

Obviously, after you leave no new contributions are paid into the scheme. But the fund that you have built up by the time that you leave can simply be left invested to carry on growing up to the time when you retire.

Instead of receiving a preserved pension from a former employer's scheme on retirement, you can transfer the pension fund which has built up to another pension arrangement (see Chapter 16).

CASE HISTORY: Hannah

If Hannah (see above) had changed jobs in 1990, she would have left behind an accumulated pension fund of £36,303.20. No further contributions would have been added to this.

Assuming that the fund continued to grow by, say, 5 per cent a year (after charges), it would have reached £56,318 by the time that Hannah retired at the age of 65. This would have bought her a pension of £3,835 a year at the annuity rate of £681 per £10,000 of fund.

How the contributions are invested

Unlike a final salary scheme, where your employer shoulders the investment risk, in a money purchase scheme you are directly exposed to the investment risk. How the contributions are invested and how well they grow are therefore extremely important to you.

With most money purchase schemes the contributions are handed over to an insurer, which invests them and will often handle the administration of the scheme as well.

The trustees of your scheme (see Chapter 17) choose the insurer and will in some cases decide in which of the insurer's funds the contributions should be placed. In other cases you can choose which fund you would like the contributions relating to you to be invested in. The choice will generally include:

- **a with-profits basis** Provided you keep your pension in this fund until you reach retirement age, this is a medium-risk option. The value of your fund then cannot fall and grows steadily as regular 'reversionary bonuses' are added. On retirement you receive a 'terminal bonus', which often represents a substantial chunk of the overall return. The size of the bonus depends on a host of underlying factors: stock-market growth, the performance of other investments held by the insurer (for example, commercial property, gilts and so on), the value of claims made against the insurer and the size of dividends paid to shareholders where the insurer is set up as a company rather than a mutual organisation. The insurer will smooth the bonuses that it pays out, holding back a bit from good years to add to bonuses in bad years. In this way your investment should grow steadily. A 'unitised with-profits' fund follows the same basic principle (see Chapter 21 for details). A with-profits fund is more risky, if you transfer your money to another pension fund or provider before reaching retirement age. In that case, you will not usually qualify for any terminal bonus, and the provider reserves the right to make a 'market value reduction' (MVR) which reduces the transfer value of the fund and can even take back some of the reversionary bonuses previously added. Because bonuses are smoothed from year to year, in a year of poor stock-market returns the investments of someone who stays in the fund could be higher than the actual value of the underlying investments (see Chart 12.1). If leavers were given the same sum as stayers, they would be getting back more than the actual value of the underlying investments. So the MVR cuts the transfer value to ensure that someone leaving does not take out more than their fair share of the with-profits fund to the detriment of the investors left behind. In general, there is no MVR if you decide to retire earlier than originally intended and you are using your fund to buy a pension
- **a unit-linked basis** Your money is invested in one or more funds of investments: for example, UK shares, international shares, property, gilts, money-market deposits and so on. The value of your 'pension pot' rises and falls directly in line with the value of the underlying investments in the fund. A fund investing in shares is

Chart 12.2: With-profits funds and the MVR

The striped columns show how an investor's pension fund grows steadily as reversionary bonuses are added.

The plain columns show the value of the underlying with-profits fund divided by the total number of investors. In effect, this is a single investor's actual share of the underlying fund. The value of the underlying fund goes up and down reflecting stock-market performance.

In most years, the value of the pension fund is less than the investor's actual share of the fund. This is because some of the profits made by the fund are not paid in bonuses. Instead, they are held in reserve to top up bonuses in the bad years. But a run of bad years can eat away the profits held in reserve. For example, in 2000 and 2001 the value of the underlying fund fell because of big falls in the stock market. By 2001, the investor's share of the underlying fund has fallen below the value of his pension fund. If the investor transferred his pension fund now, a market value reduction (MVR) would be deducted from the value of his pension fund to reduce it to the same amount as his share of the underlying fund.

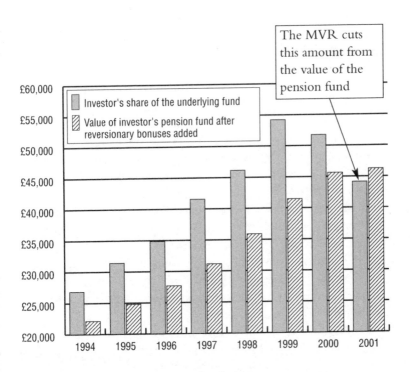

higher-risk than a fund investing in, say, gilts, and the higher-risk the fund the greater the fluctuations in value will tend to be. A fund investing in, say, money-market accounts or building-society deposits grows only modestly, as interest is added, but cannot fall in value. In practice, where there is a choice of fund the majority of pension scheme members choose a managed fund, in which the fund manager chooses a mix of investments, providing a good spread of risk and reasonable, if unexciting, returns.

Cash balance scheme

A cash balance scheme can be seen as a halfway house between a final salary scheme and a money purchase scheme. It lets your employer contain the cost of providing pensions without leaving you, the member, quite so exposed to risk as you are in a money purchase scheme.

In a pure defined benefit scheme, such as a final salary scheme, you are promised a certain amount of pension at retirement (see Chapter 11). In a cash balance scheme, you are not promised a particular pension, but instead you are promised a certain amount of cash with which to buy your pension. The amount of cash may be expressed in a variety of ways – say, as a percentage of your salary for each year of membership.

For example, if you earned £30,000 a year and the cash balance scheme promised 20 per cent of your salary for each year of membership, you would have a pension fund of £30,000 × 20% × 10 = £60,000 after 10 years in the scheme. If the annuity rate at retirement was £742 for each £10,000 of fund, you could buy a pension of £60,000/ £10,000 × £742 = £4,452 a year. (By contrast, 10 years in a sixtieths final salary scheme would have produced a pension of 10 × 1/60 × £30,000 = £5,000 a year.)

If the cash balance scheme is contributory, you pay in a certain amount each month. Your employer then pays in whatever is needed to ensure that the target cash sum is reached by retirement. If the invested contributions grow strongly, your employer will not have to pay in so much; if investment performance is weak, your employer has to pay in more. So, up to retirement, your employer is bearing the investment risk.

Once retirement is reached, the risk shifts to you. It's up to you to shop around with your cash pot to buy the best pension you can. If annuity rates are low, you'll get less for your money than you had hoped; if annuity rates have risen, you'll get a better deal.

Cash balance might be just one element in the scheme. For example, in 2003, Barclays Bank introduced a hybrid scheme with a cash balance core and a voluntary money purchase top-up alongside. Barclays pays the full cost of the cash balance part of the scheme and, if members opt to pay into the money purchase part, the bank will match the employee's contributions up to 3 per cent of salary.

Buying an annuity

On your retirement, the pension fund that you have built up is currently used to buy an annuity. At this stage money purchase employers' schemes are virtually identical to personal pensions and stakeholder schemes (which also work on the money purchase basis). The choices that you have regarding the annuity provider and type of annuity are discussed in detail in Chapter 33.

Tax-free lump sum

As with employers' final salary schemes, with money purchase schemes you can take part of your pension fund as a lump sum instead of pension. The maximum, as set out by Inland Revenue rules, is three-eighteths per year of your final salary (even though this is a money purchase scheme). The amount taken as a lump sum reduces the remaining fund, leaving less with which to buy an annuity.

More information

To get an idea of the pension you have built up so far, check your most recent benefit statement or ask for a new one. Figure 12.1 shows the sort of information you'll get. You might receive a combined benefit statement (see page 103), which includes the state pension you are expected to get. Your statements will show, in today's money, the amount of pension you might get at retirement assuming current contributions and tax relief continue.

Figure 12.1: Example of a benefit statement for a money purchase
scheme

Information at:	31/03/2004
Date of birth:	07/05/1960
Date of joining scheme:	01/04/1996
Normal retirement date:	07/05/2025

The value of your fund so far is: £32,446

Using current annuity rates, this would buy a pension at the
age of 65 of: £1,687 pa

Your future pension

The estimated value of your fund when you reach age 65
assuming your current contributions continue is: £151,207

Using current annuity rates, this would buy a pension at the
age of 65 of: £7,863

When you retire you may exchange part of your pension for cash

Chapter 13

Group personal pension schemes

In recent times, particularly since 1997, increasingly complex rules and regulations have been applied to occupational pension schemes, especially final salary schemes. The intention behind the new rules has been partly to improve the protection of scheme members (see Chapter 17), but a side effect has been to make some employers look instead to simpler, cheaper ways in which to offer their employees a pension arrangement. Group personal pension schemes (GPPSs) are an increasingly popular alternative, especially with smaller employers.

Alternative to occupational schemes

GPPSs are *not* occupational pension schemes. They are not covered by the laws relating to occupational schemes, and they are not covered by the Inland Revenue rules outlined in Chapter 10. GPPSs, as their name states, are personal pension plans offered, and often tailored, to a specific group, such as some or all of the people working for a particular firm. (They are covered by the rules and regulations detailed in Part 4 of this book.) Their status has a number of implications for scheme members:

- your employer is not obliged to pay anything into a GPPS, although many do contribute something. (This contrasts with the situation in which you arrange your own personal pension independently, when very few employers contribute anything)
- the amount that your employer pays into a GPPS on your behalf will often be a lot less than would have been paid into a final salary scheme. If you hope to build up broadly as much pension, you'll generally need to make up the difference by paying in a lot more yourself

- GPPSs work on a money purchase basis. As with all such schemes, you bear the investment risk (see Chapter 12). And with a GPPS you will generally have to make your own decisions about where to invest your contributions
- a GPPS does not automatically provide a package of benefits. Like all personal plans, the focus is on providing a pension, although the value of the pension fund will usually be paid to your dependants in the event of your death before retirement. Your employer may supplement these benefits, for example, providing life cover and/or ill-health payments from a separate scheme
- the charging structure for some GPPSs is the same as for other personal pension plans (see Chapter 21). This means that you can end up with a poor deal if you invest only small amounts, invest only for a short period or transfer to another provider. Your employer may come to some arrangement with the GPPS provider to secure a better deal on charges.

On the plus side, GPPSs are viewed as being particularly suitable for employees who work on short-term contracts and may not be able to build up reasonable benefits in traditional employers' schemes because of their frequent job moves. Because the GPPS is a personal pension plan which goes with *you* rather than a particular job, you can keep it going without any break or transfer if you change job.

Your employer may negotiate special terms with the pension provider which are particularly suitable for your type of job: for example, flexible contributions and contribution holidays if, say, your

Table 13.1: The pros and cons of group personal pension schemes

Pros	Cons
Tax advantages	Unpredictable pension and other
Employer may contribute (but does not have to)	benefits
	No guarantee that the pension will keep
Possibly, favourable terms while you're in your current job	pace with inflation during period in which it is building up
Plan continues when you change jobs	Your employer may contribute only a small amount or nothing at all
	You bear the investment risk
	You bear most or all of the charges
	Favourable terms may be lost when you change jobs

earnings tend to vary because of the availability of overtime or changes in bonuses. Such favourable terms may disappear if you cease working for your current employer.

CASE HISTORY: Doug

Doug is a programme-maker for TV. Typically, he works for broadcasting and production companies on employment contracts lasting one to three years. The main company for which he works used, at one time, to pay temporary employees a bit extra compared with permanent staff, to compensate for the fact that they received no pension benefits. More recently, it has set up a GPPS which is open to permanent and temporary employees alike (although permanent employees also have the option of joining the employer's occupational scheme).

GPPSs and stakeholder schemes

Since October 2001 employers with five or more employees must offer at least one of the following types of pension arrangement through the workplace:

- an occupational scheme
- a GPPS where, for each employee, the employer pays contributions equal to at least 3 per cent of the employee's pay, or
- a stakeholder pension scheme (Chapter 20).

Your pension on retirement

Like all money purchase schemes, the pension from a GPPS depends on a variety of factors:

- the amount, if any, paid into the scheme on your behalf by your employer. A government survey found that employers contributed to GPPS in over three-quarters of cases. Another survey of GPPSs offered by smaller employers (employing up to 250 workers) found that the employer contribution was fairly low on average, at just under 5 per cent of employee earnings
- the amount that you pay into the scheme yourself. The survey of smaller employers' GPPSs found that employees were, on average,

paying in less than 3 per cent of their earnings; this is unlikely to be enough to produce an adequate retirement income
- charges deducted from the scheme. A big slice is often taken in charges to pay commission to the financial adviser (see Chapter 22) who sets up the GPPS. Some employers arrange to pay the adviser a fee instead, which means that the charges that their employees pay are reduced
- how well the invested contributions grow
- the amount of pension that your pension fund will buy at the time when you retire. This will depend on annuity rates at that time (see Chapter 33 for more information about taking a pension from a personal plan).

CASE HISTORY: Ralph

Ralph earns £31,000 a year and belongs to a GPPS promoted at work. Ralph contributes 3 per cent of his earnings to the GPPS, and his employer adds a further 5 per cent. He has been in the GPPS for two years so far and expects to carry on with the plan until he retires in 13 years' time at age 65. By then, his pension fund is projected to have grown to £58,850, which, at present annuity rates, would mean a pension of about £4,336 a year. That's less than Ralph has worked out he needs.

Your pension if you leave before retirement

The big advantage of a GPPS is that it is linked to you rather than to your job. If you change jobs you can keep the personal plan going, although you may lose some of the terms available under the GPPS. For example, some of the charges (see Chapter 21) may be reduced when you are a GPPS member but then be increased to the normal level after you leave the shelter of the GPPS.

Any employer's contributions under the GPPS will cease when you stop working for that employer. You therefore need to consider whether your new employer will pay into it or whether you can afford to make good the lost contributions.

The decisions that you face become more complicated if the new employer offers an occupational scheme. Since 6 April 2001 you are allowed simultaneously to pay into a personal pension as well as an occupational scheme, provided you earn no more than £30,000 a year and you are not a controlling director (see Chapter 30). If you can afford it, you could carry on paying into the personal pension as well as joining your new employer's scheme. But, if you can't manage contributions to both, you'll have to choose. You'll also have to choose if you are a director or you earn more than £30,000. In most cases, an occupational scheme will be the better way in which to save for retirement. The fund that you have built up so far in the personal plan can be left to carry on growing, but check which charges will be deducted from the fund: sometimes they can eat heavily into your investment. (These complications will disappear from April 2006 when all types of pension scheme are due to be covered by a single, simplified regime – see Chapter 9.)

Alternatively, you could transfer the fund that you have built up in the personal pension to your new employer's scheme (see Chapter 25).

How the contributions are invested

With a GPPS you have the sole responsibility for deciding how the contributions are invested. The choices are just the same as for any personal pension plan (see Chapter 21).

Despite the wide choice, many people opt for managed funds, in which their contributions are invested in a broad range of investments selected by the fund manager to produce steady growth without too much risk. An extension of this option which is becoming popular, is investment in a 'lifestyle fund'. With this, the manager automatically shifts the mix of investments as you approach retirement to match your need for increasing security. For more about this, see Chapter 21.

Tax-free lump sum

GPPSs are covered by the same rules as all other personal pension plans. On retirement you can take one-quarter of the fund that has been built up (excluding any part that has been earmarked to provide contracted-out benefits, see Chapter 23) as a tax-free lump sum. The rest must be used to provide a taxable pension, as described in Chapter 19.

CASE HISTORY: Ralph

On retirement, Ralph (see above) could take one-quarter of his pension fund as a tax-free lump sum. This would mean a lump sum of $\frac{1}{4} \times £58,850 = £14,713$. He must use the remaining £44,137 to provide himself with a pension.

Figure 13.1: Example of a group personal pension plan statement

Statement date	1 January 2004
The value of your pension fund	
The value of your fund on 31 December 2003 was	£60,000
Your future pension	
The estimated value of your fund when you reach your normal retirement date is	£83,700
Using current annuity rates this would buy you a pension at age 65 of	£4,290 pa

Part of your pension at retirement may be exchanged for a lump sum.

This illustration assumes your pension once it starts to be paid will increase each year in line with inflation and when you die (whether or not you are currently married), a husband or wife will inherit half of your pension.

More information

Your employer, the pension provider or a financial adviser will be responsible for publicising the GPPS through your workplace and providing information about the scheme. If you're unsure who to contact for general information about the scheme, your Human Resources (personnel) department at work should be able to put you in touch with the right person.

The pension provider or financial adviser is responsible for advising you about the scheme and selling you a personal pension under it. There are strict rules set out in law about the information and advice that they must give you. These are the same rules that apply to all personal pension plans, which are described in Chapter 22.

If you belong to a GPPS, you'll regularly (usually once a year) receive a statement from the pension provider setting out the value of your pension fund to date. Since April 2003, the annual statement includes an illustration, in today's money, showing the amount of pension you might get at retirement assuming current contributions continue.

Once you have taken out a personal pension under a GPPS, any queries should be directed to the plan provider, not your employer. Literature about the plan should tell you who to contact. Some plan providers operate special helplines to answer your questions and provide information.

Chapter 14

Contracting out through your occupational scheme

Employees building up a state additional pension can contract out. Contracting out means giving up your state additional pension and building up a replacement pension instead through an occupational pension scheme or personal pension. The state additional pension was SERPS during the period April 1978 to April 2002 and, since April 2002, is the State Second Pension (S2P).

You can contract out using a stakeholder pension scheme to provide the replacement pension. Although the government can set different contracting-out terms for stakeholder pensions, it has not done so. Therefore, those stakeholder schemes which are personal pensions (in other words, most stakeholder schemes) are covered by the contracting-out rules in Chapter 23 relating to personal pensions. Stakeholder schemes which are occupational schemes are covered by the contracting-out rules in this chapter for occupational money purchase schemes. If you are not sure what type of stakeholder scheme applies to you, first read Chapter 20.

Contracting out means you will receive less pension at retirement from the state. Because the state will save money, it pays back part of the National Insurance contributions you and your employer are paying now. These repayments, called 'rebates', are invested in your occupational scheme or personal pension to build up the replacement pension. Whether or not contracting out is good value for you depends on the amount of state additional pension you give up, and the pension you can expect from the replacement scheme. This in turn depends on the type of scheme you use to contract out.

The state pension you give up

For an idea of the amount of state additional pension you are giving up, see Chapter 5.

Contracting out is not new. Before SERPS the government ran a state scheme called the 'graduated pension' (see page 60). You could contract out of that too and instead receive a pension from your employer's scheme.

How to contract out

In many cases, you have some choice about whether or not to contract out. But if you're an employee belonging to a contracted-out final salary occupational scheme, the choice has been made for you – the only way to rejoin S2P would be by leaving your employer scheme. That would not be worth doing just for the sake of contracting back into S2P. With a contracted-out money purchase occupational scheme, you might automatically contracted out, but some employers let individual employees choose whether or not to be contracted out.

If you belong to an occupational scheme which isn't contracted out, there are several ways in which you can contract out – and you don't have to leave your employer scheme to do so. If you're not in an occupational scheme at all, see Chapter 23. Chart 14.1 summarises your options.

How contracting out works in an occupational final salary scheme

If you're contracted out through an occupational final salary pension scheme (see Chapter 11), both you and your employer pay lower National Insurance on your earnings above the lower earnings limit. During the five years from 6 April 2002 to 5 April 2007, the rate you pay on earnings above the primary threshold (£4,745 in 2004–5) up to the upper earnings limit (£31,720 in 2004–5) is reduced by 1.6 per cent, (from 11 per cent to 9.4 per cent in 2004–5). Your employer's contribution rate is reduced by 3.5 per cent. Note that these rates apply to your actual earnings, not any earnings you are treated as having under the S2P rules. The rebate of National Insurance contributions reflects the fact that neither of you is contributing to the state additional pension during the period for which you're contracted out.

What you are promised in place of the state pension given up depends on when you contracted out.

Contracting out before 6 April 1997

During the period 6 April 1978 to 5 April 1997, contracting out meant giving up SERPS pension. For pension rights which you have built up over the period up to 5 April 1997, the occupational scheme guarantees to pay you a minimum amount of pension at retirement – a guaranteed minimum pension (GMP). It will also pay a guaranteed widow's or widower's pension – see Chapter 15. Your GMP will be broadly equal to the SERPS pension you'd otherwise have built up. But the precise amount of the GMP doesn't really matter because *you couldn't lose by contracting out through a final salary scheme in this way*. This becomes clear once you look at what happens when you retire.

At retirement, the Department for Work and Pensions (DWP) – the government department responsible for pensions – works out the

Chart 14.1: How to contract out of the state additional pension

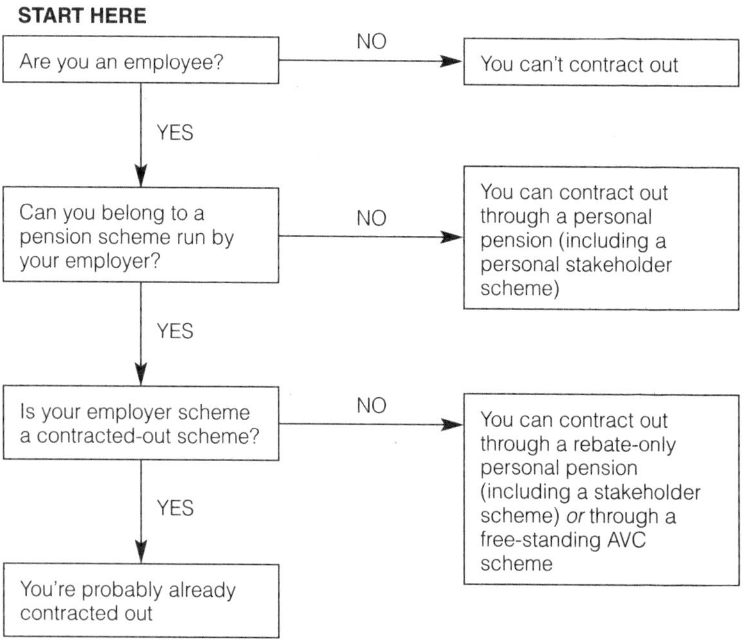

START HERE

134

full SERPS pension you would have got if you hadn't been contracted out at all. From this, it subtracts the amount of any GMPs you qualify for because of periods of contracting out. Whatever remains is the amount of SERPS pension which the state will pay you. If your GMPs are large, you'll receive only a small SERPS pension; if your GMPs are small, you'll receive a larger SERPS pension. But the GMPs plus the SERPS pension you're paid will together always equal the maximum SERPS pension you could have got without contracting out. And if your GMPs come to more than the full SERPS pension, you'll get no SERPS pension, but you'll be better off than you would have been under SERPS. A further aspect of contracting out in this way is that the DWP increases the whole pension (SERPS and GMPs) in line with inflation each year, apart from a small amount of index-linking paid by the employer scheme(s) on GMPs built up since 1988.

This system of contracting out which applied up to April 1997 meant you could not lose out and, in practice, you probably did a lot better than staying in SERPS, because most occupational final salary schemes aimed to provide pensions greater than just the GMP.

Contracting out from 6 April 1997 onwards

Contracted-out final salary pension rights built up from 6 April 1997 onwards are based on a different system. You no longer build up any GMP. Instead your employer must run a scheme which, for nine out of ten scheme members, is at least as good as a reference scheme which has been specified by the government. The main features of the reference scheme are that it must provide:

- a retirement pension at age 65 equal to one-eightieth of qualifying earnings for each year of membership since April 1997, up to a maximum pension of half average earnings. The earnings to be used in the calculation are 90 per cent of total earnings (including overtime, bonuses, etc.) above the lower earnings limit up to the upper earnings limit. Earnings for the last three years before retirement or leaving the scheme are averaged. The pension must be the same for men and for women. It can be paid before age 65, in which case it can be reduced
- a widow's or widower's pension equal to half the retirement pension built up if the scheme member dies either while working, after

retirement, or having moved on to another job while leaving the pension behind in the old employer's scheme

- annual increases to pensions, once they start to be paid, of inflation up to a maximum of 5 per cent (due to be reduced to 2.5 per cent, probably from April 2005).

The new system does not mean that every scheme has to provide pensions which are identical to those of the reference scheme, but whatever benefits are provided must be at least equivalent to the reference scheme benefits. Each scheme has to have a certificate from an actuary saying that its benefits are sufficient to pass the contracting-out test.

The switch from GMPs to the reference-scheme test changed the nature of contracting out. The reference scheme might produce

---

CASE HISTORY: Tessa

Tessa earns £50,000 a year and belongs to an occupational final salary scheme. It is a contracted-out scheme providing one-sixtieth of final salary for each year of membership payable from the age of 60; the option to swap part of the pension for a lump sum; a widower's pension of two-thirds of Tessa's pension in the event of her death before or after retirement; and pension increases, once they start to be paid, in line with inflation up to 7 per cent a year.

These benefits comfortably exceed the 'reference scheme' benefits (even if the maximum pension is swapped for a lump sum), so the scheme meets the conditions for contracting out.

Tessa reckons that this form of contracting out works to her advantage because:

- the pensionable salary used as the basis for the pension and other benefits is her whole salary. SERPS pensions and S2P do not take account of earnings above the upper earnings limit
- her pension and other benefits from the scheme should be a good deal better than a SERPS or S2P pension would have been. Even though she must pay 5 per cent of her salary into the scheme (which is 3.4 per cent more than she saves through the National Insurance rebate), the scheme seems good value.

---

benefits which are as good as or better than the additional pension given up. But it might produce worse benefits, and there is no longer any guarantee that the state will make good the shortfall.

Additional rules for contracting out from 6 April 2002 onwards

From 6 April 2002 onwards, you contract out of S2P rather than SERPS. The pensions provided by S2P for people on low to moderate earnings are higher than the pensions previously provided by SERPS (see Chapter 5). However, contracting out through a final salary scheme still works in the way described above, with the occupational scheme providing benefits at least as good as the reference scheme for most members. Asking low to moderate earners to give up an increased state pension but accept only the same pension from the occupational scheme would make contracting out fairly unattractive. To ensure that

Table 14.1: Contracting out through a final salary scheme

	Contracted-out rights built up before 6 April 1997	Contracted-out rights built up from 6 April 1997 onwards
Type of benefits you build up	Guaranteed minimum pensions (GMPs)	Pensions at least as good as those from a 'reference scheme'
Relationship to SERPS	GMPs plus remaining SERPS always equal the SERPS you would have got if you had not contracted out	None. You give up SERPS pension completely
Relationship to S2P	N/A	Low to moderate earners: you give up part of your S2P completely but still build up some residual S2P Higher earners: you give up S2P completely
Who pays pension increases	Mainly the state	The scheme
Can you lose by contracting out?	No	Possibly, though risk is small

people still have an incentive to contract out, the government introduced some special rules.

People earning less than the Band 3 threshold (£26,600 in 2004–5) – see Chapter 5 – will continue to build up some residual S2P pension even when they are contracted out. This means, at retirement, as well as getting a contracted-out pension from their occupational scheme, they will also get some S2P pension from the state. The amount of S2P they get will be less than they would have got had they not been contracted out.

For people earning between the lower earnings limit and the low earnings threshold (£4,108 and £11,600 in 2004–5), their residual SERPS pension will be based on the difference between their actual earnings and the low earnings threshold. For people earning more than the low earnings threshold up to the Band 3 threshold (£11,601 to £26,600), their residual S2P will be based on the difference between the SERPS pension they would have had if SERPS had not been abolished and the S2P they would have had if they had not contracted out.

There are no special rules for people on earnings above the Band 3 threshold (£26,600 in 2004–5) because, for them, S2P is the same as the SERPS pension they would have got had SERPS not been abolished. This means they are giving up the same amount of additional pension as they would have done under SERPS in exchange for the contracted-out pension from the occupational scheme.

Who takes over from the state?

Your employer is ultimately responsible for ensuring that enough is paid into the occupational scheme to provide the GMPs or post-April 1997 benefits, and any additional benefits promised under the scheme rules.

If the scheme is a contributory one, you will pay something towards the cost as well. But this cost forms part of your normal contributions to the scheme. These will usually be paid at a pre-set percentage of your salary (see Chapter 11). It is your employer, not you, who bears the risks of contracting out in this way. Your employer must pay extra into the scheme if the cost of providing the guaranteed benefits rises (for example, because the pension-fund investments do badly).

How contracting out works in an occupational money purchase scheme

Contracting out through an occupational money purchase scheme (see Chapter 12) – sometimes called a COMP – works quite differently. You and your employer still both pay lower National Insurance on your earnings above the lower earnings limit. But the employer scheme doesn't make any guarantees about the amount of pension it will pay you to replace the state additional pension you'd otherwise have been building up. Instead, your employer is required to guarantee that he or she will pay a set amount into the scheme which will be left to build up a fund.

The amount invested is equal to the amounts that you and your employer have saved by paying lower National Insurance – in other words, the rebate. The fund which builds up must be used to provide you with a set of benefits called your 'protected rights'. These comprise:

- a retirement pension which can be paid from age 60 onwards
- a pension for your widow or widower if you die before retirement
- a pension for your widow or widower if you die after retirement equal to half the pension that you were getting. From 6 April 1997 onwards, however, if you are single at the time when you retire you can opt for a larger pension for yourself, with no widow's or widower's pension
- increases to pensions once they start to be paid (see page 145). However, the government is proposing to remove the requirement for pension increases, probably from April 2005.

No part of the fund used to provide protected rights can be taken as a lump sum, although if more than just the National Insurance rebate is paid into the pension scheme a tax-free lump sum can be funded from the extra amount which builds up. (This rule ceases to apply from April 2006 when, under the new simplified regime – see Chapter 9 – up to a quarter of pension savings, whatever the source, can be taken as tax-free cash.)

Protected-rights benefits build up on a money purchase basis. So, as with all money purchase schemes, the amount of pension that you'll receive depends on:

- the amount invested: in other words, the amount of the National Insurance rebate
- charges deducted from the scheme. Some employers pay the administration costs separately, instead of them being deducted from the amount invested
- how well the invested rebates grow
- the rate (the annuity rate) at which the pension fund can be converted into pension. The annuity rate used for protected rights must be the same for both men and women; this is called a 'unisex annuity rate'.

How contracting out through a money purchase scheme will affect your pension prospects depends on the periods for which you have contracted out.

Contracting out before 6 April 1997

Contracting out through an employer's money purchase scheme first became possible in April 1988. From then up to 5 April 1997 the amount of the National Insurance rebate which an employer was required to invest for protected rights was a flat amount that was the same for everyone (see Table 14.2).

Where you have built up protected rights over this period, on your retirement the DWP works out the full SERPS pension that you would

Table 14.2: National Insurance rebate to be invested in a contracted-out money purchase (COMP) scheme

	National Insurance rebate as percentage of earnings between the lower and upper earnings limits	
	Each year from 1988–9 to 1992–3	Each year from 1993–4 to 1996–7
Rebate of employer's National Insurance	3.8%	3.0%
Rebate of your National Insurance	2.0%	1.8%
Total that employer was required to invest for protected rights benefits (in a contributory scheme, you might pay some of this)	5.8%	4.8%

have built up had you not contracted out at all. It then subtracts the GMPs that you would have built up if you had contracted out during this period through a final salary scheme instead of a money purchase scheme. The amount subtracted is called the 'notional GMP', and it may be more or less than the protected-rights pension that you actually receive from the contracted-out money purchase scheme. Whatever (if anything) is left after subtracting the notional GMP is the amount of SERPS pension that you'll get from the state.

Contracting out from 6 April 1997 onwards

Before 6 April 1997 National Insurance rebates were the same for everyone. But these flat-rate rebates were far more valuable to young people: their rebates would be invested for a long time and would thus produce a much bigger pension than the same rebates paid to older people, which could be invested for only a short time. As a result there was an age threshold below which contracting out seemed to represent a good deal for many people, because the protected-rights pension was likely to grow to be much bigger than the SERPS that had been given up. Above the threshold, though, it made sense for everyone to stay in SERPS, because the rebate was too small to generate enough pension to replace fully the SERPS that had been given up.

From 1997 the government tackled this problem by introducing age-related rebates. The older you are, the larger the rebate that must be invested to provide your protected rights. This makes contracting out attractive for a lot more people. However, the rebates do still flatten out at older ages, so there remains a threshold at which contracting out definitely starts to look unattractive. However, age is not the only factor. With only a modest outlook for investment returns and increasing longevity pushing down annuity rates, in 2004 many experts felt that at all ages – even if you are in your 20s or 30s – the rebates do not look large enough to give a reasonable chance of replacing the S2P benefits given up. Therefore, they were suggesting that most people would be better off staying in or returning to S2P rather than contracting out. But, if you are in a contracted-out money purchase scheme, you need to check whether you could return to the state scheme without leaving your occupational scheme. If you had to leave the scheme, you might well lose more in other benefits than you would gain from rejoining S2P.

Table 14.3 shows the age-related rebates at selected ages which your employer must pay into the contracted-out money purchase scheme to provide your protected rights. If the scheme is contributory, you may be required to pay part of this sum.

From April 1997 onwards the link between your contracted-out pension and state additional pension is completely broken. For rights built up from then, there are no longer any sums due on retirement involving notional GMPs. The position is now much simpler: while you are contracted out you completely give up all – or sometimes, part (see below) – of your state additional pension.

Additional rules for contracting out from 6 April 2002 onwards

From 6 April 2002 onwards, you contract out of S2P rather than SERPS. The pensions provided by S2P for people on low to moderate earnings are higher than the pensions previously provided by SERPS (see Chapter 5). However (mainly to avoid additional complications for the

Table 14.3: National Insurance rebate to be invested in a contracted-out money purchase scheme

Age on last day (5 April) of preceding tax year	Rebates as percentage of earnings between the lower and upper earnings limits		
	2004–5	2005–6	2006–7
15	2.6%	2.6%	2.6%
20	2.8%	2.8%	2.8%
25	3.1%	3.1%	3.1%
30	3.4%	3.4%	3.4%
35	3.8%	3.8%	3.8%
40	4.2%	4.2%	4.2%
45	5.0%	4.9%	4.8%
50	7.1%	6.4%	5.9%
55	10.5%	10.5%	10.5%
60	10.5%	10.3%	9.9%
61 or over	10.5%	10.5%	10.5%

administrators of occupational schemes), the contracting-out rebates have not been increased to take this into account. Asking low to moderate earners to give up an increased state pension but accept only broadly the same contribution to the occupational scheme would make contracting out fairly unattractive. To ensure that people still have an incentive to contract out, the government has introduced some special rules.

People earning less than the Band 3 threshold (£26,600 in 2004–5) will continue to build up some residual S2P pension even when they are contracted out. This means, at retirement, as well as getting a contracted-out pension from their occupational scheme, they will also get some S2P pension from the state. The amount of S2P they get will be less than they would have got had they not been contracted out.

For people earning between the lower earnings limit and the low earnings threshold (£4,108 and £11,600 in 2004–5), their residual S2P will be based on the difference between their actual earnings and the low earnings threshold. For people earning more than the low earnings threshold up to the Band 3 threshold (£11,601 to £26,600), their residual S2P will be based on the difference between the SERPS pension they would have had if SERPS had not been abolished and the S2P they would have had if they had not contracted out.

There are no special rules for people on earnings above the Band 3 threshold (£26,600 in 2004–5).

Who takes over from the state?

The onus is on your employer to invest the amount of the National Insurance rebates, but it is you who bears the risk of ending up with a lower pension than the S2P you give up. This is because, if your invested fund grows well, and annuity rates are favourable when you come to retire, contracting out through an employer money purchase scheme may mean that you end up with more pension than you would have done had you stayed in the state additional scheme. But, if your invested fund does badly, and annuity rates are low when you retire, you may find with hindsight that you'd have been better off staying in the state scheme. You take a gamble.

In practice, COMP schemes have proved complicated to run, and some employers have found it easier to encourage those employees who want to contract out to do so via a personal pension plan – see Chapter 23.

CASE HISTORY: Paul

Paul is 25. In May 2004 he starts work in the marketing department of a firm making office equipment on a salary of £16,000 a year. The firm has recently set up a COMP scheme which Paul has decided to join. Until now, he's made no savings for retirement apart from contributions to the state basic and S2P pensions through paying National Insurance.

To work out whether Paul's decision is a good one, various assumptions need to be made about his future earnings, future investment returns and future annuity rates.

If Paul did not contract out in 2004–5, he might build up around £70 a year of S2P in today's money. Like all state pensions, assuming current rules still apply, this would be increased each year once it started to be paid in line with inflation.

If Paul contracts out, a rebate of 3.1 per cent of his earnings between the LEL and UEL must be invested in the COMP scheme (see Table 14.3). This comes to 3.1% × (£16,000 − £4,108) = £369. If the £369 is invested and grows by 5 per cent a year, it could become £2,598 by age 65. Assuming inflation of 2.5 per cent a year, this would be worth £967 in today's money. How much pension could Paul buy with £967? Although the government is proposing that he will not have to buy an index-linked pension, bear in mind that the S2P he gives up would be index-linked. To compare like with like, assume Paul buys an annuity which will increase in line with prices up to 2.5 per cent a year and which provides a half-pension for his widow. In 2004, he could get about £390 a year of such pension for each £10,000 of pension fund, giving him a starting pension of £967 × £390 / £10,000 = £38 a year. If, instead of 5 per cent, his investment grew by 7 per cent a year, he could get a pension of about £80 a year.

In addition, Paul will also build up some residual S2P of around £21 a year even if he is contracted out. So contracting out might give him a pension of between £59 and £101 a year. Staying in S2P might give him £70 a year.

The decision is not clear-cut. If Paul is optimistic about stock-market returns, he should probably contract out. If he is cautious, he should probably stay contracted in – however, the occupational scheme might offer additional benefits that outweigh any potential loss from contracting out.

Personal pension plans

If your employer's pension scheme is not contracted out of the state scheme, you can opt to contract out on your own through a special personal pension called a 'rebate-only plan'. Details of contracting out in this way are given in Chapter 23.

If you belong to a group personal pension scheme (GPPS) offered by your employer you have your own personal pension plan. Usually it is up to you to decide whether you want to contract out, using a rebate-only plan that is technically separate from your main personal plan (see Chapter 23).

Free-standing AVC schemes

If you belong to an employer scheme that is not contracted out you can contract out independently using a free-standing additional voluntary contribution (FSAVC) scheme (see Chapter 30), instead of a personal pension. But, in practice, you'll usually do better to choose the personal pension route, because a quirk in the tax rules means that the DWP pays less into a contracted-out free-standing AVC scheme than it pays into a contracted-out personal pension.

Pension increases

After retirement, state additional pensions are increased each year in line with changes in the Retail Prices Index. If you're contracted out, the state used to continue to provide the full increase required to keep your state pension and GMPs growing in line with inflation. But this has now changed:

- for people retiring from April 1990 onwards, contracted-out occupational pensions built up over the period 6 April 1988 to 5 April 1997 must be increased by the scheme at a rate of 3 per cent a year, or by the rate of inflation if this is less. Contracted-out personal pensions built up between 1 July 1988 and 5 April 1997 must also be increased in this way. Because of the link with SERPS, the state then tops this up, so the pensions are completely (or nearly completely) inflation-proofed

- for pension rights built up from 6 April 1997 onwards, the total pension from a contracted-out occupational scheme must be increased by inflation up to a maximum of 5 per cent a year (due to be reduced to 2.5 per cent a year in the case of salary-related schemes – probably from 2005). The state no longer tops this up, and it is up to the scheme whether it makes any further increases. Note that no distinction is made between the contracted-out part of the pension and any extra amount. However, pension you build up through making AVCs or FSAVCs does not have to be increased at all. The protected rights pension from a contracted-out personal plan must also be increased by inflation up to 5 per cent a year – but not any pension you've built up in addition to the contracted-out element.

At the time of writing, new legislation was making its way through Parliament. Assuming it becomes law, compulsory pension increases for money purchase occupational pensions (whether contracted-out or not) will be abolished for pensions that start to be paid on or after a future date – likely to be April 2005. Note that this change affects pensions starting to be *paid* after the effective date not simply pensions built up after that date, so the rules outlined above will cease to apply to any part of your pension fund. Where, as is usual, your pension fund is used to buy an annuity, it will generally be up to you to choose whether or not to include any inflation-proofing. See Chapter 33 for guidance on making this choice.

More information

If you are unsure about your contracted-out status or the options open to you, get in touch with your pension-scheme administrator at work. If you're not sure who this is, ask the Human Resources (personnel) department.

Table 14.4: Free guides about contracting out

Reference	Title	From
PM7	Contracted-out pensions – your guide	Department for Work and Pensions*
	Contracting out of the state second pension	Financial Services Authority*

The contracted-out pension rights that you can expect from an occupational scheme are part of the total benefits from the scheme. They are automatically included in the figures shown in the benefit statements that you'll get. You do not need to take separate account of the contracted-out rights.

Any pension forecast from the state should take into account those periods when you have been, or are, contracted out.

Chapter 15

Other benefits from your occupational scheme

An occupational pension scheme (but not a group personal pension scheme or personal stakeholder scheme) usually automatically provides you with a package of benefits, not just a pension on retirement. Typically, these additional benefits include:

- lump-sum life cover and dependants' pensions if you die before retirement
- dependants' pensions if you die after retirement
- replacement income if you have to give up work early because of illness or disability
- a pension if you retire earlier than the normal retirement age for your scheme.

Like the retirement pension itself, these benefits are subsidised, because your employer pays some or all of the cost of providing them, and you get tax relief on any contributions that you make towards them.

Protecting your financial position in case of illness and, if you have a partner or family, providing them with security in the event of death are two of the most basic financial goals that everyone should have. The protection provided through your employer's pension scheme will help you to meet these goals.

A detailed analysis of your protection goals is outside the scope of this book. Briefly, you need to take the following steps:

- work out your income and/or lump-sum spending needs in the event of death or illness
- check what help you could get from the state (see Chapter 6)
- check what help you could get from any occupational pension schemes

- check what existing insurance cover and savings you could draw on
- arrange extra protection if there is a shortfall between your needs and the available income and lump sums. See Chapter 30 for how you may be able to do this through your occupational pension scheme or other pension arrangements.

For more information about protection planning, see *Be Your Own Financial Adviser* and *The Which? Guide to Insurance*, both published by Which? Books★. Here we outline the help you may get from an occupational pension scheme.

Death before retirement

If you belong to an occupational pension scheme, your dependants will almost certainly be entitled to benefits which are payable in the event of your death before retirement. These will usually take the form of:

- lump-sum life insurance
- sometimes a refund of your contributions to the pension scheme
- a pension for your widow or widower
- possibly pensions for your children or other dependants.

Some employers have schemes to provide some or all of these benefits even for employees who are not covered by a pension scheme run by the employer.

How much as a lump sum?

You get tax relief on the amount of money paid into the scheme to provide life cover, so naturally enough the Inland Revenue also sets limits on the amount of cover which can be provided in this way.

The general rule is that the maximum lump sum that can be paid out in the event of death must not be greater than four times the employee's final salary just before, or near, the time of death. There is also an overall cash limit on the amount of life cover for people covered by the 'post-1989 regime' for employer pensions (see Chapter 10). In the 2004–5 tax year, this limit is £408,000. This cash limit is usually increased each year in line with the Retail Prices Index. Life insurance payable from previous pension schemes and plans that you had counts towards the Inland Revenue maximum, unless the current scheme provides a lump sum of no more than twice your final salary, in which case life insurance from previous arrangements can be ignored.

The tax rules also allow the amount of your (but not your employer's) contributions to the pension scheme to be paid out as a lump sum, in addition to the main amount of cover described above. In some cases, interest is added to the repayment of contributions. The employer scheme can set its own limit, which may be lower than those set by the Inland Revenue.

In most schemes, the scheme trustees (see Chapter 17) have the right to decide who will receive the lump sum in the event of your death. (This enables the scheme administrator to make a payment quickly, without having to wait for probate. It also prevents the lump sum being counted as part of your estate for inheritance tax purposes.) In practice, the scheme will usually pay the money to whomever you have nominated on an 'expression of wish' form, though it would probably override your wishes if you'd failed to name someone – your young child, say – who had been genuinely dependent on you. You should review your expression of wish whenever your circumstances change – say, on marriage, or the birth of a child.

Problems can arise if you don't fill in an expression of wish form. In that case, the trustees would most likely pay the lump sum to your widow or widower or anyone else who was clearly dependent on you. But they might refuse to pay an unmarried partner (for example, if the trustees were unable to satisfy themselves that the partner really was in a relationship with you). In that situation, the trustees would normally instead pay the money over to your personal representatives. The lump sum would then form part of your estate and so possibly become subject to inheritance tax and delays in being paid out in accordance with your will or the intestacy rules.

Same-sex partners

Since 1 December 2003, it has become illegal for employers to discriminate on the grounds of sexual orientation. As a result, where a pension scheme pays death benefits to unmarried partners, a same-sex partner must be given the same rights as a partner of the opposite sex.

How much widow's or widower's pension?

Inland Revenue rules also limit the amount that can be paid out in pensions to a widow or widower and other dependants. The general rule is that a widow's or widower's pension must not be greater than two-thirds of the maximum pension that the employee could have had. 'Maximum' means the maximum according to the tax rules – in other words, based on the Inland Revenue definition of final salary and the number of years that the employee could have been in the scheme (or in that employment) had he or she remained in the scheme until normal retirement. If you are covered by the 'post-1989 regime' there is also an overall cash limit on the widow's or widower's pension. The limit is two-thirds of £68,000 for the 2004–5 tax year: that is, £45,333 if you would have qualified for the maximum pension. The limit is usually increased each year in line with the Retail Prices Index. Table 15.1 gives a guide to the maximum pension your widow or widower could receive depending on your salary.

The Inland Revenue's limit usually applies to the sum of benefits from all schemes or plans to which you had belonged. So widow's or

Table 15.1: The maximum widow's or widower's pension from an occupational scheme [1]

Your earnings from the employer £ per year	Maximum widow's or widower's pension £ per year
10,000	4,444
15,000	6,667
20,000	8,889
25,000	11,111
30,000	13,333
40,000	17,778
50,000	22,222
60,000	26,667
70,000	31,111
80,000	35,556
90,000	40,000
100,000	44,444

[1] If you joined the pension scheme on or after 17 March 1987, you must have been able to work for the employer for 20 years up to the time you would normally have retired for the maximum widow's pension to be payable. If you joined before 17 March 1987, 10 years' service is sufficient.

widower's pensions payable from schemes which you had belonged to in the past must generally be taken into account when working out the most that your current scheme could pay.

Once the upper limit on the widow's or widower's pension has been found, it can be increased yearly in line with the Retail Prices Index. This provides a ceiling within which the actual pension must remain. Most schemes increase widow's or widower's pensions by less than the maximum that tax rules allow.

If you were contracted out through your employer pension scheme before 6 April 1997 and it was a final salary scheme, your widow's pension must include a guaranteed minimum pension (GMP of at least half the amount of GMP you had built up (see Chapter 14), provided your widow is 45 or over, or has dependent children. There are special rules concerning increases to GMPs once they have started to be paid (see page 145).

For periods of contracting out through a final salary scheme on or after 6 April 1997, the whole widow's or widower's pension available from the scheme must be at least as good as that under a reference scheme. Broadly, it will have to at least match one-half of the retirement pension for which the scheme member would have qualified. This widow's or widower's pension must be increased in line with inflation up to 5 per cent a year (due to be reduced to 2.5 per cent a year) once it starts to be paid.

If you were contracted out through an employer money purchase scheme, the whole of your protected-rights 'fund' – see page 139 – must be converted into pension for your widow or widower.

A scheme can set its own limit on the pension it will pay provided it doesn't break the legal limit – many pay less than the Inland Revenue maximum, especially where the scheme rules have changed over the years, so you need to check your own scheme's rules and your entitlement under them. The scheme rules will also determine whether a widow's or widower's pension is payable for life – usually it is. But some schemes either stop paying, or review the position, if the widow or widower remarries.

Pension for other dependants

A widow's or widower's pension is usually paid automatically to your wife or husband, and most occupational schemes allow for the pension to be paid to someone else at the discretion of the trustees. If the trustees decide there are no eligible survivors to receive it, the money remains within the pension scheme. Often, you will be invited to complete an expression of wish form, but this will not be followed automatically because Inland Revenue rules and the scheme's own rules must be followed. In 1996 Inland Revenue rules changed to allow survivors' pensions to be paid where there was 'financial interdependency' between a scheme member and a partner rather than the previous more narrowly drawn rule that required 'financial dependency'. Interdependency allows for a situation where the survivor's standard of living depended on the joint income of the couple prior to the scheme member's death.

Pensions can also be paid to other dependants, such as children, in addition to any amount paid to a widow, widower or partner. Any one pension can't be more than two-thirds of the maximum retirement pension you could have had – this is the same as the limit applied to the widow's or widower's pension (see above).

Furthermore, all the dependants' pensions – whether for your widow or widower, partner, a child or children or some other dependant, such as an elderly relative – when added together must not come to more than the maximum amount which could have been paid to you as retirement pension.

A pension for a dependent child must cease when the child stops being dependent – for example, when the child reaches age 18, or when he or she finishes full-time education. Pensions for other dependants can continue for the rest of their lives, even if they cease to be dependent in the literal sense of the word.

Death after retirement

An employer pension scheme may also provide help for dependants in the event of your death after retirement. This can take a number of forms:

- a separate widow's or widower's pension
- pension for other dependants
- guaranteed payments of your own pension for a set number of years, if you die within that time
- possibly, a lump sum.

How much widow's or widower's pension?

As with pensions payable on death before retirement, the Inland Revenue limits the maximum pension that can be automatically provided for a widow or widower. The limit is two-thirds of the maximum retirement pension to which you could have been entitled. 'Maximum' relates to the taxman's definition of final salary, though the calculation is based on the *actual* number of years you have worked for your employer. Once it starts to be paid, the widow's or widower's pension can be increased as long as it does not exceed the maximum possible pension increased in line with changes in the Retail Prices Index.

If you're contracted out of the State Earnings Related Pension Scheme (SERPS) in the period up to 6 April 1997 through a final salary scheme, the scheme must provide a widow's pension of at least half the GMP (see page Chapter 14) that you have built up. Since 6 April 1988, there must also be provision for a GMP to be paid to widowers, provided you are receiving a state basic pension and your husband is getting either a basic pension or a state invalidity pension. There are special rules concerning increases in GMPs once they start to be paid (see page 145).

Once again, for periods of contracting out on a final salary basis from 6 April 1997 onwards, the widow's or widower's pension must be at least as good as that from a reference scheme, which requires it to be at least half of the retirement pension for which the member would have qualified.

If you were contracted out through a money purchase scheme, the protected rights must normally include a widow's or widower's pension of half the amount you had been getting in protected-rights retirement pension (see page 139).

The scheme can set its own limit on the widow's or widower's pension, and one-half of the employee's retirement pension is commonly used in final salary schemes. In many schemes, the widow's or widower's pension is based on the employee's potential retirement pension *before* any deduction is made to take account of the employee taking a tax-free lump sum (see Chapter 33).

Most large schemes pay the widow's or widower's pension for life, though some stop the pension, or review it, if the widow or widower remarries. With some schemes, you can increase the pension that your widow or widower would get by giving up part of your retirement pension – you make this decision at the time you retire. The total widow's pension (including any amount provided automatically under the scheme) must not come to more than your remaining retirement pension.

A further point to note is that a GMP is payable to a widow or widower regardless of whether the marriage took place before or after retirement. However, most employer schemes provide non-GMP pensions only for a widow or widower to whom you were married *at the time you retired* – it is not usually possible to add this benefit later if you marry after retirement.

CASE HISTORY: Joan

Joan's husband, Len, had a pension of £14,000 a year from his occupational scheme. When Len died, under the scheme rules, Joan was entitled to a pension of half of Len's entitlement but only in respect of the pension he had built up in the last 13 years of his 22 years with the employer (because the scheme had not offered any family benefits during the earlier years). Instead of getting a widow's pension of around £7,000 a year from the scheme, Joan was advised that she would get only £4,800.

Pensions for other dependants

The scheme can provide pensions for other dependants, such as an unmarried partner, children or elderly relatives. See page 152 for details of who might be eligible. No one pension can exceed two-thirds of the maximum retirement pension you could have had; and all dependants' pensions (including a widow's or widower's pension) must not, in total, come to more than the full amount of retirement pension you could have had.

Children's pensions are payable only until they cease to be dependent – say, on reaching age 18 or ceasing full-time education. Other dependants' pensions can be payable for life.

Guaranteed payment of your own pension

Your retirement pension is, of course, payable throughout your life, but it would not necessarily stop if you died soon after retirement. An employer pension scheme, in theory, can guarantee to pay your retirement pension for up to ten years, in case your death occurs before that time is up. In practice, other rules make a ten-year guarantee impractical for most schemes. But a five-year guarantee is both practical and in use in many employer schemes.

Usually, the scheme has the right to decide who should receive your pension if, after your death, it continues to be paid for the rest of a guarantee period. But, in practice, your request will usually be respected. Often, the guaranteed pension is 'rolled up' and paid immediately as a lump sum (see below). If your widow or widower is to receive periodic payments of the guaranteed pension, it will usually be paid alongside any dependant's pension she or he receives.

A lump sum

If you retire at the normal retirement date for your scheme, your employer usually won't provide you with life cover after retirement. However, if your death occurred relatively soon after retirement, the scheme might pay out a lump sum if the payment of your pension had been guaranteed (as described above), or if you'd received less in pension than the amount you'd contributed to the scheme over the years. Such a lump-sum payment is generally paid free of tax.

Early retirement due to ill-health

There are no Inland Revenue limits on the age at which you can start to receive your pension if you have to retire through ill-health. You don't have to be completely incapable of work to qualify for an ill-health pension – your health may be considered sufficiently bad if it prevents you pursuing your normal work, or if it seriously reduces the amount that you can earn. Each occupational scheme will usually set its own conditions, which may be more rigorous than the Inland Revenue rules, and the scheme will normally require medical evidence of your condition.

The tax limits on the amount of pension you can receive are much more generous than those that apply to early retirement for other reasons. The pension and other benefits must not be more than the amounts you could have had if you'd carried on working until normal retirement age (see Chapter 10) but based on your final salary at the time you have to give up work.

An employer scheme will usually set its own limits on the level of ill-health pension and related benefits, which may restrict the amounts to less than the maximum allowed by the Inland Revenue.

The rules regarding contracted-out pensions from employers' schemes (see above) also apply in the case of retirement due to ill-health.

CASE HISTORY: Ken

Ken is 55 and is having to retire early due to heart problems. The normal retirement age for his occupational scheme is 65. It's a final salary scheme paying a pension of one-sixtieth of final salary for each year of membership. Ken has been a member for 30 years and his final salary is £40,000.

Under the Inland Revenue rules regarding retirement due to ill-health the maximum pension which Ken can have is:

- **pension** $\frac{40}{60}$ × £40,000 = £26,667 a year (reduced if a lump sum is taken)
- **lump sum** $\frac{120}{80}$ × £40,000 = £60,000.

In practice, the scheme sets the benefits below the tax limits. It would pay an ill-health pension of £16,667. Under the scheme rules, part of this could be given up for a maximum lump sum of £38,000.

If you were severely ill, and not expected to live for long, the whole of the pension could be converted into a lump sum. There would be a tax charge at a rate of 20 per cent on the part which could not already be taken as a tax-free lump sum.

Choosing to retire early

For schemes set up before 14 March 1989, the tax rules normally prohibit an employer pension scheme from paying you a full pension before the normal retirement age for the scheme. For these schemes the earliest normal retirement age allowed by the Inland Revenue is either 55 or 60, depending on when the scheme was set up or when you joined it (see Chapter 10). But, in practice, most schemes set their normal retirement age later than this. In the past it was common for schemes to adopt the same ages as for the state scheme – i.e. 60 for women and 65 for men – but, to avoid illegal sex discrimination, schemes must now have equal pension ages. The most common age is now 65; the second most common is 60. The normal pension age for a scheme will usually match the normal retirement age for your employment (as set out in your contract of employment).

Under the tax rules for most pre-March 1989 schemes, the earliest age at which any pension can start to be paid is 50 for men and 45 for women (provided that the woman is within ten years of normal retirement age). However, this is due to be increased to age 55 from 2010. If you retire voluntarily before the normal age for your scheme, the tax rules say that your pension, and other benefits, must be scaled down. Broadly, your pension must not exceed one-sixtieth of your final pay for each year you've worked and the lump sum must not exceed three-eightieths – but there are alternative formulae that can be used. If you are considering early retirement, don't rely on guesswork. Ask your pension scheme to give you a statement showing how much pension you will get. If you want to check on the Inland Revenue rules (for example, because you have scope to bargain with your employer for a better pension), see the Inland Revenue manual IR12 available on the Inland Revenue* website. You should also be able to consult a reference copy at your local tax office.

The Inland Revenue rules, however, merely set a ceiling on benefits. In practice, most schemes pay less generous pensions, and other benefits, to people who choose early retirement. In particular, the scheme is likely to make a reduction (called an 'actuarial reduction') to reflect the fact that the pension will probably be paid for a longer period than a pension starting at the normal retirement age. Employers sometimes offer more generous terms where early retirement is at the request of the employer rather than being your independent decision.

If the scheme you belong to is contracted out, there are further complications. A final salary scheme is under an obligation to pay you a GMP from state pension age in respect of periods of contracting out prior to 6 April 1997. There is no provision in the rules for paying a reduced GMP from an earlier age. This does not pose any difficulty as long as your early retirement pension is at least as high as the GMP that must start to be paid when you reach state pension age. But, if your early retirement pension is lower than the GMP, the scheme would have to increase your pension once you reached state pension age.

Some schemes are happy to do that, though they might further reduce your early retirement pension to cover the cost of increasing it later on. Other schemes don't allow early retirement in this situation.

For post-April 1997 pensions from contracted-out final salary schemes, there is no problem – the contracting-out rules do allow the contracted-out pension to be paid early at a rate which is reduced to take account of the longer period for which it will be paid.

You can start to receive a protected-rights pension from an occupational money purchase scheme from age 60 onwards.

Chapter 16

Transferring out of your occupational scheme

There are various reasons why you might leave an occupational pension scheme before retirement:

- you are leaving the employer in order to take up a job with another employer or to become self-employed
- you are staying in the same job but are switching to an alternative pension arrangement run by your employer. This may be because, for example, your employer has just set up a money purchase scheme or a group personal pension scheme (GPPS) and wants to encourage members of an older, final salary scheme to switch from it
- you are staying in the same job and have independently taken the decision to switch to another new pension arrangement. (Be very careful before going down this path: you may be giving up valuable benefits which you cannot afford to replace)
- the scheme is being wound up, and you must transfer your pension rights elsewhere
- you stopped paying into the scheme some time ago but now have the opportunity to transfer to a better arrangement, for example, a new employer's occupational scheme.

If you leave an occupational pension scheme and you've been a member of it for two years or more, the scheme *must* either provide you with a pension at retirement – called a preserved or deferred pension – or allow you to transfer your pension rights to another pension scheme or plan. However, the new scheme or plan, unless it is a stakeholder scheme, is not required to accept a transfer from another scheme.

Taking a refund

If you leave a scheme that you've belonged to for less than two years, currently you're not automatically entitled to any pension rights at all. More likely, you'll get a refund of your contributions if it was a contributory scheme. You can have back only contributions which you paid *yourself* – not any contributions paid on your behalf by your employer. The trustees of the scheme have to hand over to the Inland Revenue tax on your refund, and usually the amount of the tax will be deducted from what you get. From the 1988–9 tax year onwards, the tax is paid at a special rate of 20 per cent (10 per cent in earlier years). If you're a non-taxpayer, you can't reclaim the tax; on the other hand, if you *are* a taxpayer, there's no more tax to pay. From 2006, new laws will require you to be given a choice on leaving within two years of either a refund of your contributions or a transfer value that you can pay into another scheme or plan – see Chapter 9. The advantage of a transfer value is that it reflects the contributions also paid by your employer so you do not lose the benefit of these.

There may also be a deduction – usually quite large – if you had been contracted out of the State Earnings Related Pension Scheme (SERPS) prior to 6 April 1997 through the occupational scheme. The scheme may arrange to 'buy you back' into the state scheme for the period you had been contracted out. The scheme has to pay over a sum of money – called the contributions equivalent premium – to the state, and part of this amount will be subtracted from your refund. The deduction is made before tax on the refund is worked out.

For periods of contracting-out on or after 6 April 1997, it is no longer possible to buy yourself back into SERPS on leaving a scheme, except in very limited circumstances: for example, if you have been in the scheme for less than two years but do not qualify for a refund of contributions because the scheme is non-contributory.

Your refund might include interest on your contributions – though often at a very modest rate.

The tax rules let you have a refund of contributions that you made before 6 April 1975 regardless of how long you've been a member of your occupational pension scheme, but this is unlikely to be a wise move in view of the pension rights you'd lose.

Leaving your pension behind

If you've been in an occupational scheme (see Chapters 11 and 12) for two years or more, when you leave, the scheme must provide you with a preserved pension, or let you transfer your pension rights to another pension scheme or plan.

Chapters 11 and 12 described the pension that you can expect on retirement if you leave your pension rights in the scheme. There are further guarantees that the scheme must make to you if you were contracted out.

Contracted-out pension rights

If you're contracted out through a final salary scheme which you then leave, the scheme is obliged to protect your contracted-out pension rights. How this is done depends on the period over which the rights were built up.

For contracted-out pension rights built up before 6 April 1997, you are entitled to a preserved guaranteed minimum pension (GMP) and widow's or widower's GMP. The amount of GMP you're entitled to at the time you leave is calculated and must then be increased until the time at which you reach the state pension age. The scheme can choose one of three ways in which to make the increases:

- in line with increases in national average earnings
- by a fixed amount of 6.25 per cent a year (8.5 per cent for people who left a scheme before 6 April 1988, and 7.5 per cent for leavers in the period 6 April 1988 to 5 April 1997)
- until April 1997 in line with earnings inflation up to a maximum of 5 per cent, as long as the scheme makes a payment to the state called a limited revaluation premium. From April 1997 this option is no longer available.

If, with the last two methods, the revalued GMPs fall short of GMPs increased in line with average earnings in the nation as a whole, the state makes good the shortfall through SERPS.

GMPs can be transferred to another pension scheme or plan, as long as that scheme or plan can be used for contracted-out pension rights (see Table 16.1 on page 165).

For periods of contracting out on or after 6 April 1997, you no longer build up GMPs. Instead, the scheme has to promise you a package of benefits that is at least as good as that from a reference scheme (see Chapter 14). This test applies to the whole benefit package – contracted-out rights are no longer separated from any other pension rights.

If you leave the scheme but keep your benefits there, the scheme must increase your pension, once it starts to be paid, by inflation up to a maximum of 5 per cent a year (called limited price indexation, LPI). This maximum is due to be reduced to 2.5 per cent from a date yet to be announced – probably April 2005. LPI increases apply to the whole post-April 1997 pension from the scheme.

Post-1997 contracted-out pension rights can be transferred to another scheme or plan, provided it can itself be used for contracting out (see Table 16.1).

If you have contracted out through a money purchase scheme which you then leave, the scheme must continue to provide protected rights, as described in Chapter 14. The invested rebates continue to grow, and the amount of contracted-out pension will depend on the size of the fund by retirement, as well as the other factors detailed in Chapter 14. LPI applies once the pension starts to be paid but is due to be abolished from a date yet to be announced, but probably April 2005.

Staying in touch with an employer's scheme

If you decide to leave your preserved pension with the pension scheme of an employer you've left, be sure to let the scheme know whenever you change address. You should also keep track of the benefits you can expect from the scheme at retirement (or if you decide to take a transfer at some stage). The scheme administrators of a final salary scheme are not obliged to send you benefit statements (see page 102) automatically, but you have the right to request a statement as often as once every 12 months. Once requested, the scheme administrators should provide a statement within two months. The administrators of a money purchase scheme are required automatically to send you a statement once a year.

Transferring your pension rights

Since 1 January 1986 anyone leaving an employer pension scheme who has a right to a preserved pension also has the right to take a *transfer value* instead. A transfer value is a lump sum that is judged to be equivalent to the preserved pension (and any other rights) given up. You can't receive the transfer value as cash in hand, though; it must be reinvested in another pension scheme or plan.

There are a variety of ways in which you can reinvest a transfer value – they are summarised in Table 16.1. But note that, while all employer schemes must give you the right to *take* a transfer value, there is no obligation on any scheme or plan, other than a stakeholder scheme, to *accept* your transfer value.

How much is the transfer value?

If you are switching your pension rights from an occupational money purchase scheme, the transfer value is simply the value of your fund – in other words, the contributions plus their investment growth less any deductions for charges and expenses.

If you are switching from a final salary scheme, the transfer value must be worked out by the scheme's actuary. He or she makes assumptions, for example, about future investment growth, and works back to arrive at a lump sum which, if invested now, could reasonably be expected to produce enough to pay the amount of your preserved pension at retirement (together with any other rights, such as widow's or widower's pensions, guaranteed pension increases, and so on). The figure for the lump sum is the amount of your transfer value.

What will the transfer value buy?

If you're transferring into a money purchase pension scheme or personal pension, the transfer value will simply be added to your fund and invested until it is used to provide your retirement pension or other benefits.

If you're transferring into a final salary scheme, the transfer value might be used in a number of ways, for example:

- it could be used now to 'buy' a fixed amount of pension at retirement
- it could be used now to buy 'extra years' in the scheme, so that you're credited with more years of membership than you will have in reality. Via the pension formula, these years are translated into a higher pension and other benefits. This option is most commonly found in public-sector schemes

- it could be invested as a separate fund to be used at retirement to 'buy' extra benefits in the main scheme – in a similar way to an additional voluntary contributions (AVC) scheme (see Chapter 30).

Table 16.1: What you can do with a transfer from an employer's pension scheme

Type of employer's scheme from which you are transferring	Your options [1]
Contracted out	Contracted-out occupational scheme
	Contracted-in occupational scheme [2]
	Contracted-out personal pension or Stakeholder Scheme
	Section 32 plan
Not contracted out	Contracted-out occupational scheme
	Contracted-in occupational scheme
	Personal pension or Stakeholder Scheme

[1] Note that occupational schemes and personal pensions that meet the required conditions may be stakeholder schemes.
[2] In which case, the old scheme may still pay your contracted-out pension at retirement or you may be bought back into SERPS in respect of your pre-April 1997 pension rights.

Buying extra years, in particular, often causes some confusion, because the number of years credited in the new scheme may be less than the number of years you had belonged to the old scheme. But it's easy to see why the difference arises: the transfer value from the old scheme reflects your preserved pension. In the case of a final salary scheme, this was based on your earnings when you left the scheme and the amount by which the preserved pension will be increased up to retirement. In the new scheme, your transfer value is used to 'buy' an equivalent amount of pension, but, this time, it will be based on your expected salary at retirement. Since this is generally higher than your salary on leaving the old scheme, the transfer value equates to fewer years in the new scheme than in the old. Similarly, if the new scheme offers more generous benefits (for example, better widow's pension, higher increases to pensions after retirement), your transfer value will buy fewer years in the new scheme than the old.

Transferring contracted-out pension rights

If you transfer your pension rights, any contracted-out rights must continue to be treated in a special way, although the nature of the guarantee may change. This is the case whether you are transferring from an employer scheme or a personal pension.

In general, you can transfer contracted-out rights to a new employer's occupational contracted-out scheme, to an appropriate personal pension, or to a special type of personal pension called a Section 32 contract, which is designed to preserve the guarantees inherent in GMPs.

If you transfer either GMPs or post-April 1997 pension rights from a contracted-out final salary scheme to a money purchase arrangement, you lose the right to a pension worked out according to a formula and instead switch to protected rights (see Chapter 14). For post-April 1997 pension rights, in particular, this has a number of drawbacks:

- in the contracted-out final salary scheme, part of your benefits could be a tax-free lump sum at retirement. With protected rights, there can be no lump sum

CASE HISTORY: Harriet

Harriet, aged 25, decides to leave the accountancy firm for which she has worked for four years and joins a large merchant banking conglomerate. Her new employer runs a final salary pension scheme, which will accept a transfer value from Harriet's old employer's scheme. Harriet's four years in the old pension scheme are worth a preserved pension of £1,100 a year. The actuary of the old scheme calculates that a lump sum of £4,500 would, if invested now, be enough to provide that pension. In the new scheme, it's estimated that her pay at retirement might be £36,000 (in today's money). Thus, each year in the new scheme would provide her with $\frac{1}{60} \times £36,000 = £600$. The actuary of the new scheme works out that the transfer value is just about enough to buy two years' worth of future pension. So Harriet gives up four years of membership in her old scheme for just two years in the new scheme, but the preserved pension of £1,100 a year she gives up is, in this case, virtually identical to the (2 × £600) = £1,200 a year pension she is expected to get from the new scheme as a result of the two years with which she's credited.

- a contracted-out final salary scheme does allow for a payment of pension on early retirement before reaching state pension age. Protected rights can't be paid until you reach age 60
- protected rights must buy pensions which increase by at least inflation up to a maximum of 5 per cent a year. Under the pre-April 1997 system, part of your transfer might have been non-GMPs, which could have been used more flexibly.

If post-1997 rights are transferred to another contracted-out final salary scheme, the new scheme must provide you with the same benefits as if you had been a member of the new scheme all along. This can result in better or worse benefits than you would have had from the old scheme, though of course both must meet the reference scheme test.

If the new scheme you join (or the plan you take out) is not contracted out, you can leave your contracted-out rights in the old scheme, in which case they must be preserved as described on page 162; or you could transfer any non-contracted-out rights to the new scheme and the contracted-out rights to a separate contracted-out arrangement. Alternatively, for pre-April 1997 GMPs, you can be 'bought back' into SERPS if the old scheme pays a transfer premium to the state. If you're 'bought back' in this way, you'll no longer get a GMP at retirement from the old employer's scheme; instead, you'll get a SERPS pension from the state.

Transferring to a Section 32 plan

Section 32 plans – also called buy-out bonds – are a special type of personal pension designed to accept transfer values from occupational pension schemes. The transfer value is paid into the plan and used to buy a deferred annuity (an insurance product designed to pay out an income starting at some future date). The fund which builds up is then used to provide a retirement pension and any other benefits. Section 32 plans were first introduced in 1981; since July 1988 personal pensions (see Chapter 19) have provided an alternative to them.

Section 32 plans can be used to preserve contracted-out pension rights, and can be a good idea in the case of transfers of pre-April 1997 rights from contracted-out final salary schemes. The Section 32 plan must take over the guarantee to provide a set amount of GMP at retirement. To do this, the plan provider needs to be satisfied that the transfer value is sufficient. By contrast, if you transfer from a contracted-out final salary scheme to a contracted-out personal pension, you give up your right to a guaranteed amount of pension, though you get protected rights instead. With a personal pension, you take the risk that the transfer value might provide a smaller pension than the GMP you gave up; with a Section 32 plan, the plan provider takes that risk.

Should you transfer?

Deciding whether or not to transfer pension rights from an old employer's occupational pension scheme to a new one is not easy. You need to weigh up what benefits you would be giving up from the old scheme against the benefits that you will gain from the new one. See 'More information', below, for how to go about this.

If you are moving from one public-sector job to another you may be able to take advantage of the 'transfer club'. Public-sector schemes cover, for example, teachers, NHS workers, the police and civil servants. Most public-sector schemes work on the final salary basis, and the transfer club enables years in one scheme to be added directly to years in your new scheme without any reduction to take account of earnings at the time when you left (see page 165). For example, if you belonged to the old scheme for four years, transferring means that you will be credited with four years in the new scheme.

Transferring from an employer's scheme to a personal pension is seldom a good idea, for several reasons:

- if the old scheme is a final salary scheme you'll be giving up a guaranteed pension and other benefits. The pension from a personal pension is unpredictable, depending on the amount of transfer value that you can invest, how well it grows, charges and annuity rates at the time when you retire
- you'll be giving up a package of benefits, including pensions for dependants if you were to die. Replacing all of these benefits through a personal pension could be very expensive
- the transfer value reflects the value of your fund in a money purchase scheme or the guaranteed benefits in a final salary scheme. It might not take into account any discretionary benefits (in other words, benefits to which you have no contractual right and which are paid according to decisions made by the employer or the trustees of the

scheme). These may include generous increases to the pension once it starts to be paid

- in many employers' schemes the employer pays the running costs of the scheme separately. With a personal pension the costs will all be paid out of your transfer value and the resulting fund
- even when costs are paid out of the employer's scheme's pension fund, the charges for the personal pension may be substantially greater. But you can keep costs down by choosing a stakeholder scheme (see Chapter 20).

If your occupational scheme is wound up

If your employer scheme is wound up (for example, in the event of your employer going bust, or being taken over by another firm which doesn't wish to continue the scheme), your pension entitlement from the scheme depends on the scheme's rules. Some schemes are fairly generous to members in the event of winding up, but with others, you may be *entitled* only to the minimum required under the law – i.e. the benefits that an early leaver could get. Rather than making promises about benefits, the scheme rules may give the trustees (see Chapter 17) discretion to decide what benefits over and above the legal minimum are provided, in which case you will be dependent on the health of the pension fund and the priority given to paying or increasing the benefits of different types of members – usually those currently receiving pensions will be given top priority, if funds are short.

Since 1 July 1992 regulations have come into effect which, for final salary schemes (and any schemes with a final salary element), make any shortfall in the pension fund a debt of the employer. Where the employer has gone bust, the debt will rank alongside other unsecured creditors who are owed money. This gives scheme members a better chance of getting their rights than in the past – but if the employer doesn't have the money they continue to lose out.

The position improved slightly from September 2003, when a change in the law gave all unsecured creditors a better chance of getting at least some of the money owed to them (by moving the Inland Revenue and other tax authorities down the pecking order and earmarking some funds specifically for unsecured creditors).

Despite this, the pension fund of an insolvent employer may still be short of funds if it is wound up. Where there is too little in the pension fund to finance the promised benefits, pensions legislation dictates how the available cake will be shared by setting out the order in which the promises must be met. The payments in each category in the priority order have to be met in full before moving on to meet payments in the next category. In the past, this order understandably gave very high priority to pensioners already receiving their pension but, in the process, meant that people still working might get little or nothing of their promised pension. This was disastrous, especially for people close to retiring who had no time left to build up further savings. To ease this problem, the priority order has been altered from 10 May 2004 onwards, in particular to put pensions built up but not yet in payment ahead of increases to pensions in payment. The new order of payment is:

- **costs and expenses** of the scheme and the winding-up process must be paid first
- **AVC benefits** must be met next. This is to ensure that you are not discouraged from making extra pension savings – you need to be sure that your savings are safe
- **pensions in payment** The current pensioners' income must be secure; however, future pension increases (even LPI) are further down the list. This category also includes pensions being paid to the dependants of members who have died
- **pension rights built up but not yet payable** including rights due to pension sharing on divorce, excluding any increases for inflation
- **other rights built up** including, for example, the return of contributions if you have less than two years' service, without any increases for inflation
- **increases to pensions in payment**
- **increases to pension rights built up but not yet payable**
- **increases to other rights built up**
- **whatever the scheme rules require** if there are any remaining assets to be shared out.

Pension schemes are not just wound up when the employer goes bust. Sometimes solvent employers decide to wind up their pension scheme and this has become a particular problem in recent times, with the rising cost of final salary schemes in the face of poor investment returns and the increasing longevity of pensioners. Until recently, winding up the scheme would crystallise the benefits on an early leaver basis, leaving members with smaller pensions than they had been expecting. To stop this, another change in the law was made with effect from 11 June 2003. Under the new rules, an employer who is not insolvent and winds up a scheme, is responsible for ensuring there is enough money in the scheme to buy annuities to replace in full the benefits that have been built up so far. The trustees of the scheme can agree to accept less from the employer and they might do this if, say, paying in the full amount due to the scheme would push the employer over the brink into insolvency. In that case, members might prefer to accept some reduction in their pension and other benefits in order to protect their jobs.

More information

Transferring from one occupational scheme to another

Get a benefit statement from your old scheme and an estimate of the transfer value available if you do transfer (see Figure 16.1 for an example). Take these to the administrators of your new scheme and ask them to explain what benefits you could 'buy' with your transfer value in the new scheme.

If your transfer value is very large, it may be worth getting advice from an independent financial adviser★ (preferably one who is paid by fees rather than commission – see Chapter 22 – since you are not

Figure 16.1: Example of information about your preserved pension and transfer value

Deferred pension payable at age 65: This pension is increased from the date when you left to your date of retirement, broadly in line with inflation up to a maximum of 5 per cent a year	£1,430 a year
Dependant's pension of 50 per cent of your final salary pension:	£715 a year
Child's pension of 25 per cent of your final salary pension: (Maximum 50 per cent for all dependent children)	£357.50
Alternatively, you can transfer the value of these benefits to another approved pension arrangement. The transfer value is adjusted to allow for investment conditions at the time of payment. The unadjusted transfer value at 1 April 2004 was:	£8,266

expecting to buy anything from the adviser) or a consulting actuary★. The advice may cost several hundred pounds, so it is unlikely to be economical if your transfer value is small.

Financial advisers must hold certain qualifications before being allowed to give advice about pension transfers. You can check whether they are qualified in this area by consulting the FSA Register★. (FSA stands for the Financial Services Authority, which regulates many types of financial business, including investment advice.)

Transferring from an occupational pension scheme to a personal pension

This is unlikely to be a good idea. If a financial adviser suggests this course of action be sceptical. He or she must give you the reasons for his or her advice in writing, and unless you are convinced that these are sound do not go ahead with the transfer.

The same concerns apply to a transfer from an occupational scheme to a personal pension taken out under a GPPS arrangement.

If you are contemplating going ahead with a transfer to a personal pension, contact the administrators of the pension scheme that you are leaving. Ask for a benefit statement and an estimate of the transfer value that you will receive.

The scheme's administrators or trustees cannot advise you on the merits of the personal pension that you have chosen. You will have to go to the plan provider, an independent financial adviser★ who is qualified in giving transfer advice (see above) or a consulting actuary★ for this type of guidance.

The plan provider or financial adviser will compare the benefits that you stand to receive from the employer's scheme with the benefits that a personal pension may offer. If you are leaving a final salary scheme this comparison must include a statement of the rate of growth of your personal pension fund, which you would require to match the benefits from the employer's scheme that you are giving up. Ask yourself whether this rate of growth seems realistic.

You will receive a lot of information about the personal pension; see Chapter 22 for a guide to this.

Chapter 17

How safe is your occupational pension?

How pension schemes are organised

To qualify for the various tax reliefs that apply to pension savings, a pension scheme must either be a statutory scheme or it must be run at arm's length from the employer and his or her business. This is to ensure that money set aside to provide pensions really is used for that purpose and doesn't get sucked back into the employer's business.

A statutory scheme is set up under an Act of Parliament and is the normal arrangement for most public-sector schemes – covering, for example, the police, NHS workers and civil servants. Often, these schemes are unfunded, and the pensions derive their security from the fact that future taxpayers can be called upon to pay for them.

Non-statutory schemes are nearly always set up as trusts and are bound by the various laws which apply to them. Trust law did not originally grow up with pension schemes in mind. It was designed mainly to cope with trust funds set up by families to benefit, say, children and other relatives. In the case of pension funds, the employer sets up the trust and usually decides on the initial benefits and rules (which may later be altered and adapted as the rules and law allow). The aim of the pension scheme trust is to provide pensions and other benefits (for example, on the death of a member) for the members of the scheme – the beneficiaries. The beneficiaries include not just the 'active' members (currently working for the employer) but also people receiving pensions already, people who used to work for the employer and have preserved pensions with the scheme (called 'deferred members'), people who may benefit in certain circumstances, such as wives and children, and also the employer, who is usually able to receive money from the scheme if surplus funds have built up.

Assets are handed over to the trust in the form of contributions paid by the employer, contributions from the members if it is a contributory scheme, and possibly money from the government if it is a contracted-out scheme. The assets grow through the addition of investment income and capital growth. The trustees are responsible for investing the assets in such a way that the aims of the trust can be met.

Although the trustees are responsible for the running of the pension scheme, they can employ help, and have a duty to seek specialist help when required. Commonly, trustees will appoint an administrator to handle the day-to-day business of the scheme, an investment manager to advise on investment strategy and handle the detail of the investment of the assets, an actuary to evaluate the assets and liabilities of the scheme and to advise on the necessary contribution levels, a lawyer to advise on legal aspects, and an auditor to check the accounts.

How pension schemes are regulated

The revelation in 1991 that Robert Maxwell had stolen £440 million from his employees' pension funds was a wake-up call that triggered changes in the law aimed at improving the security of occupational pension schemes. As time has gone on, different problems have emerged, laws have been amended, and in summer 2004, the UK is on the brink of yet another major shift in pension regulation designed to make occupational schemes safer and allay public fears.

Under both the existing and new regulations, the system relies basically on three pillars: a regulator, the pension trustees and the scheme advisers. If all else fails, in some circumstances, a compensation scheme kicks in.

The Regulator

At the time of writing, the Occupational Pensions Regulatory Authority (OPRA) is responsible for overseeing occupational schemes. However, OPRA has been viewed as a largely reactive regulator, responding to problems brought to its attention and to some extent getting bogged down in the detail of quite minor misdemeanours while larger problems have emerged unchecked.

To address this, at the time of writing, new legislation was making its way through Parliament, which will replace OPRA with a new

Pensions Regulator. This Regulator will be more proactive. It will take a risk-based approach to monitoring schemes, devoting more time and effort to those schemes where the risk of problems is highest or the consequences of something going wrong are greatest. The Pensions Regulator will have wide-ranging powers, from issuing improvement notices to banning trustees, freezing assets and even winding up schemes. It will also have a brief to educate and assist the people running occupational schemes or advising them and will issue codes of practice. The Pensions Regulator will oversee all types of occupational scheme and also personal pensions made available through your workplace and stakeholder schemes.

Trustees

Broadly, anyone can be a pension scheme trustee. In most schemes, the employer will be heavily represented, but there can also be outside individuals, professional trustees, staff and union representatives and, indeed, scheme members.

Since 1997, there has been a requirement that at least a third of the trustees in most schemes should be nominated by the members, but the present legislation gives the employer a route to opt out of this requirement. The new laws before Parliament at the time of writing will abolish this opt-out.

Trustees clearly have a very important role. They are responsible for the running of the scheme and, given their hands-on role at the coalface, are also best placed to spot any problems. Yet, surprisingly, to date there have been no requirements for trustees to have any particular expertise or knowledge. In good schemes, trustees have been offered training, but that has been a matter of good practice not compulsion. Again, the new laws before Parliament seek to put matters right. In future, trustees will be required to have appropriate knowledge and understanding. They can bring these qualities to the role if they are already qualified in a relevant area or they can acquire these qualities through training.

Advisers

Schemes are heavily reliant on experts, such as lawyers and actuaries. Even more than the trustees, these advisers are well-placed to spot problems because they have the specialist knowledge to understand what is going on. Therefore, there is a special duty on actuaries and auditors to 'blow the whistle' to the regulator if they suspect something is amiss and they can be fined if they fail to do so. Other professional advisers are also encouraged to expose irregularities. The new laws making their way through Parliament aim to expand the list of people who have this duty to include trustees, scheme managers, any scheme administrator, the employer and any advisers to the scheme.

Compensation

In the wake of Maxwell, a compensation scheme was established to ensure that scheme members got at least some of their benefits back if their employer was insolvent and it was discovered that the occupational pension scheme assets had gone missing because of fraud or some other crime. Under the new laws going through Parliament, this scheme is to be replaced with a broadly similar scheme called the Fraud Compensation Fund. This will cover all types of occupational scheme.

Neither of these compensation schemes help in cases where no crime has been committed but, nevertheless, the employer has gone bust leaving a gaping hole in the pension scheme assets. To address this, the new laws will set up the Pension Protection Fund. This will cover defined benefit schemes (such as final salary schemes) and will step in to cover shortfalls left once the winding-up provisions (see page 169) have shared out what funds are available. The Pension Protection Fund will ensure that pensions in payment continue to be paid in full (though increases will not be fully protected) and that, for people still working, 90 per cent of their benefits are protected, up to a set limit. The Fund will be financed through a levy paid by all defined benefit occupational schemes.

Risks in perspective

Successive changes to the law are helping to increase the security of occupational pension schemes. They should make it increasingly unlikely that anyone has to face the shock and misery of losing their pension. Devastating though that experience is, it should be borne in mind that the number of pensioners who have lost their occupational pension is small as a proportion of the total number of pension scheme members, and the risk of retiring on an inadequate income is much greater than the risk of loss by saving this way. It is important to keep the risks in perspective and not to be deterred from joining an employer's scheme. You can help to minimise the risks of something going wrong by taking an active interest in your scheme: read the documents and reports you are sent, ask questions if you don't understand or if you want further information, and consider becoming a trustee.

Part 4

Your options when there is no
occupational pension scheme

Chapter 18

Your pension options

This section of the book is aimed at you if you cannot join an occupational pension scheme through your job. This will be the case if:

- you are self-employed
- you are an employee but your employer does not run an occupational scheme
- you are an employee but you are not eligible for your occupational scheme
- you are an employee and you belong to a group personal pension scheme (GPPS) promoted through work
- you are an employee and you belong to a personal stakeholder pension scheme either arranged through your workplace or organised by yourself (see Chapter 20)
- you run your own business and have not yet thought about the pension options open to you (which include setting up your own employer's scheme, see Chapter 27).

This section will also be useful if you belong to an occupational pension scheme, but you want to use a personal pension or stakeholder scheme either to contract out of the state additional pension scheme (see Chapter 23) or to top up your retirement savings (in which case, see also Chapter 28).

If you are self-employed or there is no pension scheme open to you through your job, do not ignore saving for retirement. There are many demands on your money, especially in the 'family years' of life, when you probably have a mortgage to pay, have the costs of raising and educating children, need a reliable (often expensive) car and so on. Sometimes these other financial goals will have to take priority, but you should start saving for retirement as soon as you can.

> **Warning**
> If you can join an occupational pension scheme at work, this will nearly always be the best way to save for retirement. Do not be persuaded to save through a personal pension or stakeholder scheme *instead*. However, a personal pension or stakeholder scheme can be a good way of topping up your occupational pension.

This is especially important if you are self-employed. Employees, including directors of their own companies, are contributing to the additional state pension – see Chapter 5 – which will top up their basic state pension (see Chapter 4). But self-employed people are not covered by the additional state scheme. If you do nothing about your pension, all you will have to retire on is the state basic pension and means-tested state benefits. Under the present rules these guarantee a single pensioner a minimum income of little more than £100 a week. Could you live comfortably on that?

Do not be an ostrich

There's no point burying your head in the sand. Maybe you've skimped on protecting your income in the event of illness in the hope that prolonged illness will not strike you. That's a gamble, but it may pay off: after all, many people do stay healthy throughout their whole working life. But retirement is different. A few people die young, but the majority live to a ripe old age and will retire at some stage. There is no 'if' about retirement planning: you are looking ahead to a period of life which you must treat as a certainty. Retirement will arrive and you will need an income to live on.

Start saving early

As described in Chapter 3, the emphasis these days is on making your own savings for retirement. The state will continue to provide a safety net, but only at a very minimal level. And bear in mind the risk that the state system may change yet again (see Chapter 7), in which case the safety net could become even skimpier.

The earlier you start to save for retirement the less onerous it will be. If you delay too long it may even become impossible to catch up.

Table 18.1 illustrates the effect of delaying the start of your pension savings.

The amounts shown in Table 18.1 are at 2004 rates; both the amount that you must pay in and the income that you'll need will be a lot larger in terms of future money because of the impact of rising prices. The precise figures vary according to the assumptions made; we have assumed that your pension fund will grow by a fairly conservative 1.5 per cent a year more than inflation after deducting charges, and that at age 65 you buy an annuity giving you a pension which increases each year in line with inflation. If you think that investments will perform better (quite likely) and/or that annuity rates will be higher than in 2004 (perhaps doubtful), the picture will not be quite so gloomy.

The important points to note about Table 18.1 are that delaying the start of your pension savings increases both the amount that you must pay in each year in which you do save and the total that you must save overall if you are to reach the same target pension.

Table 18.1: The amount that you may need to save to provide each £10,000 a year of pension (at 2004 prices) by the age of 65

Age at which you start to make regular contributions	Monthly contribution required [1]
20	£190
30	£282
40	£456
50	£877
60	£3,037

[1] This is the monthly contribution in the first year. We have assumed that the contributions increase each year in line with increases in your earnings, and that earnings increase by 1.5 per cent a year more than prices.

Where to save

The following chapters look at the options open to you if you cannot join an occupational pension scheme and have to fund a pension alone. You can opt for dedicated pension arrangements (such as personal pension plans and stakeholder schemes) or ordinary savings routes, but preferably those which give you good tax advantages, such as

Individual Savings Accounts (ISAs) – see Chapter 32. If you run your own company there are some special types of employers' schemes that you can set up for yourself: Chapter 27 outlines these.

Dedicated pension schemes and plans, and investments such as ISAs, are especially efficient ways to save if you are a taxpayer. But personal pensions and stakeholder schemes have advantages even for non-taxpayers.

Chapter 19

Personal pensions

Personal pensions are a way of making your own pension arrangements by saving, usually with an insurance company, though unit trusts, building societies, banks or friendly societies are also allowed to offer these pension plans. (Although banks and building societies do market plans, these are invariably run by life insurance companies either owned by the bank or society, or for whom the bank or society acts as an agent.)

Whatever type of organisation you save with (here called the plan provider), it invests your money to build up a cash fund. At retirement, the fund is used to provide your pension.

Personal pensions can be used for contracting out of the additional state pension scheme – this aspect of the plans is dealt with in Chapter 23.

All personal plans function on a money purchase basis (see page 187). This means that they work much like many other forms of saving: you pay money in, leave it to grow and eventually take the proceeds, in this case in the form of a pension.

As such, a personal pension gives you your own 'savings pot' and is therefore very easy to understand (in contrast to, say, a final salary employer's scheme, see Chapter 11). But the drawback with all money purchase schemes is that there are no guarantees. You do not know how much pension you'll end up with.

It's hard to predict what pension you'll get from a personal pension plan because there are many unpredictable factors involved. One of the most important is how well your invested contributions grow. If the investments perform well, you'll get a better pension than if they perform badly. Another factor is the amount of pension that you can 'buy' with your fund on retirement. This depends on annuity rates at the time when you retire (see Chapter 33). If annuity rates are low, you'll end up with a worse pension than if they are high. The key point to note is that you bear the full investment risk when you save for your retirement using a personal pension. Table 19.1 summarises the main advantages and disadvantages of saving for retirement using a personal pension.

Personal pensions first went on sale on 1 July 1988. Before that date, you might have taken out an earlier type of personal plan called a 'retirement annuity contract'. (You can no longer start a new retirement annuity contract, though you can still pay contributions into an existing one.) These earlier plans are covered by different rules from personal pensions concerning contribution limits, benefits, and so on. For an outline of the rules for retirement annuity contracts, see page 196.

Money purchase occupational schemes (see Chapter 12) are allowed to opt out of the rules that normally apply to occupational schemes and to be covered instead by the rules for personal pensions. If you belong to a scheme which goes down this route, the rules described in this section of the book will govern the amount you can pay in contributions, the benefits you get, and so on. At the time of writing, few if any schemes had made the switch.

> **Stakeholder pensions**
> Some personal pensions are stakeholder pensions. This means they meet certain conditions about low charges and flexibility (see Chapter 20), but in other respects they are no different from other personal pensions and are covered by the rules described in this Chapter.

Who qualifies?

Nearly everyone under the age of 75 can take out a personal pension. Since April 2001 you do not have to have any earnings to be eligible. This has opened up the plans to children, people running a home, carers and other people who do not work. The only people who cannot have a personal pension (unless used only to contract out) are:

- controlling directors who already belong to an occupational pension scheme
- employees earning more than £30,000 a year and who already belong to an occupational pension scheme.

Table 19.1: The pros and cons of personal pension plans

Pros	Cons
Tax advantages	Unpredictable pension and other benefits
Bonus if you are a non-taxpayer	No guarantee that the pension will keep pace with inflation during the period when it is building up
Simple concept	You bear the investment risk
Can carry on when you change jobs	You must usually pay the full cost of providing the pension and other benefits [1]
	Charges are sometimes high
	Charges are often complicated [2]
	Can be inflexible and poor value if you stop the plan early or transfer your fund to another pension arrangement [2]

[1] If you're an employee investing through a group personal pension scheme (see Chapter 13), your employer may pay in something. When an employee has arranged the personal plan independently, the employer usually does not contribute. If you're self-employed, you pay the full cost.
[2] But not if you choose a stakeholder scheme.

Subject to the contribution limits (see page 191), you can contribute to more than one personal pension at a time.

How much pension?

All personal pension plans work on a money purchase basis. This means that the pension you'll receive depends on:

- the amount that you paid into the scheme
- charges deducted by the plan provider
- how well your invested contributions grow
- annuity rates at the time when you retire.

The upshot is that you can't, in advance, be sure of how much pension you'll get.

A personal pension can also provide benefits for your dependants, such as pensions for a widow or widower, other partner or children (see Chapter 24). Using the plan to provide dependants' benefits reduces the amount to be used for your retirement pension. Similarly, you 'pay' extra (by receiving a lower pension at the start of your retirement) for a pension which increases after retirement – for example, by a fixed amount each year, or by enough to match inflation.

Tax-free cash at retirement

As with occupational pension schemes, you can usually take part of the proceeds from a personal pension as a tax-free lump sum at retirement. Doing this reduces the amount of pension you get – but, generally, taking the cash is worthwhile. If you can't manage on the reduced pension, you could use your tax-free cash to buy a purchased life annuity – see Chapter 33. How much tax-free cash you can have depends on the type of personal plan that you have and when you first started it. The limits are shown in Table 19.2.

You can't take any tax-free cash from a personal pension being used to contract out of the state additional pension scheme (see Chapter 23).

Pension increases

You decide whether to have a pension which is paid at a single flat rate or one which increases year by year at the time you want to start taking your pension. If you choose a pension which does include some built-in increases, the starting level of the pension will be lower – see Chapter 33. Under current rules, a pension from a personal plan used for contracting out of the state additional pension must be increased in line with inflation up to a given limit though this is set to change (see Chapter 23).

Table 19.2: How much tax-free cash you can have

Type of plan and when started	Maximum amount of tax-free cash
Started on or after 1 July 1988 and before 27 July 1989	One-quarter of pension fund (except amounts to be used to provide dependants' pensions) [1]
Started on or after 27 July 1989	One-quarter of pension fund (except amounts to be used to provide 'contracted-out' [2] pensions) without any overall maximum

[1] Strictly speaking, a £150,000 overall cash limit per plan applies to lump sums taken from personal pensions started before 27 July 1989. In practice, the limit has no significance because, first, a cluster of plans could be arranged rather than a single plan and, second, the plan-holder can switch to another plan (which will not be subject to the cash limit) at retirement using the 'open market option' – see Chapter 33.
[2] See Chapter 23.

CASE HISTORY: Jack

Jack is saving for retirement using a personal pension plan. If, by retirement, he builds up a fund of £143,000, he could choose to take up to one-quarter of the fund – in other words, £35,750 – as a tax-free lump sum. If he did this, based on annuity rates in June 2004, he'd be left with a level pension of £7,958 a year instead of a full pension of £10,610 a year.

When is the pension paid?

You don't have to stop work in order to take a pension from a personal pension. However, the Inland Revenue lays down rules which prevent you taking your pension too early in life. Normally, you can start your pension at any age from 50 onwards (due to increase to 55 by 2010), but earlier ages apply to some occupations – see Table 19.3.

Inland Revenue rules prohibit you from paying into a personal pension plan after reaching age 75, and that is the latest age at which you can start to draw your pension. Within the Inland Revenue age limits, the organisation providing the plan may have its own rules about the normal pension age. It's rare that a plan has a single fixed pension age. With some plans, you choose your own retirement age at the time

Table 19.3: Occupations with early retirement ages

Age	Occupation	Age	Occupation
35	Athletes	40	Cricketers
	Badminton players		Golfers
	Boxers		Motor cycle riders
	Cyclists		Motor racing drivers
	Dancers		Speedway riders
	Footballers		Trapeze artists
	Models		Divers
	National Hunt jockeys		
	Rugby League players	45	Flat-racing jockeys
	Squash players		Non-commissioned Royal
	Table tennis players		Marine Reservists
	Tennis players		
	Wrestlers		

you first take out the plan, though you may be able to change your mind later on. Other plans are even more flexible, and let you leave your decision until you're ready to start taking the pension. You can increase your scope for flexibility by having several pension plans and starting your pension from each at a different age. For example, you might have four plans with pension ages of 60, 61, 62 and 65. From 6 April 2001 onwards, providers can offer personal pensions that, although set up as a single plan, offer multiple retirement dates, so you use part of the fund to buy an annuity on one date, a further part on another date, and so on. Having some flexibility is important because annuity rates may be low at the time you would have liked to start taking a pension. Since the level of annuity rates then affects the pension you get throughout your whole retirement, it might be better to put off starting all or part of your pension in the hope that rates will rise again. At the time of writing, the government is consulting on other ways to make annuities more flexible.

The later you start taking your pension, the longer your pension fund is left invested and, usually, the longer you carry on making contributions. Since you'll be older when the pension starts (and your life expectancy will be lower – see Chapter 1), the pension provider can expect to pay out the pension for a shorter period. This means that, the later you start receiving it, the greater your pension is likely to be. Conversely, if you retire early, your pension will be smaller.

Since July 1995 it has been possible to put off buying an annuity but still take an income direct from the pension fund you have built up – a process called 'income drawdown'. You take any tax-free lump sum as normal, at the time you start taking an income, and you must eventually switch to an annuity by the time you reach age 75. This can be a useful option if annuity rates are low at the time you retire and you expect them to rise in future. It can also be useful if you need the lump sum but do not really want the pension income – you must take some income, but the minimum is less than an annuity would have provided. See Chapter 33 for more details.

What do you pay?

You can choose whether to take out a personal pension (sometimes called a regular premium plan) which requires regular payments – monthly – or a plan which requires only a single lump-sum contribution (sometimes called a single premium pension plan). There may be a minimum contribution – for example, £20 a month or £200 a year with a regular payment plan, or £1,000 with a lump-sum plan.

Most regular payment plans let you increase your contributions – either by a fixed amount each year, or in line with price or earnings inflation. Increases may be automatic, or optional. Generally, you should consider increasing your payments regularly, so that your pension savings don't fall back in terms of today's money. You may also be able to make extra one-off payments to your regular payment plan.

Many regular payment plans also allow you to reduce your payments, or miss a limited number of payments without penalty – though you may have to pay extra for this option. Chapter 21 looks, among other things, at the pros and cons of regular payment plans versus lump-sum plans.

If your personal pension is a stakeholder scheme, the minimum contribution may not be greater than £20 (whether paid as a regular contribution or a single lump sum). In addition, stakeholder schemes may not lock you into a regular pattern of payments – it's up to you when and how often you pay.

Limits on what you pay

The Inland Revenue limits the amount of pension contributions you can make which will qualify for tax relief. Nearly everyone can contribute at least £3,600 a year in total to all their personal pensions and stakeholder schemes. This is the before-tax-relief (gross) contribution limit. Subtracting basic-rate tax relief makes the limit £2,808 a year. If you are earning, you may be able to contribute more than this.

The earnings-related contribution limits are set as a percentage of your net relevant earnings. If you're an employee, this means your total before-tax pay, including the value of most taxable fringe benefits (for example, a company car). If you're self-employed, net relevant earnings basically means your profits for tax purposes. The limits tell you the maximum before-tax-relief amount that you can pay into your personal plan. Table 19.4 shows the percentage contribution limits.

In addition to the percentages listed in Table 19.4, there is an overall cash limit on the amount of earnings which can be taken into account in working out your contribution limit. In the 2004–5 tax year, the proposed earnings limit is £102,000. This means, for example, that

CASE HISTORY: Ryan

Ryan is 45 and finance director of a small knitwear firm. In the 2004–5 tax year he contributes £8,500 (before tax relief) to his personal pension. He receives basic-rate tax relief of £1,870 (22 per cent of £8,500) automatically, by handing over just £6,630 to the insurance company which runs his plan. But Ryan pays higher-rate tax of 40 per cent on at least £8,500 of his income, so he can claim additional tax relief of £1,530 (40 per cent of £8,500 less the basic-rate tax relief already given). The total after-tax-relief cost to him of the £8,500 contribution is only £5,100 (£8,500 less basic-rate relief of £1,870 and less higher-rate relief of £1,530).

someone aged 55 earning £150,000 a year can contribute at most 30 per cent of £102,000, which comes to £30,600. This works out at just 19 per cent of his or her earnings. The earnings limit is usually increased each year in line with changes in the Retail Prices Index. Table 19.5 shows the earnings limits which applied in earlier years.

The net relevant earnings used as a basis for your contributions in any particular tax year do not have to be the earnings for that year. You can choose net relevant earnings from any of the previous five tax years as a basis for your contributions. You are then treated as if you have that level of earnings for each of the five years following the basis year unless you opt to have a subsequent year treated as your basis year. You can base contributions on the basis year even if your actual earnings for the tax year in which you are making contributions have fallen or you have no earnings at all in that year.

You do not have to pay contributions yourself. Anyone can pay contributions on your behalf. And you can pay contributions into someone else's plan. For example, an employer can pay into an employee's plan, a husband can pay into a plan for his wife, a disabled person can pay into a plan for a carer, a parent or grandparent can pay into a plan for a child. Any contributions paid into your plan by someone else count towards the contribution limit for the year. If you're using a personal pension plan to contract out of the additional state pension scheme (see Chapter 23), amounts used for contracting out don't count towards the contribution limit.

Table 19.4: Tax-relief limits on contributions to personal pensions

Age at the start of the tax year (6 April)	Contribution limit as a percentage of your earnings	Contribution limit for each £1,000 of your earnings
Up to 35	17.5%	£175
36 to 45	20%	£200
46 to 50	25%	£250
51 to 55	30%	£300
56 to 60	35%	£350
61 to 74	40%	£400
75 and over	you can no longer contribute	

Table 19.5: Earnings limits and impact on contributions to personal pensions

Tax year	Earnings limit £	Maximum contribution for person aged up to 35 £
1988–9	No limit	17.5% of earnings
1989–90	£60,000	£10,500
1990–1	£64,800	£11,340
1991–2	£71,400	£12,495
1992–3	£75,000	£13,125
1993–4	£75,000	£13,125
1994–5	£76,800	£13,440
1995–6	£78,600	£13,755
1996–7	£82,200	£14,385
1997–8	£84,000	£14,700
1998–9	£87,600	£15,330
1999–2000	£90,600	£15,855
2000–1	£91,800	£16,065
2001–2	£95,400	£16,695
2002–3	£97,200	£17,010
2003–4	£99,000	£17,325
2004–5	£102,000	£17,850

CASE HISTORY: Jane

Jane, who is married to Ted, is not working at present. She is a full-time mum bringing up their two children, aged three and one. Jane has no income of her own at present, so cannot herself afford to make pension contributions. But, to ensure that Jane is still building up a reasonable pension, Ted pays £2,808

193

a year into Jane's stakeholder pension scheme. This is equivalent to £3,600 less basic-rate tax relief at 22 per cent (22% × £3,600 = £792). The scheme provider claims back the tax relief and adds it to Jane's scheme. Even though Ted is a higher-rate taxpayer, he cannot claim any extra relief on the contributions because they are being paid into someone else's pension scheme, not his own.

CASE HISTORY: Ahmed

Ahmed, aged 38, started his own business in 2001. The table shows his net relevant earnings for the tax years 2001–2 to 2006–7:

Tax year	Earnings for the tax year	Basis year for pension contributions	Earnings on which contributions based	Maximum contributions for the tax year
2001–2	£42,000	2001–2	£42,000	£8,400
2002–3	£40,000	2001–2	£42,000	£8,400
2003–4	£36,000	2001–2	£42,000	£8,400
2004–5	£38,000	2001–2	£42,000	£8,400
2005–6	£46,000	2005–6	£46,000	£9,200
2006–7	£39,000	2005–6	£46,000	£9,200

In 2004–5, he could make maximum contributions to his personal pension of 20% × £38,000 = £7,600. However, he has another option, which lets him contribute more. He can choose any of the five preceding years as his 'basis year'. He had no net relevant earnings before 2001 (because he belonged to an occupational scheme) and picks 2001–2 as his basis year. This means for the five years following 2001–2 – in other words from 2002–3 up to 2006–7 – he can base his contributions on earnings of £42,000. His maximum contribution in each of those years is 20% × £42,000 = £8,400.

In fact, Ahmed uses 2001–2 as his basis year only until 2004–5. In 2005–6, his earnings are £46,000. Since these are higher than his earnings in 2001–2, he opts for 2005–6 to be his new basis year. This means that for the five years following 2005–6 – in other words from 2006–7 up to 2010–11 – he can base his contributions on earnings of £46,000. His maximum contribution in the years up to 2009–10 is 20% × £46,000 = £9,200. In 2010–11, the maximum is higher (25% × £46,000 = £11,500) because he reaches age 46.

Tax relief on your savings

You get tax relief up to your highest rate of income tax on the amount you contribute to your personal pension. This means, for example, that a taxpayer paying tax at a 22 per cent rate in 2004–5 can contribute £100 to a plan at a cost of only £78. The cost to a 40 per cent taxpayer of contributing £100 would be only £60 after tax relief.

You get basic-rate tax relief automatically by paying only the after-tax-relief amount into your plan. You get this relief even if you do not pay any tax on your income. In other words, for non-taxpayers, the relief is a bonus contribution added to your plan. The lower 10 per cent rate of income tax is ignored, so you'll get tax relief at the full basic rate even if you paid only 10 per cent tax on all, or part, of the income you're now paying into your plan. If you're a higher-rate taxpayer, you have to claim the extra tax relief due. You can make the claim for additional tax relief on your personal pension contributions either through your tax return, or by using Form PP120, which you can get from your tax office.

If you make payment towards someone else's personal pension, as normal you deduct basic-rate tax relief from the contribution before handing it over to the plan provider. But, if you are a higher-rate taxpayer, you cannot claim any extra tax relief on contributions to a plan for someone else.

Going over the contribution limits

In general, if you pay more into a personal pension than the tax-relief rules allow, your excess contributions will be returned to you as soon as the overpayment is spotted. If you're an employee and both you and your employer contribute to the plan, any overpayment will be repaid to you rather than to your employer.

Benefit of hindsight

Using the carry-back rule, you can have a contribution that you pay in one tax year treated as if it has been paid in the previous year. You must have enough unused tax-relief limit for the previous year to cover the amount carried back. You get tax relief at the rates which applied in the earlier tax year.

Carrying back contributions can be particularly useful if you're self-employed or run your own company, because the delay in making your pension contributions for a particular year gives you time to make up the accounts for that year and to assess your tax position. But bear in mind that you can, in any case, base your contributions on earnings in an earlier basis year – see page 192.

Carrying back is also advantageous if tax rates change, and relief is available at a higher rate in the year to which you carry back than in the year in which the contribution is paid. If you want to use the carry-back rule, you must pay the contribution by 31 January following the end of the tax year to which you want to carry it back. For example, if you want to carry a contribution back to the 2003–4 tax year, you must pay it by 31 January 2005. You must tell your tax office you are using the carry-back rule either at or before the time you make the payment. You can tell your tax office either by saying so on your self-assessment tax return or by completing form PP43, available from your tax office. You'll also need to fill in form PP120 to claim the tax relief.

If you're an employee, you'll get any higher-rate tax relief either through the Pay-As-You-Earn (PAYE) system or by cheque. If you are self-employed, how you receive any higher-rate tax relief depends on where you are in your tax-payment cycle at the time when you make the claim. Chart 19.1 on page 202 sets out the position if you pay a contribution in the tax year 2004–5 but opt to carry it back to 2003–4, bearing in mind that self-employed people pay their tax as follows:

- two payments on account made on 31 January during the tax year and on 31 July following the end of the tax year. Each payment is set at half the tax bill for the previous year
- a balancing charge or repayment made on 31 January following the end of the tax year. A charge is made if the two payments on account came to less than the actual bill for the tax year. A repayment is made if the two payments on account came to more than the actual bill for the tax year.

Note that when a contribution is carried back to a previous year it does *not* reduce the payments on account for the following year.

Retirement annuity contracts

A retirement annuity contract is a type of personal pension arrangement that was available before 1 July 1988, the date on which personal pensions first went on sale. You can no longer start a new retirement annuity contract, but, if you already have one, you can continue to pay into it. Retirement annuity contracts are covered by different rules from those applying to personal pensions.

Who qualifies?

Retirement annuity contracts (also called Section 226 or Section 620 plans) were available to the self-employed and employees who were not covered by an occupational pension scheme. You have to have earnings to be eligible to pay into a retirement annuity contract.

How much pension?

The pension is worked out on a money purchase basis, so it depends on:

- the amount you pay into the contract
- charges deducted by the contract provider
- how well your invested contributions grow
- annuity rates at the time you retire.

At retirement, you can shop around for the best annuity rate (see Chapter 33), but if you transfer your pension fund to another company, you will be switching from a retirement annuity contract to a personal pension (since retirement annuity contracts can no longer be newly sold). This means your benefits will become subject to the rules for personal pensions instead of retirement annuity contracts. In particular, this will affect the lump sum you can have (see overleaf).

A retirement annuity contract can also provide benefits for your dependants (see Chapter 24). This reduces the amount available to provide your own pension.

Tax-free cash at retirement

You can take part of the proceeds of your contract as a tax-free lump sum at retirement. Doing this reduces the amount of pension you get, but taking the cash is usually worthwhile. If you can't manage on the reduced pension, you could use the cash to buy a purchased life annuity – see Chapter 33.

The maximum cash you can take is three times the remaining pension – see the case history below. If you started your contract between 17 March 1987 and 30 June 1988, there is also an overall cash limit on the lump sum of £150,000. However, the limit applies to each separate contract, so was usually avoided by arranging the plan as a cluster of many different contracts instead of just one.

If you shop around at retirement and switch to another provider to get the best annuity rate (see Chapter 33), you will be transferring from a retirement annuity contract to a personal pension. This will alter the maximum lump sum you can take: when annuity rates are high, it will reduce the lump sum you can get, but when annuity rates are low the maximum lump sum from the personal pension is likely to be higher than that from the retirement annuity contract.

CASE HISTORY: Geoff

Geoff is about to retire. He has built up a pension fund of nearly £104,000 in a retirement annuity contract to which he has contributed for over 30 years. He can either take a pension from the contract of £7,700 a year, or take a lower pension and up to £18,936 as a tax-free lump sum. If he takes the maximum lump sum, his pension will be reduced to £6,312 a year. The maximum lump sum is calculated so that it is three times the remaining pension, in other words 3 × £6,312 = £18,936.

If Geoff had to transfer to another provider to get the best annuity rate, his pension fund would become subject to the rules for personal pensions instead of retirement annuity contracts. The maximum lump sum he could take would be a quarter of the pension fund (25% × £104,000 = £26,000). This is higher than the maximum he can take from the retirement annuity contract.

Pension increases

At the point of retirement, you decide whether to buy a flat-rate pension or one which will increase as retirement progresses – see Chapter 33.

When is the pension paid?

You normally cannot start to take your pension before age 60. There are some exceptions, for example, if you retire through ill health (see

Chapter 24) or if you have an occupation for which an earlier retirement age has been officially recognised – see Table 19.3 for agreed retirement ages under 50 and Table 19.6 for ages between 50 and 60. You must start taking your pension by age 75.

Table 19.6: Occupations with early retirement ages between 50 and 60

Age	Occupation	Age	Occupation
50	Croupiers	55	Airline pilots
	Money broker dealers		Brass instrumentalists
	Newscasters		Distant-water trawlermen
	Offshore riggers		Inshore fishermen
	Royal Navy Reservists		Money broker dealer directors
	Rugby League referees		NHS psychiatrists
	Territorial Army members		Nurses, midwives, etc.
			Part-time firemen
			Singers

What do you pay?

At the outset, you will have chosen whether to take out a regular premium contract requiring payments, say, every month or a contract which requires only *ad hoc* lump sum contributions. With a regular premium contract, there may be penalties if you miss the payments.

Most regular premium contracts let you increase your contributions. Generally, you should consider increasing your payments regularly so that your pension savings keep pace with inflation and do not fall back in terms of today's money.

Limits on what you pay

The Inland Revenue limits the amount of pension contributions you can make which will qualify for tax relief. The limits vary according to your age and are set as a percentage of your net relevant earnings – see Table 19.7. If you're an employee, this means your total before-tax pay, including the taxable value of most fringe benefits. If you're self-employed, it means your profits for tax purposes. The limits tell you the maximum before-tax-relief amount you can pay into your contract.

Contributions for a particular tax year are based on your net relevant earnings for that year. (There is no basis-year option like that applying to personal pensions.) However, see the carry-forward and carry-back rules below.

Unlike the rules for personal pensions, there is no overall cash limit on the amount you can pay. However, the percentage of earnings allowed with retirement annuity contracts is lower. This means a very high earner can pay more into a retirement annuity contract than to a personal pension, but people on lower levels of earnings may be able to pay more into a personal pension. If you contribute to both a retirement annuity contract and a personal pension, as well as meeting the rules for each type of scheme, your combined contributions to both must not exceed the limits for personal pensions (see page 191).

Table 19.7: Tax-relief limits on contributions to retirement annuity contracts

Age at the start of the tax year (6 April)	Amount of relief as a percentage of your earnings	Amount of relief for each £1,000 of your earnings
Up to 50	17.5%	£175
51 to 55	20.0%	£200
56 to 60	22.5%	£225
61 to 74	27.5%	£275
75 and over	you can no longer contribute	

Tax relief on your savings

You get tax relief up to your highest rate on the amount you pay into a retirement annuity contract. You pay in the full contribution without deducting any tax relief and claim the relief due through your tax office. Either use Form PP120 from your tax office or make the claim through your tax return.

Going over the contribution limits

Excess contributions can be left invested in a retirement annuity contract, but they will not qualify for tax relief, and the eventual proceeds will be treated as investment income rather than pension.

Carry-back and carry-forward

The carry-back rules allow you to have contributions paid in one tax year treated as if they had been paid in the previous year. You must have

CASE HISTORY: Leonard

Leonard saves for retirement mainly through a retirement annuity contract which he took out back in 1956 (when they were first launched). He also started a personal pension in July 1988. Leonard is now 65 and wants to contribute as much as possible to his plans to boost his income once he retires. His earnings in 2004–5 are £43,000. He can contribute up to 27.5% × £43,000 = £11,825 to his retirement annuity contract and up to 40% × £43,000 = £17,200 to his personal pension. But his total contributions to both plans must not exceed the personal pension limit – i.e. £17,200.

He decides to pay the full £11,825 into his retirement annuity contract, which leaves him £17,200 – £11,825 = £5,375 to pay into his personal pension.

enough unused contribution limit for the previous year to cover the amount carried back. If you had no net relevant earnings that year, you can carry the contribution back two years (but no further). In either case, you get tax relief at the rates which applied in the earlier tax year.

Carrying back contributions in this way can be particularly useful if you run your own business and there is a delay in making up your accounts, and consequently in finding out how much you can contribute to your pension. It is also advantageous if tax rates in the earlier year were higher than they are now.

To use the carry-back rules, you must pay the contribution by 5 April of the year following the one to which you are carrying back (or the second year following, if you are carrying the contribution back two years). For example, you must pay the contribution by 5 April 2005 if you wish to carry it back to the 2003–4 tax year. You need to tell your tax office that you are carrying back the contribution either by completing Form PP143 or by giving details in your tax return. If you are an employee, tax relief will normally be given through your PAYE code or by cheque. Chart 19.1 shows how the tax relief will be given if you are self-employed.

You can go over the contribution limit for any tax year by using the carry-forward rules. These are useful if you need to boost the amount of pension that you hope to receive from your contract. See Chapter 31 for details.

Chart 19.1: When you get tax relief if you use the carry-back rules

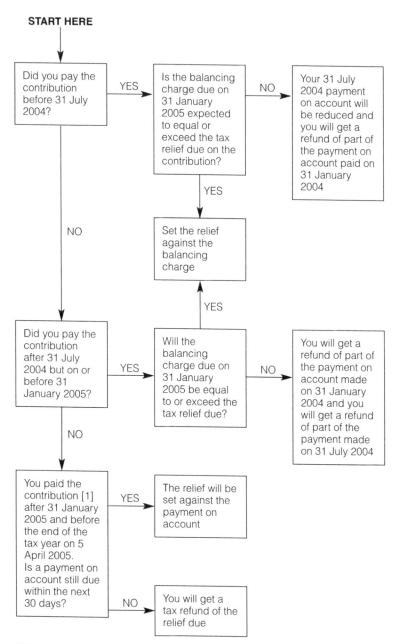

START HERE

Did you pay the contribution before 31 July 2004?
— YES → **Is the balancing charge due on 31 January 2005 expected to equal or exceed the tax relief due on the contribution?**
— NO → **Your 31 July 2004 payment on account will be reduced and you will get a refund of part of the payment on account paid on 31 January 2004**
— YES → **Set the relief against the balancing charge**

(Did you pay the contribution before 31 July 2004?) — NO ↓

Did you pay the contribution after 31 July 2004 but on or before 31 January 2005?
— YES → **Will the balancing charge due on 31 January 2005 be equal to or exceed the tax relief due?**
— NO → **You will get a refund of part of the payment on account made on 31 January 2004 and you will get a refund of part of the payment made on 31 July 2004**
— YES → **Set the relief against the balancing charge**

(Did you pay the contribution after 31 July 2004 but on or before 31 January 2005?) — NO ↓

You paid the contribution [1] after 31 January 2005 and before the end of the tax year on 5 April 2005. Is a payment on account still due within the next 30 days?
— YES → **The relief will be set against the payment on account**
— NO → **You will get a tax refund of the relief due**

[1] Applies only to contributions to retirement annuity contracts

CASE HISTORY: Jean

Jean is 50, and works as a self-employed graphic designer. To keep matters simple, she chose her accounting year to coincide with the tax year. The only drawback is that she doesn't know until after the end of the tax year what her profits and tax position for the year were. She doesn't want to find that she's paid more than the tax rules allow into her retirement annuity contract, so she has committed herself to paying fairly low regular premiums of £4,000 a year (before tax relief), which she hopes to top up when she can.

Business turned out to be fairly good in 2003–4, and Jean decides to pay extra into her contract. In October 2004 she makes an extra lump-sum contribution of £3,000 and asks her tax office to carry this back to the 2003–4 tax year. Her profits for 2003–4 were sufficient for Jean to qualify for tax relief at 22 per cent on the full £3,000, that is, relief of £660.

Jean has made tax payments on account on 31 January 2004 and 31 July 2004 of £2,923 each, based on her final tax bill for 2002–3. But the £5,846 that she has paid is more than the £5,346 which is actually due for the year (before taking account of the pension contribution), so she is due to get a balancing refund of £5,846 – £5,346 = £500 on 31 January 2005.

Tax relief on her £3,000 carried-back contribution is given by revising the two payments on account she has already made. Each payment is reduced by $\frac{1}{2}$ × £660 = £330 to £2,923 – £330 = £2,593. Jean therefore receives a refund by cheque from the Inland Revenue for £660.

Special rules for doctors and dentists

If you're a GP or dentist working in a practice, you count as self-employed for tax purposes. But, unusually, you're eligible to contribute to an occupational pension scheme – the National Health Service (NHS) Superannuation Scheme. At the same time, you can contribute to a personal pension or retirement annuity contract, and there are special rules to work out how much you can contribute. As a GP or dentist, you have a choice:

- you can pay into the NHS scheme but give up all tax relief on these contributions. In this case, all your earnings count as net relevant earnings (see page 191); the tax-relief limit for personal pension contributions or retirement annuity contract contributions is then worked out in the normal way. This option can be attractive, because you can effectively base *two* pensions on the same earnings

- you can pay into the NHS scheme and receive tax relief as normal on these contributions. Multiplying the NHS scheme contribution by 16⅔ gives a figure for the earnings which are covered by that scheme. Subtracting this amount from your total earnings leaves the amount of net relevant earnings which can be used as the basis of working out contributions to a personal pension or retirement annuity contract.

If you're a dentist or a GP, you may decide not to join the NHS scheme – or to leave it if you already belong. In that case, you could use all your earnings as a basis for contributions to a personal pension or retirement annuity contract in the normal way. But the NHS scheme is a good one, and you're likely to do better by joining it.

If you belong to the NHS scheme, you can make additional voluntary contributions (AVCs) – see Chapter 30 – as long as your total contributions don't exceed the normal limit applying to an employer's scheme, which is 15 per cent of your earnings. Your AVCs can be made either to the NHS AVC scheme or to a free-standing AVC scheme. If you do make AVCs, the rules for working out your possible contributions to a personal plan are more complicated than those outlined above. Note that, because doctors and dentists count as self-employed people, the normal rules allowing simultaneous contributions to an occupational scheme and personal pension (see page 186) do not apply.

CASE HISTORY: Derek

Derek is a 31-year-old doctor earning £30,000 a year from a thriving group practice. In the 2004–5 tax year, he pays tax at the basic rate of 22 per cent. He pays £1,000 a year into the NHS scheme; this has a 6 per cent contribution rate, so multiplying by 16⅔ gives an estimate for the amount of Derek's earnings which are covered by the NHS scheme. This figure is £16,666. Derek would like to take out a personal pension plan as well. He has two options:

- he can receive tax relief of £220 (22 per cent of £1,000) on the contribution to the NHS scheme. This means that he'll have net relevant earnings of

£30,000 – £16,666 = £13,334 that can be used as a basis of his contributions to a personal plan. His maximum contribution would be £2,333, which would qualify for £513.26 tax relief. In total, he'd be contributing £3,333 to his pension savings with total tax relief of £733.26

• alternatively, Derek could give up the £220 tax relief on the NHS scheme contribution. In this case, his full £30,000 earnings would be eligible as a basis for contributions to a personal plan. His maximum contribution would be £5,250, which would qualify for tax relief of £1,155.

If Derek wants to make relatively large savings for retirement, the second option looks promising. But he should weigh up whether he'd do better by making AVCs to the NHS scheme or a free-standing AVC scheme (see Chapter 30), instead of taking out a personal plan.

More information

Plan providers and financial advisers can give you details about particular pension plans, and may be able to help you make your pension choices – see Chapters 21 and 22. See Chapter 35 for what to do if you have a problem concerning a personal pension, which the plan provider or your adviser can't resolve.

Table 19.8 lists some useful general information booklets about personal pensions.

Table 19.8: Information about personal pensions

Booklet/leaflet	Published by
PM1 A guide to your pension options	Department for Work and Pensions*
PM4 Personal pensions – your guide	Department for Work and Pensions*
PM5 Pensions for the self-employed – your guide	Department for Work and Pensions*
PM8 Stakeholder pensions – your guide	Department for Work and Pensions*
IR78 Personal pensions	Inland Revenue*

Chapter 20

Stakeholder pension schemes

The government has praised occupational pension schemes, which it sees as being, in partnership with the state, 'one of the great welfare success stories'. But not everyone can join an occupational scheme. For example, your employer may not offer a scheme, you may not be eligible to join one, you may change jobs too frequently to make joining one worthwhile, or you may be self-employed.

When you can't join an occupational pension scheme, your main alternative for retirement saving is a personal pension. But, in the past, personal pensions gained a reputation for being:

- inflexible
- high-charging
- unnecessarily complicated
- poor value for money.

Many have offered a particularly bad deal if you had only small amounts to save.

A new deal

Against this background, in April 2001 the government introduced the stakeholder pension scheme. This is not a new type of pension scheme; it is a set of conditions that can be applied to either personal pensions or money purchase occupational schemes. If the conditions are met, the scheme can use the name 'stakeholder', and you can be confident that the scheme is straightforward and offers good value for money.

Even if you decide against taking out a stakeholder scheme, the conditions provide a good benchmark against which to compare other schemes or plans, to check whether they too offer value for money. If you choose a non-stakeholder scheme or plan, make sure you understand how it differs, and that you are happy to accept those alternative conditions.

Table 20.1: The pros and cons of stakeholder pension schemes

Pros	Cons
Tax advantages	Unpredictable pension and other
Simple	benefits
Low running costs	No guarantee that pension will keep
Value for money	pace with inflation during the period of
Easy to transfer/can carry on if you	build up
change jobs	You bear the investment risk
	Employers do not have to contribute [1]

[1] Unless it is an occupational stakeholder scheme

What's special about stakeholder schemes?

A pension scheme can be called a 'stakeholder scheme' only if it meets certain conditions:

- **low charges** Charges must total no more than 1 per cent a year of the value of your pension fund (but due to be increased to 1.5 per cent from April 2005). This must cover all the costs of running the scheme and managing your investments. The cost must include information and basic advice. If there is a fee for more detailed advice, this must be set out in a separate contract and charged separately
- **low and flexible contributions** The minimum contribution must be no higher than £20, whether as a one-off payment or a regular contribution. You can't be required to make contributions at regular intervals. It's up to you when or how often you pay
- **portability** You must be able to transfer out of a stakeholder scheme into another stakeholder scheme or another pension arrangement without penalty. Stakeholder schemes must accept transfers from other stakeholder schemes and other pension arrangements
- **simplicity** The scheme must include a default investment option which determines how your money is invested if you don't want to choose an investment fund for yourself. This will often be a tracker fund (see page 215) though, under new rules due to take effect from April 2005, it will generally be a lifestyle fund (see page 218)

- **keeping you informed** The scheme provider must give you a benefit statement at least once a year showing you in straightforward terms the value of your rights under the scheme. If the scheme's charges alter, you must be informed within one month of the change.

Who can join a stakeholder scheme?

Stakeholder schemes can be personal pensions or occupational money purchase schemes and, apart from meeting the stakeholder conditions above, they are covered by the normal rules for those arrangements. As described in Chapter 19, from April 2001 onwards, nearly everyone is eligible to have a personal pension and, if they so choose, this can be a stakeholder scheme.

Occupational money purchase schemes that meet the conditions can also register as stakeholder schemes. The main difference between an occupational stakeholder scheme and a personal stakeholder scheme is that you can belong to the former only while you are working for the particular employer, whereas personal stakeholder schemes are not usually linked to a particular job.

Since October 2001, employers with five or more employees who do not already offer a pension arrangement through work have to give you access to a stakeholder scheme through your workplace. In most cases, this will be a personal stakeholder scheme.

Even employees who already belong to an occupational pension scheme can often take out a stakeholder scheme to top up their savings (see Chapter 30). The only group that cannot have a stakeholder scheme (unless used only to contract out) comprises people who:

- already belong to an occupational pension scheme which is not itself a stakeholder scheme, and
- are either controlling directors or earn more than £30,000 a year.

Your stakeholder pension on retirement

All stakeholder schemes work on a money purchase basis. This means that the pension that you will receive on retirement will depend on:

- the amount paid into the scheme
- the tax reliefs available
- the charges deducted

- how well the invested contributions grow
- annuity rates at the time when you start taking the pension.

The amount paid in

See Chapter 19 for the contribution limits applying to personal pensions, including those that meet the stakeholder conditions. If the scheme is to be contracted out, see Chapter 23. See Chapter 10 for the limits on what you can pay into an occupational money purchase scheme, including those that qualify as stakeholder schemes, and Chapter 14 if it is a contracted-out scheme.

Chapter 30 gives details of the circumstances in which members of occupational pension schemes can also pay up to £3,600 a year into a personal stakeholder scheme.

Tax reliefs

- You will get tax relief on your contributions.
- If you are a non-taxpayer paying into a personal stakeholder scheme, you get a bonus equal to basic-rate tax relief added to your savings.
- Capital gains from investing the contributions are tax-free. Some investment income is tax-free but not income from shares, unit trusts and similar investments.
- Part of the pension fund can be taken as a tax-free lump sum (but not any part used for contracting out).

Charges

Charges are limited to a maximum of 1 per cent a year (due to rise to 1.5 per cent from April 2005) levied as a percentage of your pension fund. However, some personal pensions that are not stakeholder schemes charge less than 1 per cent a year, particularly where you have built up a substantial pension fund or you are making very large contributions.

How your savings are invested

See Chapter 21 for information about how personal pensions can be invested, and Chapter 12 for details of investments for occupational money purchase schemes.

Options on retirement

You normally use your pension fund to buy an annuity on retirement (see Chapter 33).

Why choose anything other than stakeholder?

If your employer offers an occupational pension scheme, this is usually the best way to save for retirement, not least because your employer must contribute a substantial part of the cost. So, generally, it makes sense to join an occupational scheme whether or not it has stakeholder status.

When it comes to personal pensions though, if stakeholder schemes are low-charging, flexible and such good value for money, why would anyone choose an ordinary personal pension? It's a good question and, in general, anyone newly starting a personal pension would do well to consider a stakeholder scheme. But here are two reasons why you might still opt for a non-stakeholder personal pension:

- **greater investment choice**. Some stakeholder schemes offer a limited range of investment funds. If you want more exotic options, you'll probably need to look elsewhere. And, if you want to choose your own investments, you'll need a self-invested personal pension which does not come in the stakeholder variety
- **even lower charges**. Although stakeholder schemes must by definition have low charges, some non-stakeholder personal pensions charge 1 per cent a year or less. They may not be registered as stakeholder schemes because they fail to meet one of the other conditions, such as the no-more-than-£20 minimum contribution. If you're planning to invest more than that anyway, you might not be bothered by the lack of stakeholder status. But you need to check very carefully that there are no unacceptable non-stakeholder terms, such as hefty penalties if you want to transfer your plan.

The picture is different if you already have a personal pension that you started before 6 April 2001. You might already have paid the bulk of any high charges and so have nothing to gain now by switching to a stakeholder scheme. And, as described in Chapter 25, you could crystallise hefty surrender charges if you did transfer.

However, if you were advised to take out a personal pension after 31 March 1999, under guidance issued by the financial regulator, your adviser should have taken care to sell you a plan which would not cause you any 'material disadvantage' if you later switched to a stakeholder pension scheme. 'Material disadvantage' was not defined but seems likely to include surrender penalties on transfer out of the personal pension. If you do now transfer from a personal pension started after 31 March 1999 and find you are facing penalties, consider making a complaint about the advice you were given (see Chapter 35).

How safe are stakeholder schemes?

When you have a stakeholder scheme that is a personal pension, you are protected by the financial regulatory system described in Chapter 26. The safety of occupational schemes is discussed in Chapter 17.

In addition, whether it is a personal pension or an occupational scheme, every stakeholder scheme must be registered with the Occupational Pensions Regulatory Authority (OPRA★). OPRA is responsible for seeing that all the stakeholder conditions and rules are met. OPRA has the power to impose sanctions on schemes that breach the rules. OPRA is due to be replaced shortly by a new Pensions Regulator (see page 174).

More information

For a broad outline of stakeholder pensions, see PM8 *Stakeholder pensions – your guide*, published by the Department for Work and Pensions (DWP).★ See also the FSA★ fact-sheet, *Stakeholder pensions and decision trees*.

Chapter 21

Choosing a personal pension

There's a huge choice of personal pension plan providers and literally hundreds of individual plans to choose from. But in the past many plans were poor value for money, particularly if you wanted to save regularly (rather than invest lump sums from time to time).

Better-value plans have become more widespread, largely due to action by both the government and the regulator for personal pensions, the Financial Services Authority (FSA). In particular, the introduction of stakeholder schemes from April 2001 onwards has made the market for pensions more competitive and persuaded many providers to offer a better deal than they did in the past.

This chapter outlines the features that you should look out for when choosing a personal pension plan. Chapter 22 looks at how to take out a plan and where to get advice.

How do you want to save?

Most plan providers offer both regular contribution plans and single lump-sum contribution plans. Often, you (or you and your employer, if he or she's contributing to your plan) have to invest at least a given amount – for example, £20 a month or £200 a year with a regular contribution plan, or £500 or £1,000 with a single contribution plan. Most regular contribution plans will accept extra one-off payments, though once again there may be a minimum amount for these, such as £250 or £500.

The majority of regular premium plans will let you increase your contributions if you want to. With some plans you can arrange to increase your payments automatically each year by a set amount.

An important feature to look out for with a regular premium plan is whether you can miss one or more payments without penalty. This can be important if you have a temporary hiccup in your earnings or your circumstances change, and can be useful if, say, you want to take a career break. You may need to pay extra for a 'waiver of premium' option that allows you to miss payments if your earnings fall because of illness or redundancy.

This feature may be part of the package when you've taken out your plan under a group personal pension scheme (GPPS, see Chapter 13). Most plan providers also offer plans which will accept just the payments from the government, if you want to use a personal plan simply for contracting out of the State Second Pension (see Chapter 23).

If you choose a stakeholder pension scheme, the minimum contribution – whether as a regular payment or as a lump sum – may not be set higher than £20. In addition, the scheme cannot lock you into a pattern of regular payments. It's up to you when and how often you pay and, if you do choose to make regular contributions, you can miss them without penalty.

Regular payments or lump sum – which is best?

A regular payment plan can be useful in providing an element of discipline to your saving, and in helping you to save a large amount, but in manageable chunks. Regular payment plans are suitable mainly for people in employment who receive a steady income.

At one time, a regular premium plan let you lock into a fixed level of charges, but those days are long gone, and nowadays all plans give the provider flexibility to increase charges during the life of the plan. So, don't look solely at what you'll be paying now, look also at what you might have to pay in future. At one time, most regular premium plans were suitable only if you were sure that you would be able to keep up payments into the plan for many years to come. This is because the plan provider pays out a large chunk of the costs of setting up the plan at the outset (called front-end charges). These are mainly the costs of paying commission to the adviser or salesperson who brought in the business. If you keep the plan going for a long time these costs are effectively spread out. But if you stop the plan early or transfer your savings to another plan the plan provider recoups the costs by charging you a surrender penalty. These penalties can be severe, even ten years into the plan, and if you stop or transfer within the first few years your fund will often be less than you have invested. See page 221 for more about charges. Good advice has traditionally been that you should not start a regular contribution plan unless you are sure that you can keep up the payments. Nowadays, though, you can opt for a stakeholder scheme which gives you complete flexibility.

If you opt for a regular contribution plan that is not a stakeholder scheme, check what flexibility the plan gives you – for example, it can be very useful to be able to make an extra *ad hoc* payment into the plan if you have a windfall. Equally, it can help to minimise hardship if you're able to miss contributions without penalty, or reduce the amount you pay. Lump-sum plans give you far more flexibility, since you just take out a plan whenever you want and have funds available.

If you run your own business, or you're an employee whose income varies a lot, you may find single premium plans more suitable than regular premium ones. But you'll have to impose your own discipline on your savings habit. Also, you'll have to accept whatever terms apply to each plan when you take it out, so you can't 'lock into' favourable terms in the way that you may be able to do with a regular payment plan.

If you chose a flexible arrangement but need the discipline of regular payments, setting up a direct debit or standing order to transfer automatically monthly or yearly payments from your bank account should help.

How your money is invested

There are a number of different ways in which the money in your plan can be invested. Some plans *always* invest just one way, others give you a choice. The broad methods of investment are described below.

Choosing your own investments

Plans which let you choose your own investments are called Self Invested Personal Pensions (SIPPs). You build up your own fund of investments comprising assets that you've chosen yourself. Regulations place some limits on your choice, but the range is wide and can include UK shares, gilts, and property, among others. In practice, a 'do-it-yourself' pension plan is likely to be uneconomic unless you have a large sum to invest.

Unit-linked, unit trust and similar plans

Unit-linked plans are offered by many insurance companies. Your money is allocated to units whose value is linked to a specific fund of investments. Your return depends on the price of your units; this rises and falls in line with the value of the underlying investments.

Plans operated by unit trusts and open-ended investment companies (OEICs) – and, to a large extent, investment trusts – work in a similar way, with the value of your pension pot rising and falling in line with a fund of underlying investments in which you have units or shares. These types of plan have been much less common in the past than those run by insurance companies.

Whether insurance-based, unit-trust-based and so on, unitised plans offer you a choice of different types of investment funds and unit trusts, investing in, for example, UK shares, foreign shares, gilts, and so on. A managed fund or mixed-unit trust invests in a broad spread of different investments. You can usually choose to invest in more than one fund at once, but there may be a minimum investment for each one. Generally, you can switch between the different funds or different trusts after you've started the plan. Sometimes one or two switches a year are free.

Tracker funds

With most unitised funds, the fund manager tries to select the underlying shares or other investments that he or she believes will give the best returns. This involves continuously monitoring the relevant markets and being prepared to switch from stock to stock and from one type of investment to another as conditions change. There is, of course, no guarantee that the fund manager will succeed in outguessing the market – indeed, there is some evidence to show that this so-called 'active fund management' does not beat the market at all. The downside to active fund management is the costs involved in paying for so much input from the fund managers and the charges for the frequent sales and purchases of investments. As a result, some funds have opted to work in a much more passive manner.

With a tracker fund, the main input from the fund manager is when the fund is first set up. The underlying investments are selected to mimic a particular market as described by a given stock–market index

– e.g. the FTSE 100 Index or S&P 500. The fund is then left to track that market with no attempt being made to identify and switch to expected best performers. These 'index' or 'tracker' funds have been turning in very creditable performances and generally benefit from much lower charges.

With-profits plans

These are offered by insurance companies and a few friendly societies. Your money is invested by the plan provider in a broad spread of investments – shares, gilts, property, etc. Your return depends largely on how well the investments grow, but also on other factors, such as the provider's profits from other parts of its business, its level of expenses, etc.

Your return is in the form of bonuses: reversionary bonuses are added to your plan regularly – often yearly; a terminal bonus is usually added at the time you convert your investment fund into pension. The bonuses are not directly linked to the performance of the investments in the underlying fund. In good years, some of the profits are kept back in reserve and used to boost reversionary bonuses in years when investment performance is poor. This is a process called 'smoothing'. Once a reversionary bonus is added to your plan, it cannot be taken away (provided you keep the plan going until retirement), so your plan should always be on a growing trend. But the level of future bonuses isn't guaranteed. Plan providers are usually cautious about increasing reversionary bonuses, and reluctant to cut them. However, many insurance companies have cut their reversionary bonus rates in recent years on the back of falling stock-market values. Particularly during a prolonged downturn, all providers are likely to have to cut bonuses, but those who will be worst hit are generally the companies that have the lowest reserves. Just like a household, having something in reserve for a rainy day improves a company's financial strength and this is an important aspect to check out when choosing a with-profits plan.

The level of terminal bonus can vary greatly, and can amount to a sizeable proportion of your plan – for example, as much as half or even nearly three-quarters of the total return. The greater the proportion of your return that is left to the terminal bonus the more risk you are taking on. This is because the terminal bonus is in no way guaranteed until the point at which you receive it: in other words, when the plan matures. Statements showing how well your plan has grown so far may include an estimate of the terminal bonus based on current bonus rates, but this is only an indication of what you may get. If stock-market conditions are poor when your plan matures it's quite likely that the terminal bonus rate will be cut.

If you transfer your pension plan before it reaches maturity, you usually miss out on any terminal bonus and you could even lose some of the reversionary bonuses which have already been added to your plan. This is because the provider usually reserves the right to impose a market value reduction. For an explanation of why this happens and how it works, see page 121.

Many with-profits plans are organised on a unitised basis. Your money is allocated to units in the with-profits fund. The value of the units increases in line with declared bonuses. However, instead of charges being implicit within the bonus, they are levied separately, using the normal structure which applies to unitised funds (see page 222). This makes unitised with-profits funds a little more transparent than the traditional with-profits arrangement.

Bond-based funds

These are a particular type of unitised fund. The underlying investments are corporate bonds, preference shares and gilts (British government stocks), all of which are collectively known as fixed-interest investments.

A single bond offers a fixed income and usually a set capital gain (or loss) payable at a fixed point in time, although before then the bond can be sold in the market at whatever market price then prevails.

A fund investing in bonds does not offer the same guaranteed returns, because the fund manager will constantly be buying and selling different bonds. However, because of the nature of the underlying bonds, the fund as a whole provides a reasonably stable return. This will tend, over the long term, to be less exciting than the return on shares, so bond-based funds are not usually a good idea if you are a long way from retirement. But as retirement approaches it may be sensible gradually to switch your investments away from more volatile equities to more stable bonds in order to lock into past growth.

Deposit-based schemes and funds

Deposit-based schemes can be offered by banks and building societies but seldom, if ever, are. Deposit administration plans, which work basically like deposit accounts, are run by a handful of insurance companies. A cash fund or money-market fund as an option within a unit-linked plan is similar and much more common. Your money is invested in an account to which interest is added periodically. The amount of your capital can't fall and grows as the interest is added, but the level of future interest rates isn't guaranteed.

Lifestyle funds

These are a relatively new concept. When you start your pension plan, your money is invested in a fund which takes into account your attitude towards risk and the length of time that you have until your planned retirement date. A mix of shares, bonds and deposits is chosen to reflect those factors and is then automatically adjusted as time goes by. For example, if you take out the plan when you are in your thirties, are planning to retire at the age of 65 and are comfortable with a reasonably high level of risk, your fund may initially be invested entirely in shares. When you are around the age of 50, the fund manager may start to switch some of your investments into bond-based funds. By the time that you are 60, a quarter of your fund may be in bonds. During the last five years before your retirement the manager may also start shifting your investments into deposits, and by retirement your fund may be made up of, say, no shares, three-quarters bonds and one-quarter deposits.

You will have avoided the worry of making investment decisions, and the lifestyle fund will have exposed you to stock-market growth when you were investing for the long term. It will have locked in your returns by shifting to more stable investments as the point at which you intend to withdraw your fund approaches.

Which type of plan?

As the lifestyle fund demonstrates, your choice of investment depends largely on how much risk you're willing to take, and the length of time to go until you need your pension. In general, to have the chance of a higher return, you'll need to take more risk. Unit-linked plans, where the amount of your investment can fall as well as rise, are generally more risky than with-profits plans, where your investment increases but can't normally fall back. Bond-based funds are medium risk. Deposit-based schemes and funds are the least risky, since the amount of your capital can't fall, and because interest rates tend to be more steady than the terminal bonus rates on with-profits policies. But the deposit-based schemes and funds will tend to give the lowest returns and are vulnerable to inflation.

It's essential that long-term retirement savings should be invested so that their value at least keeps pace with inflation. If you're a long way from retirement, you should probably be looking mainly at share-based unit-linked investments, as these give you the best chance of beating inflation and of getting a good return over the long term. Choosing a managed fund or mixed trust is less risky than going for more specialised funds or trusts. If you prefer a lower risk strategy, or you are within, say, 10 or 15 years of retirement, consider investing part of your money on a unit-linked or unit-trust basis and part on a with-profits basis or in bond-based funds. When you're within a few years of retirement, a mix of bonds and deposit-based schemes and funds can be a way of protecting your past investment growth from falls in stock-market prices.

Charts 21.1 and 21.2 demonstrate how various types of pension plan and unit-linked funds have performed. They show the value in June 2004 of £1,000 invested either five or ten years previously, net of fund charges and with income reinvested.

The first point to note is that whatever type of fund you choose there is usually a big difference between the best and the worst performers. Unfortunately, this knowledge is of little help to you, since you cannot know in advance which funds will turn out to be the best, especially when you are investing over the very long term. Academic studies consistently confirm that past performance is no guide to the future. You may want to ignore consistently badly performing funds, but there is no evidence to suggest that today's top performers will be the winners in five, 10, 20 or more years' time.

The second point that the charts clearly demonstrate is that higher returns go hand in hand with greater risk. The charts are arranged so that the highest risk funds are on the left, with risk reducing as you move towards the right of each chart. If you could have picked out the best performers in each group, you would have got a better return from

Chart 21.1: Past performance of personal funds over five years

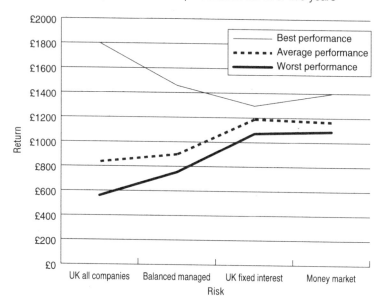

Chart 21.2: Past performance of personal funds over ten years

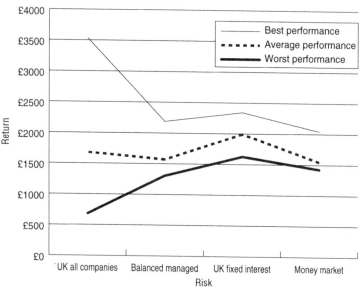

Source: *Money Management*, June 2004

the UK all companies (share-based) fund than the balanced managed (mix of shares, bonds, etc.) fund; you would have done better with the balanced managed fund than with the gilt fund; and you would have done better with the gilts than with the money-market (deposit) fund. The same is true if you look at the average funds for each sector.

But the risk is demonstrated by the difference between the best and worst performers in each sector, which is lowest for the money-market funds and highest for the equities. If you'd had the misfortune to choose the worst-performing UK equity fund you would have done a lot worse than by choosing the worst-performing money-market fund: indeed, over five years you would have ended up with even less than you had originally invested.

Risk also varies over time. This is not shown by the charts, but if you could look at similar charts for many different periods you would see that the average return from the money-market funds would not change much from time period to time period. But as you move up the risk scale the returns would be more volatile, so that the average return on UK equities would show much greater variation from one time period to another.

Fees and charges

With deposit-based schemes, the rate of interest offered will reflect the expenses incurred by the plan provider, though sometimes there are separate charges that you must pay too – for example, an administration fee. Similarly, the level of bonuses earned under a traditional with-profits plan incorporates an allowance for expenses – though again you'll usually have to pay a separate policy fee or administration charge as well.

The position with all unitised plans is quite different: there are generally fewer hidden expenses. Instead, you pay a variety of explicit charges. Unit-trust charges are relatively simple, but the plans offered by insurance companies often have a very complicated charging structure. Table 21.1 summarises charges you may come across.

Overall, the most important factors determining the size of your pension will normally be investment performance and annuity rates at the time when you retire. A higher-charging plan will not necessarily provide the lowest pension. Clearly, however, the investments will have to work a lot harder in order to overcome the handicap of higher

Table 21.1: Charges for unit-linked and unit-trust plans

Name of the charge	Description
Charges commonly applied to unitised plans	
Bid-offer spead	The difference between the higher offer price at which you are allocated or buy units and the lower bid price at which you cash them in. Typically, the spread will be around 5–6%
Exit charge	A charge when you withdraw your investment, usually levied only during the first few years. Most commonly used by some unit trusts where they have no bid-offer spread
Management charge	A yearly charge set against the investment fund or unit trust to cover the costs of managing the underlying investments. Typically, this might be about 1% or 1.5% of the amount of the fund or trust
One-off administration charge	There might be a single charge at the outset of the plan, or deducted from the first year's payments
Additional charges often applied to insurance-based plans	
Policy fee and/or administration charge	A deduction made at regular intervals to cover the costs of the paperwork, etc., involved in setting up and running the plan
Unit allocation	A given percentage of each payment is allocated to units. The percentage may be lower in the earlier years of the plan, and it may be lower if you pay monthly, say, rather than yearly. Don't be misled by allocations of over 100%: it sounds as if you're being credited with more money than you've paid in but this isn't so – it may mean 100% of the money left after a policy fee or administration charge has been deducted, or you may be getting a refund of part of the management fee
Capital units	You may be allocated 'special' units, especially in the first year or two of the plan, which have a much higher management charge – for example, 3% or 5% of the amount of the fund. You usually carry on paying this higher charge throughout the life of the plan
Surrender charges	You're likely to be credited with only part of the value of your plan if you stop paying into it, or transfer it, in the early years

Note: unit-linked plans may charge you if you switch your contributions and/or invested money from one fund to another, though the first switch, or two, each year is usually free. Switching unit trusts will be expensive if you have to sell units in one trust and buy units in another. But some unit-trust plans make use of 'umbrella funds' – the trust is split into a number of different funds between which you can switch either free or at low cost.

charges, and it is extremely unlikely that any investment policy can make up for the worst charges. The message is clear: shop around and avoid plans with high charges.

When can you retire?

The tax rules normally allow you to take the proceeds of a personal pension plan at any age from 50 (due to rise to 55 by 2010) to 75. But protected rights from a contracted-out plan (see Chapter 23) can't be taken before age 60. Within these limits, the plan may set its own rules.

With some plans, you have to choose a retirement date at the time you first take out the plan, though there will be no penalty if you retire after that date. But there may be a penalty if you retire earlier, so it's probably best to choose the earliest possible date at the outset, even if you subsequently change your mind. Many plans don't insist on a set retirement date, but let you choose near the time. You don't have to stop work to be able to take a pension from a personal pension. This means that you could ease back on work but maintain your income by starting to take a pension before you fully retire. Having several personal pensions with different pension ages can add to your retirement flexibility. Since April 2001 onwards the tax rules allow providers to offer multiple retirement dates within a single plan.

A plan which allows you to defer taking an annuity but to draw an income direct from the plan (see Chapter 33) also gives you a wide margin of flexibility, because the income you draw from the fund can range from the amount an annuity would have provided down to roughly a third of that sum.

Pension choices

There are different types of pension that you can choose: a level pension, one which increases by a set amount each year, or one which increases in line with price inflation – usually up to a certain limit, such as 5 per cent a year. The options open to you are looked at in detail in Chapter 33.

You don't have to make your choice about these features at the time you take out the plan, as long as the plan gives you an open market option – all personal pension plans used for contracting out must give you this option, and most other plans do too. The open market option allows you to take your fund to another plan provider (which must be an insurance company or friendly society) at the time you want to start taking your pension. So you can leave your shopping around for a pension until then. However, at the time you start the plan, you should check whether there will be any penalty if you exercise your open market option at retirement. For example, a penalty might be in the form of a retirement bonus which you get only if you stay with the original plan provider.

More information

The FSA publishes tables comparing personal pensions and also those which qualify as stakeholder schemes. If you have access to the Internet, you can check these by visiting the FSA consumer website★. You can also get print-outs of the tables by calling the FSA Consumer Helpline★. Specialist magazines are another useful source both of information about plans generally and of surveys comparing the different plans which are available; an added advantage is that surveys usually give details of how to contact the providers for more information. Some magazines are available through newsagents, and with many you can arrange a subscription, or obtain single copies, direct from the publisher. Specialist magazines that run regular surveys of pension plans include *Money Management*★ and *Pensions Management*★. *Which?* magazine★ also publishes regular articles about personal pensions, including comparative surveys of many of the plans available. Copies of *Which?* are kept by many public reference libraries.

If you're already interested in the plans offered by particular providers, you can get information about them direct from the providers. The telephone book may have the address and phone number of a local branch or office. If not, your local library should be able to find details of the head office for you. Many providers have websites where you can find details of their pension plans. Some websites even let you apply online.

You can take out a plan directly from the provider without having any advice at all. But, if you are not clear about what you want or confident about taking out a plan, it would be a good idea to consult a financial adviser. This could be an adviser working for the company itself, in which case you'll normally just get advice about that company's products. However, during 2005, the rules are due to

- whether you have a husband or wife
- whether you have children, and their ages
- your regular financial commitments (such as mortgage payments, household bills, and so on) and your likely commitments in retirement
- your intended retirement age
- your likely entitlement to state pensions
- details of any pension scheme that is open to you through your workplace
- details of any previous employer's schemes from which you're entitled to a pension at retirement
- details of any personal pensions that you already have
- details of any life insurance you currently have
- details of any other savings and investments
- how much you can afford to pay into a pension plan
- whether you want to transfer any funds from previous pension schemes or plans into a new plan
- what features you want your plan to have
- your attitude towards investment risk
- likely changes to any of the above.

The only situation in which less information would be sufficient is where your intention is only to contract out of the State Second Pension through a rebate-only plan (see Chapter 23). In this case, the plan provider needs to know only your age and sex, employment status, earnings, details of any scheme open to you through your workplace, and your attitude towards investment risk.

Once the salesperson has got to know you, he or she must recommend to you only suitable products from the company's wares – if none is suitable, he or she must tell you so. He or she should help you to make your decision in the light of the options open to you (so, for example, if you could join an excellent occupational scheme and it would be unlikely that a personal pension could beat it, the salesperson should tell you that none of his or her products is suitable for you).

A salesperson for one company within a group of related companies might be unable to sell the full range of that group's products. If he or she recognises that the product of another company within the group might be suitable, he or she can offer to arrange for you to meet with the salesperson for that other company. For example, a life-insurance salesperson might arrange contact with the unit-trust arm of the same group.

When you have agreed to a deal, you'll be given or sent detailed information about the product (see page 235). You'll also receive a suitability letter (formerly called a reason-why letter), setting out why the adviser has given you the advice that he or she did, and a cancellation notice which tells you that you have the right to withdraw from the deal within 14 days of receiving the notice. After 14 days, you're committed to the contract.

Execution-only business

You forgo some of the protection of the Financial Services and Markets Act if you voluntarily opt to do business on an execution-only basis. This will generally be the case if you invest through a coupon in an advertisement, in response to a mail shot or with a direct-sales-only company. Because you have agreed to invest without the benefit of any advice, the plan provider or adviser is under no duty to get to know you or to offer suitable advice. Therefore, you have only yourself to blame if things go wrong. In the light of this, you should be very wary of taking out a pension plan on an execution-only basis.

Going to a tied agent

Getting in touch

You'll see tied agents' advertisements in, say, local newspapers, trade directories and the *Yellow Pages*. You may be on an agent's mailing list as a result of having shown interest in some of their other products, or you may be on a mailing list which the agent has bought from an outside source. You'll also find tied agents in your high street. Most banks and building societies are tied agents. Other such agents include small firms operating under a variety of names, such as 'insurance and pensions adviser', 'insurance consultant', 'pensions consultant' and 'financial adviser'.

The selling process

Tied agents can sell and advise only on the products offered by the single company to which they are tied. In the past, that meant the products of just one provider, because of a rule called 'polarisation'. Under polarisation, advisers had to choose either to sell one company's wares or be totally independent – they could not sell products from a handful of companies. But polarisation is in the process of being abolished.

Already, for stakeholder pension schemes and, from 2005, for other personal pensions (and certain other investments), the company to which an adviser is tied is allowed to adopt into its range the products of other providers. These may be sold alongside the company's own pensions or the company might not have any pensions of its own and just market the plans and schemes of other providers.

The change has been made to increase consumer choice. Many consumers tend to go to their bank or building society for financial advice because it is a familiar outlet. In the past, banks and building societies almost all sold the products of a single provider – often their own insurance arm – so you really didn't get much choice at all. From 2005, it is expected that at least some banks and building societies will adopt a wider product range so that you do have several competing products to choose from. And other firms – not just banks and building societies – can opt for this course too.

You will need to check whether you are being offered the products of one provider or several – the initial disclosure document will tell you which applies. You should also make sure you are happy with the choice offered – it will still be fairly limited and, if you want a bigger choice, going to an independent adviser is likely to suit you better.

Tied agents are regulated by the same rules that apply to a company's own salespeople (see page 228), and the company is ultimately responsible for the conduct of its agents. So if you deal with tied agents, they must make clear to you their status and the company that they represent. They must follow the 'know your customer' and 'suitable advice' rules. If you invest through a tied agent, the plan provider will send you details of the product, a suitability letter and a cancellation notice, giving you 14 days to back out of the deal.

Going to an independent adviser
Getting in touch

If you're unsure which plan provider's products will suit you, it's best to seek help from an independent adviser rather than from a company salesperson or tied agent.

For a list of independent financial advisers (IFAs) in your area, contact IFA Promotion★, the Institute of Financial Planning★ or the Society of Financial Advisers★. Many IFAs are paid by commission from the provider whose products they sell (see below), which could, in theory, sway the advice that they give you. But, from 2005 (when polarisation is abolished), any adviser calling itself 'independent' must offer you the choice of paying by fees if you want to.

Many accountants, solicitors and actuaries give financial advice. They must be independent in accordance with the rules governing their professions.

The selling process

As the name suggests, independent advisers are independent of any particular company and must base their advice on the products of the full range of companies in the market.

An independent adviser is bound by the 'know your customer' rule, explained on page 228, and you should expect him or her to investigate all the areas outlined there. An independent adviser must recommend the most suitable product for you from the range available. In practice, the adviser does not have to look at every product on the market for every customer; he or she must make regular surveys of the market to identify the best products but doesn't need to make a special survey for each customer; the adviser is allowed to identify the 'best' product for an identifiable group – for example, all people in a given age group who want rebate-only pension plans – rather than seeking out a product afresh for each new customer.

If you invest through an adviser, the plan provider will usually send you details of the plan (see page 235) and a cancellation notice – see page 230. You have 14 days to back out of the deal. The adviser must also send you a suitability letter stating why he or she has given you the advice he or she did.

How salespeople and advisers are paid

Salespeople employed by a particular company may be paid by salary, bonuses, commission on sales, fringe benefits (such as a car), and so on. Tied agents usually receive commissions on the sales that they make, and they may be able to claim back from the company certain expenses associated with running the business. Most independent advisers receive commission on the sales that they make (but, from 2005, will have to offer the option to pay by fees). In one way or another, the commission payments to salespeople, agents and independent advisers are met out of charges or expenses on the investment to which you agree. Some advisers charge you a fee for their services and, in this case, commissions they receive may be used to reduce the fee you pay, or the commissions may be paid over to you. Solicitors and accountants always charge fees and may keep any commissions they receive only with your consent.

Payment by commission raises the possibility of some conflict of interest. One potential problem arises with independent advisers. Plan providers compete for the clients of independent advisers, in part by offering better commission deals than their rivals. Yet, the adviser who is your agent is supposed to advise you with reference only to your circumstances – not to the amount of commission he or she will earn. There is clearly a temptation for an independent adviser to recommend the products of the company that will pay the most commission. Some don't pay commission to the middleman at all, so there's a risk that these plans might be overlooked.

Even where salespeople and tied agents are able to sell only the products of one company, the temptation of commission payments could persuade them – as well as independent advisers – to recommend their customers to invest more than they really wanted to, to recommend a higher-commission product in preference to one which might be more suitable for the customer, or to recommend a product when in fact none of the products available is suitable. You should be on your guard against these problems. Work out for yourself how much you want to invest, make sure that you know what you want and check that the recommended product meets your requirements. When you get the suitability letter, read it and make sure you agree that the reasons set out in the letter were the ones you discussed, and that they seem to provide a sound basis for your investment. If you are not happy, consider using your cooling-off period to pull out of the deal.

If you use a solicitor, accountant or other fee-based adviser, the problems are less likely to arise.

Since 1 January 1995 you must be told in advance what commission the salesperson or adviser stands to make if you invest in the products they are recommending. Details will be given in the product details you're sent. From 2005, you must also be given a *Guide to the Cost of our Services* on first contact. This sets out whether you will pay by fee or commission, how much you typically might pay and, if payment is by commission, the market average, so you can compare what your adviser will get with what other advisers get. Once again, because this document contains important information required by the regulator, it carries the Key Facts logo (see page 227).

If the amount of commission looks high compared with that on other products or on other companies' products, query the amount. A product that pays high commission is likely also to have high plan charges (and can be the main reason for high surrender charges). High charges do not necessarily mean that the product is undesirable, but clearly it is going to have to work a lot harder than a low-charging plan to overcome the handicap of high charges. Can the salesperson or adviser explain why that plan is expected to perform so much better than a low-charging one? If he or she can't, or if the explanation is unconvincing, take your business elsewhere.

Competition is very intense these days, and, if pressed, many advisers will agree to share their commission with you. Because of the tax rules applying to pension plans, it is not usually possible actually to hand over a cash sum to you, as it might be with a different sort of product. However, if the adviser will give up part of the commission, it can be ploughed into your plan and used to enhance the terms or benefits.

Advertisements

The FSA has drawn up comprehensive rules to control the way investments are advertised. They include:

- an advertisement must give the name of the advertiser and, usually, the name of the regulating body (see Chapter 26), too
- the nature of the investment must be clear. If full details are not given, the advertisement must say how you can get them
- references to past performance must not be misleading, must follow a standardised format and must include appropriate warnings that past performance is not a guide to the future
- projections and illustrations, if used, must be worked out in a set way (see below)

- if the value of your investment can go down as well as up – for example, as with unit-linked investments and unit trusts – there must be a warning to this effect.

Information about plans

When you first approach a plan provider or a middleman for information about pension products, you will probably be offered literature about the products, usually in the form of a brochure. Either in the brochure or along with it, you must be given details of certain key features of the plan in question. These must include:

- a description of the plan, including the payments which would be required and which, if any, of the benefits are fixed
- if your investment would be unit-linked, details of the funds available
- if your investment would be on a with-profits basis, a description of how the bonuses are worked out
- the risk involved – for example, whether the original value of your capital can fall as well as rise
- a guide to the transfer value of the plan during the first five years, should you decide to switch to another plan
- the effect of charges and expenses on your investment.

The information given in the key features will be based, where necessary, on realistic examples. If you decide to go ahead and invest in the plan, the rules require that you be sent broadly the same information again but, this time, including calculations that are based on your specific situation and decisions about, for example, how much to invest. This information must be sent by the plan provider, unless it can reasonably assume that your adviser has provided the information instead. Where applicable, the important information must also include the note about how much commission your adviser is to receive for arranging the plan for you (see page 232). The investor-specific key features includes an illustration (or projection) of the possible benefits which you might get from the plan at retirement age.

During 2005, key features documents will be replaced by Key Facts documents. These will include broadly the same information as key features, but in a clearer format and in a way that makes it easier to compare one product with another. Similarly, the illustration will be replaced by a Key Facts Example – see Figure 22.1.

The Key Facts Document and Example contain important information that will help you decide whether the product is suitable for you and whether it offers a good deal compared with other products you consider. So that you can spot these documents easily, they bear the Key Facts logo (see page 227).

A major difference between the key features document and the new Key Facts Document is that, for all types of personal pension and stakeholder scheme, the Key Facts Document gives you an idea of how much your pension might be worth at the time you retire *in today's money*, in other words, after stripping out the effect of inflation on the buying power of money. For example, in Figure 22.1, the pension fund might grow to £67,200, which might buy a pension of £5,320. But that pension would have only the same buying power as an income of £2,880 today if prices had risen by 2.5 per cent a year on average between now and retirement. You want your pension in order to support your desired lifestyle in retirement, so the buying power of the pension is the all-important figure. For more about the impact of inflation, see Chapter 32.

Another important point to note about both the key features and Key Facts documents is that the example of how much your savings might be worth by retirement is just that: an example. It is based on assumptions. It is assumed that:

- your savings qualify for certain tax reliefs. It is assumed that the current reliefs and tax rates will continue into the future, but in reality they might change
- your savings grow at a particular rate – usually 7 per cent, but typically your money is invested in stock market investments, such as shares and bonds, whose value can go down as well as up and which might grow by more or less than the assumed growth rate
- charges are deducted from your savings at a particular rate – usually the same as the provider's current rate of charges. But the provider usually has a lot of freedom to change the charges in future, so the actual rate could turn out to be different, and
- the pension fund can buy a pension at retirement at a particular annuity rate. Usually, the current rates are used, but these could have changed a lot by the time you retire.

Nobody can see into the future and, by retirement, your savings might have done a lot worse or a lot better than the amount shown in the

Figure 22.1: Extracts from a Key Facts Example

What do I pay in this example?

You pay	£78.00
Basic rate tax rebate	£22.00
Total payment	£100.00

Does this example show me what I'm going to get back?

- No. The value of the investments in your plan may go up or down or stay the same. And our charges could change too. So we cannot predict what you will get back.
- But our example can show you how charges could reduce what you might get back.

Let's assume:

- you decide to invest 100% of your payments in the balanced managed fund.
- we do not change the level of charges we take and the tax rebate remains the same (not guaranteed), and
- the investments in your plan grow at a steady rate of 7% each year (not guaranteed).

The later years At the end of year	You would have paid in (inc. tax rebate)	What you plan would be worth without charges	What your plan would be worth after charges
10	£12,000	£17,196	£16,060
15	£18,000	£31,240	£28,400
20	£24,000	£50,980	£45,000
25	£30,000	£78,560	£67,200

What would a fund of £67,200 give me if I retire at age 65?

- You must use your fund to buy an annuity to give you an income.
- If we make some assumptions, we can give you an idea of how much income you could get with a fund of £67,200.

Let's assume:

- you choose to have your income paid monthly from the day you retire
- you choose to have the same income paid out each year
- inflation from now until you are 65 averages 2.5% a year (not guaranteed), and
- at age 65, annuity rates are based on an interest rate of 54.% (not guaranteed).

You could use this to get:

A tax-free lump sum of:	£16,820	A yearly income of (before tax):	£4,000	What this income would be worth in today's money	£2,160
OR A tax-free lump sum of:	£0	A yearly income of (before tax):	£5,320	What this income would be worth in today's money	£2,880

example. 'What then is the point of the example?' you might ask. The answer is to help you plan ahead. You have to make decisions now about how much to save for retirement and the example, albeit that it could be way off, gives you a starting point for deciding how much to put aside. However, it will be essential that you check the actual progress of your savings at regular intervals (and the provider will send you yearly statements for this purpose) to see if you are on track and to top up your savings if necessary. Chapters 28 to 32 will help you do this.

The key features documents for a stakeholder pension scheme include a set of stakeholder decision trees, and these are provided separately alongside Key Facts Documents. The trees are flow diagrams that take you step-by-step through a sequence of questions designed to establish whether it would be appropriate for you to consider a stakeholder scheme. They are very broad-brush, and you will still need to make the decision for yourself about whether a stakeholder scheme is suitable and which provider's scheme to choose.

The decision trees were introduced because the maximum charges for stakeholder schemes are relatively low at just 1 per cent a year (due however to rise to 1.5 per cent from April 2005). Many providers and advisers argued that such low charges would not be enough to pay commission to an adviser selling such schemes. As a result, stakeholder schemes were thought likely to be sold largely on a no-advice (execution-only) basis. That left consumers on their own, and, to ensure some help was to hand, stakeholder decision trees were introduced. The rules also allow for people who are not financial advisers to help you work your way through the decision trees. Such helpers could be someone at work, such as a union representative, or staff at a citizens' advice bureau. But this help does not count as advice, and you have no grounds for complaint against the person who helped you if later on you reckon you made the wrong decision about taking out a stakeholder scheme.

In the event, not all stakeholder schemes are being sold on a no-advice basis. Some providers have managed to pay commission to advisers within the 1 per cent charging ceiling. Some employers have footed the bill separately for advice to be given at the workplace. And you have the option of choosing a fee-based adviser, who should be happy to recommend non-commission-earning products.

Comparing personal pensions

You can shop around before you buy. The Key Facts Documents will help you compare one pension plan with another, in particular, showing you the impact of different charges.

Before starting to shop around, it's a good idea to narrow your choice by using surveys published from time to time by, for example, *Which?*★ magazine and *Money Management*★ that compare the features of different plan and schemes. The Financial Services Authority★ publishes comparative tables comparing personal pensions and also stakeholder pension schemes from different providers.

If you don't fancy shopping around yourself, get an independent financial adviser (IFA★) to do the job for you.

Self-defence for shoppers

Though the Financial Services and Markets Act provides some very important areas of protection for the investor (see Chapters 17 and 26) – and a limited degree of compensation if things do go wrong – no law can stop the really determined fraudster. You should also take your own protective measures:

- do your homework. Work out roughly what your needs are. Read up to give yourself a broad idea of what's available to meet those needs
- have handy the information you'll need – for example, a recent pay slip, forecast of your state pension, booklet for your employer's pension scheme, and so on
- get advice if you need it. With pension problems, solutions are rarely cut and dried, so don't rely on just one adviser – compare the advice of two or three
- don't deal with advisers who are not authorised. Don't deal with providers who are not authorised. Check their status through the FSA Register★ *before* you do business with them
- check whether an adviser charges fees. Ask what commissions the adviser will receive
- avoid salespeople and advisers who don't ask enough questions – they can't give sound recommendations if they are ignorant of your circumstances

- get everything in writing – make notes of telephone calls, confirm the contents of meetings in a follow-up letter
- read literature and documents, especially those which carry the Key Facts logo (see page 227). Make sure you understand them before you agree to invest
- avoid paying money to an adviser. Instead, make cheques payable direct to the plan provider – even if you have to write several cheques for different providers
- keep on file all the information – brochures, notes of meetings, and so on – which formed the basis of your decision to take out a plan.

Chapter 23

Contracting out through a personal pension

If you are an employee and you have not already contracted out of the state additional pension scheme through your occupational pension scheme (see Chapter 14), you can make your own decision to contract out through a personal pension.

This chapter does not apply to you if you are self-employed. You do not belong to the state additional pension scheme, and you therefore cannot contract out of it.

If you are a director of your own company you count as an employee and, unless you have already contracted out, you are a member of the state additional pension scheme. If you have not made any pension arrangements yet, or you save through a personal pension, you can contract out using a personal plan, as described in this chapter. But there are also other options open to you when it comes to saving for retirement (see Chapter 27).

Note that personal pensions, including those that qualify as stakeholder schemes, can be used for contracting out. But you cannot contract out using a retirement annuity contract.

The pension you'll get

A personal pension that is used for contracting out is separate from any other pension plan that you may have. It is sometimes called a rebate-only plan or an appropriate personal pension. It accepts only a rebate of National Insurance contributions which have been paid by you and your employer. But if you don't belong to an occupational pension scheme your contracted-out plan can form part of a personal pension package which receives contributions greater than just the rebate. On its own, a contracted-out plan will not provide enough income to support a comfortable retirement. It is therefore very important to make additional savings as well.

All contracted-out personal pensions work on a money purchase basis, so the rebate is invested and used to provide you with protected-rights benefits. These are:

- a retirement pension which can be paid from age 60 onwards
- a pension for your widow or widower if you die before retirement
- a pension for your widow or widower if you die after retirement equal to half the pension that you were getting. But, from 6 April 1997 onwards, if you are single at the time when you retire you can opt for a larger pension for yourself, with no widow or widower's pension
- increases to pensions once they start to be paid but this requirement is set to be abolished probably from April 2005.

Note that none of the protected-rights pension fund can be taken as a lump sum under current rules, but this is due to change when the new simplified pensions regime starts from April 2006 (see Chapter 9). You will then be able to take up to a quarter of your pension savings as a tax-free lump sum, regardless of the type of pension scheme or plan.

The amount of pension that you'll get by contracting out in this way depends on:

- the amount invested in the plan, in other words, the size of the rebate (see page 246)
- charges deducted from the plan (see page 245)
- how well the invested rebate grows (see page 245)
- annuity rates at the time when you reach state pension age. The rules require the same rate to be used for both men and women. This is called a unisex rate.

The treatment on retirement of protected rights from a personal pension is the same as the treatment of protected rights at retirement from an occupational money purchase scheme (see Chapter 14). For rights built up before 6 April 1997, the Department for Work and Pensions (DWP) works out the full SERPS pension that you could have built up and then subtracts notional guaranteed minimum pensions (GMPs) corresponding to periods when you were contracted out. Depending on how well your personal plan has performed, the notional GMPs may be greater or smaller than the actual pension your plan provides.

For rights built up on or after 6 April 1997, the link with SERPS and now S2P is broken. In other words, while you were contracted out, you did not build up any SERPS pension at all. And, if you contract out now, you completely give up all – or in some cases, part (see below) – of your S2P. Therefore, contracting out through a personal pension means that you could end up with more or less than if you'd stayed in the state scheme.

Pension increases

After retirement, state additional pensions are increased each year in line with changes in the Retail Prices Index. If you're contracted out, the state used to continue to provide the full increase required to keep your SERPS and notional GMPs growing in line with inflation. But this has now changed:

- for people retiring from April 1990 onwards, contracted-out personal pensions built up over the period up to 5 April 1997 must be increased by the scheme at a rate of 3 per cent a year, or by the rate of inflation if this is less. Because of the link with SERPS, the state then tops this up, so the pensions are completely (or nearly completely) inflation-proofed
- for pension rights built up from 6 April 1997 onwards, the protected-rights pension from a contracted-out personal pension must be increased by inflation up to 5 per cent a year – but not any pension you've built up in addition to the contracted-out element
- assuming proposals being debated by Parliament at the time of writing become law, for pensions started from 6 April 2005 onwards, there will be no requirement for the pension to increase after it starts to be paid. It will be up to you whether to choose an annuity with built-in increases or not (see Chapter 33).

Should you contract out?

The question you need to answer is: will the pension that you can build up through investing your National Insurance rebate in a personal pension be enough to replace the state additional pension that you are giving up? Answering the question is not straightforward, and depends on a range of factors:

- your sex
- your age
- the impact of charges
- your view about future investment performance
- your view about future annuity rates
- the size of the rebate.

In the next few pages, each factor is considered in turn. But, taking them all together, many experts feel that, given the current modest outlook for investments and likelihood that annuity rates will worsen over time, the rebates presently on offer are not high enough to make contracting out worthwhile, whatever your age or sex.

Your sex

Men and women, on average, don't benefit equally from S2P. Any woman born before 6 April 1955 will have a lower state pension age than a man. Also, women in their mid-60s can expect to live some three or four years longer than a man of the same age. So, supposing a man and a woman had identical entitlements to state additional pension at the start of their retirements, the woman could expect to receive her pension for between three and eight years longer than the man. If the woman were currently in her late 40s or older, she could expect to receive considerably more additional pension than the man. A younger woman would not do quite as well, but would still tend to do better than the man. Despite this difference in the total amount of pension a man and a woman can expect to receive, the rebate to be invested in a personal pension is identical for a man and a woman who earn the same. Yet, other factors being equal, the woman is giving up more additional pension than the man. The upshot of this is that contracting out is more likely to be attractive to men than to women.

Your age

State additional pensions are worked out according to a formula, but a contracted-out money purchase pension – such as that provided by a personal pension – depends to a large extent on how the invested rebates grow. If you're young, you have a long time until you reach pension age: your rebates will be invested for a longer period, and should grow by more than the rebates of an older person, who'll reach retirement sooner.

Until April 1997 the same rebates were paid into your personal pension regardless of your age. This made contracting out look increasingly unattractive the older you got. However, since 6 April 1997 rebates have been age-related. This means that they increase as you get older in an attempt to maintain the attractiveness of contracting out. If the rebates were perfectly matched to age, there might be little reason to stay in or return to S2P. But, in order to contain costs, the government has capped the rebates; hence, in 2004–5, for a man aged 54 or over or a woman aged 49 or over contracting out looks particularly unattractive.

The impact of charges

Charges have a direct impact on what you will get back from your contracted-out personal pension. Charges are looked at in more detail in Chapter 21, but it is relevant here to draw attention to flat-rate fees. The amount invested in a contracted-out personal pension is often very small. Therefore, any flat-rate charge can take a high proportion of the investment. For example, a plan fee of £10 each time a contribution is made is just 1 per cent of a £1,000 investment but rises to 10 per cent of a £100 investment. High flat-rate charges can make a small plan completely uneconomic.

Flat-rate fees can also be a problem if you contract out just for a few years and then rejoin the state scheme. Your contracted-out plan is left invested until retirement but if flat-rate fees continue to be taken out of the plan at regular intervals, the value of the pension fund can be badly eroded.

The problem is avoided if you contract out using a stakeholder pension scheme. Flat-rate fees are not allowed. Charges will only be levied as a percentage of your fund, and are in any case capped at a maximum of 1 per cent a year (due to be increased to 1.5 per cent a year from April 2005).

Your view about future investment performance

With contracted-out personal pensions, investment performance will play a large part in determining how large or small your eventual pension will be. If you're optimistic on this score, and expect your invested rebates to grow well, contracting out will tend to be an attractive option. If, on the other hand, you take a more cautious view of likely investment growth, you'll be more attracted to staying in the state scheme.

Your view about future annuity rates

When you want to start your pension, you take the fund that has built up and buy an annuity with it. How much pension you get for your lump sum depends on annuity rates at that time. For many years now, annuity rates have been tending to fall. A major reason for this is that people are tending to live longer – life expectancy (in other words, how long you are expected to live) from birth seems to be increasing by about one year every decade.

If people live longer but still retire at the same age, their pensions have on average to be paid out for longer. This means, for the same lump sum as before, you will be offered less pension each year.

If you expect annuity rates to keep on falling, you should assume that whatever pension fund you build up will buy less pension in future than it does now. So, unless rebates increase, contracting out is going to look increasingly less attractive.

The size of the rebate

The size of the rebate is set by the government on the advice of its actuary. (An actuary is a professional whose skills lie in assessing probabilities and likely future values from statistical and other data.)

The rebates are usually set for five years at a time and then revised. The most recently published rebates take into account the change in the state scheme from SERPS to S2P. SERPS pensions were based on a single tranche of your earnings above the lower earnings limit (LEL) up to the upper earnings limit (UEL) – £4,108 up to £31,720 in 2004–5 – and, reflecting this, there was a single rebate of National Insurance contributions paid on earnings between those limits. S2P is different: your S2P is worked out by dividing earnings between the LEL and UEL into three bands, and a different percentage of each band counts towards your pension – see Chapter 5. The rebates payable from April 2002 onwards follow this pattern, so you get different rebates on different slices of your earnings.

Aligning the rebates and the way S2P is worked out makes it more likely that the contracted-out pension you get will be broadly similar to the state pension you give up. But this will not be true for employees earning more than the LEL but less than the low earnings threshold (£11,600 in 2004–5). This group is treated for S2P purposes as if they have earnings equal to the low earnings threshold – but the rebates are based on their actual earnings, and so will fall short of the amount likely to build up a pension equal to the amount of S2P they would have had. To tackle this problem, the government has introduced special rules that mean employees in this group continue to build up a residual S2P even when they are contracted out. The residual S2P is less than the S2P they would have got had they not been contracted out and is based on the difference between their actual earnings and the low earnings threshold.

Table 23.1 sets out the rebates for selected ages for 2004–5. The rebates for the remaining years to 2007–8 are similar but not identical for all ages.

Table 23.1: Examples of National Insurance rebates to be invested in a contracted-out personal pension plan for 2004–5 Tax Year

Age on last day (5 April) of preceding tax year	Rebates as percentage of earnings between these limits:		
	Lower earnings limit and low earnings threshold [1]	Low earnings threshold and Band 3 threshold [2]	Band 3 threshold and upper earnings limit [3]
2004–5 tax year 15	8.4%	2.10%	4.2%
20	8.8%	2.20%	4.4%
25	9.2%	2.30%	4.6%
30	9.6%	2.40%	4.8%
35	10.2%	2.55%	5.1%
40	10.6%	2.65%	5.3%
45	12.0%	3.00%	6.0%
50	16.0%	4.00%	8.0%
55	21.0%	5.25%	10.5%
60	21.0%	5.25%	10.5%

[1] £4,108 to £11,600 in 2004–5.
[2] £11,601 to £26,600 in 2004–5.
[3] £26,601 to £31,720 in 2004–5.

Special tax rules apply to the rebate paid into a personal pension. You are given tax relief on the part of the rebate which represents your own National Insurance contributions. This part of the rebate is 1.6 per cent of your earnings above the lower earnings limit up to the upper earnings limit – it remains the same whatever the size of the age-related rebate for which you qualify. Tax relief is given only at the basic rate – even if you're a higher-rate taxpayer. You don't receive the tax relief directly; instead, it's paid by the DWP into your personal pension plan along with the rebate. In 2004–5 the tax relief represents another 0.45 per cent of your earnings between the upper and lower earnings limits. There's no tax relief on any part of the rebate which represents National Insurance contributions paid by your employer.

CASE HISTORY: Ryan

Ryan, who is 45, earns £21,000 a year and is a basic-rate taxpayer. His employer operates a group personal pension scheme (GPPS), which Ryan joined several years ago. Ryan has independently taken the decision to contract out of S2P by taking out a rebate-only personal pension in addition to the personal pension that he has through the GPPS.

Ryan pays nothing directly into the rebate-only plan, but after the end of each tax year the Department for Work and Pensions (DWP) hands over the rebate and tax relief to the plan provider. The amount paid by the DWP for 2004–5 is:

Rebate of National Insurance on earnings from LEL to low earnings threshold = 12.0% × (£11,600 – £4,108)	£899.04
Rebate of National Insurance contributions on earnings from low earnings threshold up to £21,000 (since this is less than the Band 3 threshold) = 3% × (£21,000 – £11,600)	£282.00
Basic-rate tax relief on Ryan's share of the rebate 22% relief on 1.6% × (£21,000 – £4,108)	£76.23
TOTAL	£1,257.27

CASE HISTORY: Gloria

Gloria is 55. She earns £25,000 a year and is currently in the S2P scheme but is thinking about contracting out through a personal pension. If she contracts out in 2004–5, she will be giving up about £140 a year of S2P in today's money. However, she would get a National Insurance rebate paid into her personal pension as follows:

Rebate on earnings from LEL to low earnings threshold = 21% × (£11,600 – £4,108)	£1,573.32
Rebate on earnings from low earnings threshold up to £25,000 (since this is less than the Band 3 threshold) = 5.25% × (£25,000 – £11,600)	£703.50
Basic-rate tax relief on Gloria's share of the rebate = 22% relief on 1.6% × (£25,000 – £4,108)	£94.28
TOTAL	£2,371.10

She gets an illustration from the pension provider of how much pension the rebate might provide if it were invested in a personal pension for the five years until she reaches the state pension age of 60. On the basis of 1 per cent a year growth over and above inflation, she could expect a pension that would grow each year in line with inflation starting at about £111 a year. Assuming higher growth of 3 per cent a year over and above inflation, the pension would start at around £123 a year. On either basis, the pension she might get is less than the S2P she would be giving up. To get a pension equal to the S2P she is giving up, the invested rebate would need to grow by around 7½ per cent a year more than inflation. Gloria thinks that would be wildly optimistic and decides to stay contracted in to the S2P scheme.

More information

You may feel that the decision about whether to be contracted in or contracted out of the state additional scheme is reasonably clear for you, but if you're unsure about whether it is worthwhile for you, you may want the help of a financial adviser.

Your employer (try the personnel or pension administration department, if there is one) may be able to put you in touch with a pension plan provider or independent adviser. This is particularly likely if there is already a group personal pension scheme (GPPS) at work: it may be part of the GPPS deal that you have access to advice on contracting out. Note that your occupational pension scheme administrator and the trustees of any occupational scheme are unlikely to be authorised to give this type of advice themselves.

An adviser will supply you with a Key Facts Example (or a key features illustration) of the pension that you may get as a result of investing the rebates. This will be similar to the example/illustration described in Chapter 22. However, a slightly different method is used to work out the pension you might get at retirement in today's money. Instead of using an investment growth rate that includes growth due to inflation and then stripping out the effect of inflation, an example/illustration for a rebate-only personal pension or stakeholder scheme is worked out using investment growth over and above inflation (called the 'real growth rate'). Regulations state that the growth rates used must be 1 per cent and 3 per cent a year. They mean that you are assuming your invested rebates will grow by 1 or 3 per cent a year more than the amount needed to compensate for inflation. Bear in mind that these are just examples to help you plan ahead – in reality, the invested rebates might grow by more or by less.

Once you have contracted out through a personal pension, you will receive a statement each year. This tells you how much has been received from the DWP and paid into your plan, the value of your plan to date and the amount of pension in today's money that this might provide.

Chapter 24

Other benefits from a personal pension

Unlike an occupational pension scheme, a personal pension does not automatically provide you with a package of benefits. It's up to you to decide what benefits you want, and then you must pay for them. The range of extra benefits includes:

- lump-sum life cover for dependants if you die before retirement
- a pension for widow, widower or other partner, or a limited lump sum, if you die after retirement
- a waiver of contributions if you are unable to work because of illness or disability
- a pension paid early if you are too ill to work.

Death before retirement

A contracted-out personal pension (see Chapter 23) *must* allow for a widow's or widower's pension to be payable if your widow or widower is aged 45 or over, or is younger than 45 but qualifies for child benefit. The pension would be whatever amount can be bought by the fund built up through investing the contracting-out rebates (together with tax relief and incentive payments, if applicable). Your widow or widower has an open market option, which gives her or him the right to shop around for a different pension provider rather than stay with the original plan provider.

The pension *may* cease if your widow or widower remarries while under the state pension age, or ceases to be eligible for child benefit and is still under the age of 45 – but this depends on the terms of the contract at the time of death; it may provide for continued payment of the pension in these circumstances.

A contracted-out widow's or widower's pension built up before 6 April 1997 must be increased each year in line with inflation up to a maximum of 3 per cent a year. For post-April 1997 contracted-out pensions the increase must be inflation up to 5 per cent a year but for pensions starting on or after 6 April 2005 this requirement is due to be dropped and the pension will not have to increase at all . If you have no widow or widower, the fund built up by the invested rebates can be paid to another dependant or, failing that, paid to your estate, or to someone you nominate.

With personal pensions, other than contracted-out plans (or the contracted-out element of a plan), you can arrange for a pension to be paid to your widow, widower, children and/or other dependants in the event of death. With a retirement annuity contract, the amount of money that has built up in your fund is the only limit on the size of the pension, or pensions, that can be paid. With a personal pension, there is also a restriction that the total of pensions for dependants must not come to more than the amount of retirement pension which your fund could have bought if you could have retired at the time of death.

How much of a lump sum?

If your plan doesn't include any arrangements for paying pensions to dependants, or if you have no dependants, a lump sum can be paid from your plan. With a retirement annuity contract, this is the amount of your accumulated fund. With a personal pension, the lump sum is either the accumulated fund, or could be equal to the return of contributions together with reasonable interest and bonuses. The lump sum can be paid to anyone you nominate – there is no requirement for the recipient(s) to be financially dependent on you.

How much life cover?

If you started the life insurance policy before 6 April 2001, you can use up to 5 per cent of your net relevant earnings (see page 191) to pay premiums for a life insurance used to pay out a lump sum if you die before age 75. You could take out this insurance through your personal pension even if you were not also making contributions towards a pension itself. However, this rule has now changed. If you started the life insurance policy on or after 6 April 2001, you can use up to 10 per cent of the actual contributions you make to pay the premiums for life cover. This means you must also be contributing towards your pension.

You get tax relief at your highest rate on the premiums, but the amount you pay counts towards your overall contribution limit for personal pensions (see Chapter 19). So, if you want to pay the maximum possible towards your pension, you may do better to arrange separate life insurance outside your personal pension arrangement.

When connected to a retirement annuity contract, the life insurance is called a Section 621 policy. When connected to a personal pension plan, it is called a Section 637 policy. Basically, these two policies are the same.

Death after retirement

With the exception of contracted-out plans, you must choose at the time you start to take your pension which death benefits you want to have as part of your plan. They might include:

- a guarantee that your pension will continue for a set period, in case death occurs within that time
- the equivalent of any guaranteed pension paid as a lump sum
- a pension for your widow or widower
- a pension for other dependants.

Pension guarantee

You can arrange for your retirement pension to carry on being paid for a set period after the date of your retirement, in case your death occurs within that time. The guarantee period can't be longer than ten years. You can nominate the person who will receive your pension if you die within the period – or the lump-sum equivalent of it. The recipient doesn't have to be financially dependent on you.

How much pension for your dependants?

A contracted-out personal pension must allow for a widow's or widower's pension as described in Chapter 23. The sum of any pensions for your widow, widower and/or other dependants from a plan which is not contracted out must not come to more than the amount of pension that you were receiving.

If you want your widow or widower to receive a pension, apart from any contracted-out pension, in the event of your dying after retirement has started, you must make this choice at the point of retirement. Generally, you need to buy a suitable annuity – see Chapter 33 for more about this.

Retiring due to ill-health

If you have to retire because of ill-health, you can start to take a pension from a personal plan at any age. You don't have to be entirely incapable of work but, if you're under age 50 (due to rise to 55 from 2010), you must be ill to the extent that you're judged incapable of carrying out your normal work, or work of a similar nature for which you're trained or otherwise suited. The plan provider will need medical evidence of your condition.

There are no tax restrictions on the pension you can get. But the problems remain that your pension fund will be smaller because less has been paid in and the investment has had less time to grow, and that your pension will be more expensive because it may have to be paid for longer. There are two 'extras' which can be included in personal pensions which would help to overcome these problems:

- **waiver-of-premium benefit** If you're ill for longer than a given period – say, six months – you no longer have to pay the contributions towards your regular payment plan, but the plan continues to grow as if the contributions had been made and invested. Most personal plans offer this benefit, usually as an option
- **permanent disability insurance** If you're expected to be permanently incapable of carrying on your work (or similar work) because of ill-health or disability, this insurance guarantees that your ill-health pension from the plan will be at least a minimum amount. Though this benefit is allowed under the rules for personal pensions, it is seldom, if ever, offered at present.

With both these options, you would have to pay for them by contributing extra towards the plan. The extra amount paid qualifies for tax relief in the same way as the rest of your contributions, but it eats into your overall contribution limit (see Chapter 19), which means you can put aside less through the plan for retirement. With a personal pension, tax rules prevent more than a quarter of your total contributions being used to provide waiver-of-premium benefit and permanent disability insurance.

Don't confuse permanent disability insurance with permanent health insurance (now more commonly called income protection insurance). The latter provides you with an income if your earnings stop because of illness, even when the illness is temporary and you're expected to recover from it. Permanent health insurance can't be included within a personal pension, and premiums that you pay for permanent health insurance don't qualify for tax relief.

Chapter 25

Transferring a personal pension

Unlike an occupational pension scheme, you can usually take a personal pension with you if you change jobs or employment status. But there may be other, better options open to you, so you should check what happens if you stop paying into your plan and/or transfer the accumulated fund.

Changing jobs

If you have a single lump-sum contribution personal pension, changing jobs has no effect at all on the plan. And, if you have a regular contribution personal pension, you can usually keep your plan going without any alteration if you change jobs. There are three exceptions:

- if you have a contracted-out personal pension (see Chapter 23) for which you cease to be eligible. This would happen if you switched from being an employee to self-employed status instead. It would also happen if you decided to join a new employer's scheme which was itself a contracted-out scheme. In both cases, you would not be able to continue claiming the National Insurance rebate for your personal pension

- if you have a (non-contracted-out) personal pension for which you cease to be eligible. This would happen if your new employer runs an occupational scheme which you decide to join and you are either a controlling director or you earn more than £30,000 a year (see Chapter 30)

- if your old employer has been paying some or all of the contributions to your personal pension. You'll need to investigate whether you can keep the plan going with lower contributions, with contributions from your new employer, or by paying in more yourself.

If you do have to stop paying into your personal pension, you can't get back any money already paid into it, except as a pension (and any tax-free lump sum for which you're eligible). To do this, you must have reached at least the earliest pension age recognised by the tax rules and the plan provider.

If you stop paying into a regular contribution personal pension, usually your fund continues to be invested, and it carries on growing as before to provide your eventual pension and any other benefits. Alternatively, you can transfer the fund to another pension plan or scheme – for example, you might want to invest it in your new employer's scheme (assuming the scheme will accept your transfer). Likewise, you can transfer the fund built up in a single-contribution personal plan, if you wish.

If you have to stop paying into a regular contribution plan, the eventual pension will of course be smaller than originally expected, because you'll have put less money into the plan. However, if you stop paying in the early years, the most severe effect could be due to charges. There are a variety of charges (see Chapter 21). These give the plan provider its profit margin, and cover its costs which are usually particularly heavy when the plan is first set up. If you keep up the plan as originally intended, the charges are effectively spread over a long period of time and have a proportionately small impact on your overall return. But, if you stop the plan in the early years, a large chunk of the charges will often be set against your fund – which is as yet relatively small. This can drastically reduce the amount in your plan and, in some cases, can reduce your fund to nothing. With some plans, charges continue to erode the value of your fund after you've stopped paying in, thus reducing it further. So you'll need to look at the terms of your particular plan very carefully in this situation in order to decide whether any value remaining should be left invested in the plan or transferred elsewhere.

You will avoid these problems if you have a stakeholder pension scheme. Under the conditions for stakeholder status, there can be no penalty charges if you stop your scheme early. Ongoing charges can only be levied as a percentage of your fund and can come to no more than 1 per cent a year (due to rise to 1.5 per cent a year from April 2005).

Your right to transfer

Even if you're not changing jobs, you don't have to contribute to the same personal pension until your retirement. You can stop contributing to it and leave the money that has already built up in it invested in the plan. Alternatively, you can transfer your money to another personal pension or to an occupational scheme, if that scheme agrees to accept the transfer.

Both retirement annuity contracts and personal pensions must allow you to transfer your pension rights to another plan or scheme. The amount that you can transfer (the transfer value) is your accumulated fund less any charges.

Bear in mind that you can no longer start a retirement annuity contract anew. This means that if, for example, you were not happy with your current contract provider and wanted to switch to a new one, you would have to transfer from a retirement annuity contract with the old provider to a personal pension with a new one.

The penalties for stopping your plan early or taking a transfer value can be hefty. They may take the form of surrender charges (see Chapter 21), or you might be losing the right to a 'loyalty' bonus paid only if you continue the plan for a set period or until retirement. Surrender charges are often very severe if you stop or transfer a plan in the early years – the value of your plan may be less than the amount paid in contributions, and, if you stop the plan in the first year or so, it may well be worth nothing at all. However, these problems are avoided if you have a stakeholder scheme.

If your pension fund is invested on a with-profits basis, you may also face a market value reduction (see page 121) if investment conditions are poor at the time you decide to transfer.

Beware, too, of continuing flat-rate charges eating into a plan that you have left invested. A percentage charge obviously varies with the value of the plan. But a flat-rate charge is the same whether your plan is growing or static and has a proportionately large impact on a plan that is small. This is not a problem with stakeholder schemes, since they are not allowed to levy flat-rate charges.

Transferring contracted-out pension rights

If you transfer your pension rights, any contracted-out rights must continue to be treated in a special way, although the nature of the guarantee may change.

In general, you can transfer contracted-out rights to an occupational contracted-out scheme or to another contracted-out personal pension.

More information

If you want to switch your personal pension to another plan or to some other pension arrangement, ask the plan provider for the available transfer value. If you plan to transfer into another personal pension, ask the new provider for an example/illustration of how much pension your invested transfer value might buy at retirement (see Chapter 23). If you want to transfer into an occupational scheme, check whether the scheme will accept the transfer value and, if so, what benefits it will buy. Compare the possible benefits from the new pension arrangement with the expected benefits you will be giving up in the old personal pension.

Chapter 26

How safe is your personal pension?

Personal pensions are covered by the investor-protection legislation embodied in the Financial Services and Markets Act 2000.

One-stop regulation

Investments are policed through a system of self-regulation. This means that, instead of the government intervening directly, the job has been delegated to a private-sector body which is responsible for registering investment businesses, settling rules, monitoring compliance with the rules and enforcing them. When the system started in 1988 there were several self-regulating bodies at the helm. Following two bouts of rationalisation, there is now just one, the Financial Services Authority (FSA★), which is answerable ultimately to the Chancellor of the Exchequer.

Authorisation

Under the current system, it is illegal for most financial firms, including pension providers and financial advisers, to operate in the UK unless they are authorised by the FSA or specifically exempt from authorisation.

Firms which are based in another European Economic Area (EEA) country and subject to their home-state regulation are automatically deemed to be authorised. EEA countries are the member states of the European Union plus Iceland, Liechtenstein and Norway.

The main exemptions from authorisation are:

* firms acting as agents for another firm (called the 'principal'). The principal is responsible for its agents, so it is the principal rather than the agent that needs to be authorised

- members of certain professions (lawyers, actuaries and accountants) whose investment activities are regulated by their trade body, provided that body has been granted status as a Designated Professional Body★.

Before buying a pension or taking advice, always check against the FSA Register★ that the firm you are dealing with has the correct authorisation or exemption.

How personal pensions are regulated

The parliamentary act sets out the broad framework of financial regulation, including the need for every relevant business to be authorised to carry on business in the UK. The detail is contained in rules drawn up and administered by the self-regulating body. The FSA rule books run to thousands of pages and, among other things, they set out:

- who is fit and proper to undertake financial business
- requirements for the business to be solvent
- how business must be conducted
- how clients' money and assets must be handled
- what information should be disclosed to the client and how
- the need to keep client records
- the need to employ compliance officers in each business in order to ensure that the rules are kept
- procedures with which the regulator can check up on compliance
- complaints' procedures
- disciplinary procedures.

The regulator has teeth. It can, and does, revoke the authorisation of firms which persistently or seriously break the rules. It can, and does, impose very large fines for breaches of the rules. The FSA also issues guidance to firms on how the rules should be interpreted and changes that interpretation as and when experience or circumstances suggest that a different direction is needed in order to protect consumers.

The FSA has a wide remit not only to regulate financial business but also to educate the public about personal finance. This makes sense, because much of the selling of financial products takes place in private and on a one-to-one basis between adviser and consumer. This type of situation is notoriously hard to police, and the person best placed to defend themselves against mis-selling and bad advice is you, the consumer.

Too good to be true?

This paints the regulatory system in a very rosy light. But in practice it has encountered various problems. For example:

- it has proved very difficult to stop fraudulent firms from setting up as investment advisers and, though the system has shown some success in catching the fraudsters, this has often been only after investors' money has been lost
- the cost of self-regulation is high and particularly hard for small firms to bear.

The most persistent problem in recent years has been the mis-selling of personal pensions to people who might have been better off leaving their pension savings with an employer's scheme. A survey commissioned by one of the FSA's predecessors found that, in more than nine out of ten cases, salespeople had not followed the proper rules and regulations. The sorry saga of Equitable Life has also undermined public confidence, though the regulatory failures there mainly pre-date the current system.

There have been calls for an end to self-regulation, with some experts saying that the regime is flawed. But most continue to support the self-regulatory system. The amalgamation of all the former regulatory bodies into the FSA – one super-regulator – which gained its full powers on 1 December 2001 has strengthened the regulatory system.

Despite any uncertainties, it is once again important to keep a clear perspective. The risk of ending up poor in one's retirement is very real, so it is essential that you do save for retirement. If you have the option of joining an occupational scheme, be very wary of choosing a personal pension instead – do not take sales patter at face value. If a personal pension is the only pension arrangement open to you, you can minimise the risks of being sold a dud, if you do your homework first – see Chapters 21 and 22. And, by choosing a stakeholder scheme – or a personal pension that conforms with most of the stakeholder conditions – you can avoid the high charges and lack of flexibility that have dogged personal pensions in the past.

Chapter 27

Directors of own company

If you run your own business as a self-employed person, your pension options are strictly limited to those described in Chapters 19 and 20. But if you run your own business as a company, you have in addition a number of other useful opportunities open to you; the pros and cons of each are summarised in Table 27.1.

As a company director you are an employee, but your company is the employer. You can therefore set up your own occupational pension scheme, of which you can become a member. This is not only useful for retirement provision, but also gives you scope for tax planning.

Your own occupational scheme

As a company, you can set up an occupational pension scheme, and there are two ways of doing this on the small scale appropriate to a business:

- an executive pension scheme
- a small self-administered scheme (SSAS).

Since these are employer's schemes, the Inland Revenue limits already outlined in Chapter 10 currently restrict the benefits which you can take. This in turn restricts the size of the fund that can be built up and, therefore, the contributions which can be paid into the schemes. But, provided you don't breach these limits, with both types of scheme you have enormous flexibility to vary the amount paid in each year. Contributions can be paid either wholly by the employer (i.e. the company), in which case they qualify for relief from corporation tax, and are only limited to the extent of the Inland Revenue benefit limits; alternatively, they can be paid partly by the employee (e.g. you as company director), in which case that part qualifies for income tax relief – employee contributions are covered by the rules described in Chapter 10.

Making payments to your pension scheme as a way of limiting your tax bill is all very well, but it's not a lot of help if the money is then locked away until you retire. Here is the other major planning feature of these schemes – the pension scheme can make loans to the company provided they are made on commercial terms. An SSAS can also invest in, or purchase assets from, the company within given limits, and a common transaction is for the SSAS to buy the company premises and lease them back to the company.

Executive pension schemes

These are insurance-based schemes which can cover just one person or a group of people. They are commonly used by family companies to provide the directors with pensions, but they are also used by larger companies to offer retirement benefits to a select group of employees. You hand over the contributions to an insurance company, which invests them on your behalf. The fund which builds up is used to provide retirement pensions and any other benefits, such as life insurance and dependants' pensions. The benefits can be closely tailored to suit each member of the scheme. Up to a half (or sometimes a quarter) of the fund can normally be lent back to the company. Contributions by the company are assumed to continue on a regular basis, but, since 1987, the employee contributions don't have to be regular.

Small self-administered schemes

These are covered by special Inland Revenue rules. There must be fewer than 12 members, and the fund can't just be invested with an insurance company. Usually an actuary, insurance company or investment manager will – for a fee – run the SSAS on your behalf. The fees are sufficiently high that generally the SSAS route is not economic for small pension funds of less than, say, £100,000. As with executive plans, part of the fund – up to one half (a quarter in the first two years) – can be lent back to the company on commercial terms. The SSAS can also invest in the company and buy assets – such as the headquarters building – from it. To prevent abuse, the Inland Revenue imposes various rules on these schemes, including the compulsory appointment of a pensioneer trustee – an independent person whose main role is to prevent the SSAS simply being wound up and the assets (which have had the benefit of tax relief) being distributed to the members.

Table 27.1: Pension arrangements for family companies

	Executive pension scheme	Small self-administered scheme	Personal pension plan
Suitable for relatively small contributions	Yes	No	Yes
Flexible benefit package	Yes	Yes	No
Opportunity to save the company tax	Yes	Yes	Yes, to a limited extent
Opportunity to save the employee tax	Yes	Yes	Yes
Company can borrow from pension fund	Yes	Yes	No
Pension fund can invest in company or buy assets from it	No	Yes	No
You have control over how the pension fund is invested	Some	Yes	Some
Suitable if you don't have much time to monitor the company pension arrangements	Yes	No	Yes

Part 5

Boosting your pension

Chapter 28

Do you need to boost your pension?

Chapter 8 looked at the pension gap after taking into account the amount of retirement income that you may get from the state. If you belong to an occupational pension scheme or are contributing to a personal pension (or retirement annuity contract) you will already have gone some way towards closing that gap.

Are you on track?

You should periodically (say, once every three years and whenever your employment or pension circumstances change) check your pension savings against your target retirement income in order to see if you are on track.

If you are on track, well and good. If not, increase your savings as soon as you can in order to bring yourself back on target. If you delay, you may find that the only option is to lower your sights and settle for less than the ideal retirement income.

How to check your pension target

Your first step should be to collect together all the necessary paperwork. This includes:

- a recent forecast of your state pension (or recent combined benefit statement)
- a recent benefit statement from a current occupational pension scheme
- recent deferred-benefit statements from any previous occupational pension schemes
- statements and examples/illustrations from any contracted-out personal pensions

- statements and examples/illustrations from any other personal pensions or retirement annuity contracts. Include plans that you may have taken out through a group personal pension scheme at work.

If you do not have recent statements and examples/illustrations, order them from the appropriate place (see the *More information* sections in earlier chapters of this book).

Some of the above statements for occupational schemes or personal pensions might be 'combined benefit statements' – see page 103. In that case, they will show your expected state pension as well as the occupational or personal pension. If more than one of the statements is a combined one, make sure you count your state pension once only. If you get a combined statement, you do not need to get a state pension forecast separately.

Using the information in the statements and illustrations, complete the Calculator in Table 28.1 on page 274. Work through the Calculator with the aid of the notes given below. The figure that you arrive at is your pension gap. If it is zero or negative you are on track for your retirement target. If it is more than zero you need to boost your pension savings.

If you find the Calculator too daunting, take your paperwork to a financial adviser and ask him or her to work out whether you are on track. However, for most people, it is now relatively simple to estimate the pension you might get at retirement. This is because, since April 2003, all pension statements are required to show the amount of pension you might get at retirement based on various assumptions *in today's money*. So all you have to do is take the relevant figures from your statements, slot them into the Calculator and do some simple adding and subtracting.

The Calculator is geared up mainly to work out your pensions gap if you intend to retire at or around state pension age (65 for most people, slightly younger for some older women). You can use it to check the position if you intend to retire at other ages if you make the following adjustments:

- **Step 2: your state pension** If you intend to retire early, you will have to manage without any state pension until you reach state pension age, so set amount B to zero to check your income in the early years of retirement. If you intend to retire late, consider deferring your state pension to earn extra – see page 280 – and put the higher amount in box B
- **Step 4: your occupational pension** If you intend to retire early, your occupational pension will be reduced – see Chapter 15 for

guidance. If you intend to retire late, it might be increased – check your scheme booklet

- **Step 5: your personal pension or stakeholder scheme** If you intend to retire early, your pension will be lower; if you retire later, it will be higher. Ask the pension provider for a statement showing the pension you might get given a different retirement age.

Using the Calculator in Table 28.1

Step 1: Your target retirement income
Go back to Chapters 1 and 2 and decide what income you could comfortably retire on. Don't worry about inflation: this is the income that you want on retirement but in today's money.

Step 2: Your state pension
Take these figures from the information given on the Retirement Pension Forecast that you obtained by completing form BR19 (see Chapter 4) or from a combined benefit statement. Use the figures for the pension that you are forecast to receive by state pension age.

Step 3: Pension gap before private savings
Subtract B from C to find your pension gap before taking into account your private savings for retirement. This is the shortfall you would have if you relied on just the state pension (though you might be eligible for means-tested state benefits to top this up if it were your only income).

Step 4: Your current occupational scheme
Take the figure from your benefit statement that shows your expected pension at retirement in today's money. This assumes that you carry on building up a pension through this scheme until the retirement age shown. It should include the pension produced by additional voluntary contributions (AVCs) you have paid to an in-house added years scheme. If you pay into another type of in-house AVC scheme, you will probably receive a separate statement from that scheme.

Step 5: Your current personal pension, stakeholder scheme or AVC scheme
Take the figure from your benefit statement that shows your expected pension at retirement in today's money. This assumes that you carry on building up a pension through this plan until the retirement age shown.

Step 6: Past occupational schemes

Take the figure from your benefit statement that shows your expected pension at retirement in today's money. This reflects the pension rights you had built up at the time you left the scheme.

Step 7: Past personal pensions, stakeholder schemes or AVC schemes

Take the figure from your benefit statement that shows your expected pension at retirement in today's money. But check carefully the basis for this figure. If it assumes you make no further contributions to the plan, well and good. If it assumes you carry on contributing but you do not intend to do this, instead take the size of your pension fund now and use Table 28.2 to convert this into the amount of pension it might provide in today's money at retirement. Put the resulting figure in the Calculator.

Step 8: Pension from other savings and investments

You don't have to save for retirement using just pension schemes and plans. They do tend to be the most tax-efficient way to save, but they are fairly inflexible. If you have other savings or investments already built up and definitely earmarked for retirement, use Table 28.3 to convert their value now into the amount of pension in today's money that they might provide at retirement. Put the resulting figure in the Calculator. See Chapter 32 for guidance.

Step 9: Total pension from your savings

Add together amounts D to H.

Step 10: Your pension gap

Subtract amount I from amount C. If the result is zero or less, you currently seem to be saving enough to achieve the retirement income you want and amount J is zero. Check the position regularly – say, once every three years – to make sure that you are still on track.

If the result of C minus I is greater than zero, put that amount in box J. Amount J is your pension gap and it tells you that you need to boost your savings if you are to retire with the income you want.

Special situations in which you might need to boost your pension

Early retirement from choice or redundancy

Retiring early has three effects on your pension that conspire to reduce the amount that you'll receive:

* less is invested in the scheme or plan, because contributions are paid for a shorter time
* the invested contributions have less time to grow, so your pension fund is smaller
* the pension must be paid for a longer time, so the amount of pension that you'll receive each year is reduced.

If you are saving on a money purchase basis (for example, through an occupational money purchase scheme or a personal pension), these effects feed directly through to your pension savings: your pension fund is smaller, and you will face a lower annuity rate at the point of retirement compared with retiring at a 'normal' retirement age of, say, 65.

If you are saving through a final salary scheme, it's your employer who directly bears the brunt of these effects. But they affect you indirectly, because the scheme will normally include rules to reduce your promised pension if you retire early. A common adjustment made is to reduce your pension by 6 per cent for each year that you retire early. This means that retiring five years early, at age 60, say, would reduce your pension by nearly a third; retiring ten years early, at age 55, say, would reduce your pension by well over half.

A further factor to bear in mind is that any state pensions cannot be paid before state pension age and most contracted-out pensions before age 60. If you retire earlier than that, then you will have to fill your income gap in some other way until the state and contracted-out pensions kick in.

If you work for an employer, you can sometimes get a better-than-normal pension deal if you opt for early retirement at a time when the employer is looking for redundancies.

In most cases, early retirement is an expensive goal. If you are determined to retire early you must be prepared to save extra during your working life.

Table 28.1: Calculator: the pensions gap

		Example	Your figures
Your desired yearly income in today's money (see Chapters 1 and 2)	A	£28,000	
The amount of pension that you can expect from the state (see Chapters 4 and 5) *State retirement pension forecast or combined pension statement*	B	£4,576	
Your pension gap in today's money before taking into account your own savings for retirement. A–B (round up to nearest £1,000)	C	£24,000	
Pension you can expect from an occupational pension scheme to which you currently belong (see Chapters 10 to 14) *Benefit statement*	D		
Pension you can expect from a personal pension/stakeholder scheme/AVC scheme to which you currently contribute (see Chapters 19 and 20) *Benefit statement*	E		
Pension you can expect from former employer's occupational pension schemes (see Chapters 11 and 12) *Benefit statement*	F		
Pension you can expect from personal pension/stakeholder scheme/AVC scheme to which you no longer contribute (see Chapters 19 and 20) *Benefit statement*	G		
Pension you might be able to fund from other savings and investments (see Chapter 32) *Annual statement*	H		
Total pension expected from your own savings for retirement. D+E+F+G+H (round up to nearest £1,000)	I		
Your pension gap (see Chapters 29 to 32). C–I	J		

Table 28.2: To convert a pension fund into pension

This Table shows for each £1,000 in your pension fund today the amount of pension it might buy at retirement, assuming that between now and retirement the invested fund grows at 7 per cent a year. Charges are deducted at 1 per cent a year and inflation averages 2.5 per cent a year.

Years until retirement	Value of fund at retirement in today's money	Yearly amount of index-linked pension in today's money that this fund might provide for									
		A man retiring at age					A woman retiring at age				
		55	60	65	70	75	55	60	65	70	75
0	£1,000	£37	£43	£52	£65	£84	£34	£39	£46	£57	£71
5	£1,183	£43	£51	£62	£77	£99	£40	£46	£55	£67	£84
10	£1,399	£51	£60	£73	£91	£118	£47	£55	£65	£79	£100
15	£1,655	£61	£71	£86	£107	£139	£56	£65	£77	£94	£118
20	£1,957	£72	£85	£102	£127	£165	£66	£77	£91	£111	£140
25	£2,315	£85	£100	£120	£150	£195	£78	£91	£107	£131	£165
30	£2,738	£100	£118	£142	£177	£230	£93	£107	£127	£155	£195
35	£3,239	£119	£140	£168	£210	£272	£109	£127	£150	£183	£231
40	£3,831	£140	£165	£199	£248	£322	£129	£150	£178	£217	£273

Table 28.3: To convert non-pension savings into pension

This Table shows for each £1,000 of your savings or investments today the amount of pension they might buy at retirement, assuming that between now and retirement the investments or savings grow at 6 per cent a year. Charges are deducted at 1 per cent a year and inflation averages 2.5 per cent a year.

Years until retirement	Value of fund at retirement in today's money	Yearly amount of index-linked pension this fund might provide for									
		A man retiring at age					A woman retiring at age				
		55	60	65	70	75	55	60	65	70	75
0	£1,000	£37	£43	£52	£65	£84	£34	£39	£46	£57	£71
5	£1,128	£41	£49	£59	£73	£95	£38	£44	£52	£64	£80
10	£1,272	£47	£55	£66	£82	£107	£43	£50	£59	£72	£91
15	£1,435	£53	£62	£75	£93	£121	£49	£56	£67	£81	£102
20	£1,619	£59	£70	£84	£105	£136	£55	£63	£75	£92	£115
25	£1,827	£67	£79	£95	£118	£154	£62	£71	£85	£103	£130
30	£2,060	£75	£89	£107	£133	£173	£70	£81	£96	£117	£147
35	£2,324	£85	£100	£121	£150	£195	£79	£91	£108	£132	£166
40	£2,622	£96	£113	£136	£170	£221	£89	£103	£122	£148	£187

Divorce

With around a third of all marriages ending in divorce, many women who had left pension decisions to their husbands are suddenly faced with the question of whether they will be financially secure in their retirement. Special rules ensure that divorced women (and men) can qualify for a basic state pension even if their own National Insurance record is insufficient, but the situation regarding other pensions is more complex.

If your marriage ends in divorce before you reach state pension age and you do not remarry before you reach that age, you can qualify for a basic state pension based on your own and your former husband's (or wife's) contributions record. Similarly, you can use your former husband's (or wife's) record if your marriage ends after you have reached state pension age. The rules are complicated, and you can choose between different formulae for calculating the pension, so get advice from The Pension Service★.

Since 1 July 1996, courts must take pension rights into account when making orders relating to the finances of a divorcing couple. There are various orders the court can make, and you can voluntarily include similar arrangements in a divorce settlement.

The ways in which the courts might take account of any pension rights are described below. For ease of expression, we have assumed the wife is being compensated for loss of the husband's pension rights, but the same options apply if a husband requires compensation from the wife. The options are:

- giving the wife a bigger share of other assets to offset the loss of her interest in the husband's pension
- giving the wife a lump sum to compensate her for the loss of specific benefits, such as the right to receive a widow's pension
- earmarking part or all of a future tax-free lump sum payable on the death of the husband for payment to the ex-wife
- making it mandatory for the husband to swap part of his pension for a tax-free lump sum at retirement and earmarking part or all of that lump sum for the ex-wife
- earmarking part of the husband's pension (either a future pension or one currently being received) to be paid to the wife, or
- 'pension-sharing' – in other words, transferring part of the husband's pension rights now to the wife.

For divorce proceedings started before 1 December 2000, only the first five options were available to the courts. For divorce proceedings started on or after 1 December 2000, the courts have the further option of pension-sharing, and this is a popular option.

Under pension-sharing, the value of the husband's pension rights is calculated. This is essentially the same as the transfer value that would be used if the pension were being transferred from one scheme or plan to another (see Chapters 16 and 25). Part of that value is transferred to the wife to fund her own pension. The value of the husband's rights is reduced by the sum transferred. The transfer can be made in either of two ways:

- **internal transfer** The money stays in the same pension scheme to which the husband belongs, and the wife becomes a member of the scheme. She gets pension rights in accordance with the rules of that scheme
- **external transfer** The money is moved to another pension scheme, generally chosen by the wife. This might, for example, be a stakeholder scheme or an employer's occupational scheme to which the wife already belongs. She will then get a pension in accordance with the rules of the new plan or scheme.

If the husband works in the public sector – for example, the police, NHS, Civil Service, or much of the teaching profession – usually only an internal transfer is allowed. This is because many public-sector pension schemes are unfunded (in other words, instead of pensions being paid from an accumulated pension fund they are paid out of money raised from taxpayers). That means any external transfer would also have to be paid for by taxpayers. The government was reluctant to risk an immediate tax burden caused by transfer payments from these schemes, so drew up the rules to prohibit external transfers in the case of unfunded public-sector schemes. Where (less commonly) a public-sector scheme is funded – for example, the local authority superannuation scheme – external transfers must be offered.

Where the husband is a member of a private-sector scheme which is funded (as is normally the case), external transfers must be offered and internal transfers may be available. An unfunded private-sector scheme does not have to offer external transfers.

The court can direct that a very wide range of pension rights be shared, including any SERPS pension or S2P, additional voluntary contributions and contracted-out pension rights. But pension-sharing cannot apply to the state basic pension (which is already subject to special rules on divorce – see above), state graduated pension, widow's and widower's pensions and lump-sum death benefits.

The husband's pension and other benefits are normally treated as if they have not been reduced when it comes to working out how much extra he can pay into the scheme to top up his benefits. However, by concession, the reduction due to the pension-sharing is recognised if he earns less than a quarter of the earnings limit (in other words, ¼ × £102,000 = £25,500 in 2004–5) and he is not a controlling director.

The pension and other benefits received by the wife are ignored when it comes to working out how much she can pay into a pension scheme.

Chapter 29

Boosting your state pension

There are several ways in which you might be able to increase the pension you will get from the state.

Basic pension

If your Retirement Pension Forecast from the Department For Work and Pensions (DWP, see Chapter 4) shows that you will qualify for a reduced level of state basic pension, you may be able to increase the amount that you'll receive by paying voluntary Class 3 National Insurance contributions. But you can go back for only six years to fill any gaps in your record.

If you are going back just two years, you pay contributions at the rate that applied in the earlier year. If you go back further, you pay at

Table 29.1: Rate at which you usually pay Class 3 contributions in 2004–5

Year to which the contribution is being backdated	Weekly rate	Cost for a whole year
2003–4	£6.95	£361.40
2002–3	£6.85	£356.20
2001–2	£7.15	£371.80
2000–1	£7.15	£371.80
1999–2000	£7.15	£371.80
1998–9	£7.15	£371.80
1997–8 or earlier	You cannot fill these gaps	

the rate current for the year in which the payment is made. Table 29.1 shows the amount you would have to pay in 2004–5.

Married women's reduced rate contributions

If you're one of the women who is still paying National Insurance at the married women's reduced rate (see page 44), is it worth switching to full-rate contributions instead? In paying at the lower rate (4.85 per cent in 2004–5 of earnings between the lower and upper limits and 1 per cent on earnings above the upper earnings limit), you give up your rights to certain state benefits, including the right to build up your own basic state retirement pension (and you can't belong to the state additional pension scheme). Instead, you must rely on your husband's National Insurance record. The maximum state basic pension you can receive based on his record is £47.65 in the 2004–5 tax year. If your husband's National Insurance record would qualify him only for a reduced basic pension, then the amount which you receive would also be reduced by the same proportion.

In deciding whether to switch to full-rate National Insurance, you have to weigh up the pension (and other state benefits) you'd gain against the extra National Insurance you'd have to pay. The answer will depend on your own and your husband's circumstances. For many older women the switch would generate little or no state basic pension, given that you need contributions for at least a quarter of your working life before you start to get any basic pension at all. However, switching means you would start to build up the state additional pension. Since April 2002, with the introduction of S2P, the state additional pension offers a particularly good deal to people on low earnings (see Chapter 5).

It's important to make the right choice, because once you switch to the full rate of National Insurance, you can't ever switch back to the reduced rate. Your local tax office can advise you; leaflet CA13 *National insurance for married women* contains details of how to make the switch.

Earning extra by putting off your retirement

The state pension age is currently 65 for men and 60 for women. But you can choose not to start your pension then. By delaying the start of your state pension you will receive an enhanced amount once it does start to be paid. You must defer the whole of your state pension (basic pension plus SERPS, S2P and any graduated pension), and the whole pension benefits from the increase. Any pension for a wife based on the husband's contributions must also be deferred if the husband makes this choice.

You can put off starting to receive state pension for up to five years at present. Your eventual pension will be increased during that time by 7.5 per cent for each year you put it off. You can't defer taking state pension for longer than five years, as it becomes automatically payable at age 65 for women and age 70 for men. If you're under that age but you've already started to receive your pension, you can stop taking the pension and, thus, qualify for the increase until you reach 65 or 70, as applicable.

Suppose you decide to put off taking your pension for a year – will it be a good deal? If you gave up a full basic pension for the 2004–5 tax year, you'd lose £79.60 a week or £4,149 (including the Christmas bonus) for the year. At the end of the year, you'd start to receive your pension, but at an increased rate. The increase would be 7.5% x £79.60 = £5.97 a week or £310 a year. You would benefit from this increase throughout the remainder of your retirement and, because the state pension is increased each year in line with prices, the value of the increase would maintain its buying power year after year. Dividing the £4,149 you gave up by £310 comes to 13⅓. This tells you that you would need to survive for just over 13 years to make the deal worthwhile.

The trade-off is the same, however long you defer your pension under the current rules – in other words, you need to survive 13⅓ years to make it worthwhile. Table 29.2 shows the life expectancy of men and women at various ages beyond state pension age. They suggest that, under the current rules, deferring the state pension is worthwhile for a single man up to age 68 and a single woman up to age 72. If a married man has a wife claiming state pension based on his contributions, her pension is increased as well as his and so deferment could be worthwhile until she reaches age 72.

Whether or not deferring your pension will be worthwhile will also depend on your relative tax rates, both at the time you would give up the pension and at the time you would start to receive it again. If you expect your tax rate to fall in future, then deferring your pension now to earn a higher rate later on is more likely to be a good idea.

Finally, bear in mind that the discussion above has considered the position of an *average* man or woman. If your health is poor, you are less likely to benefit from deferring your pension.

Table 29.2: How many years a retired person can expect to live on average after deferring their state pension

Age now	Man	Woman
60	n/a	23.2
61	n/a	22.3
62	n/a	21.5
63	n/a	20.7
64	n/a	19.8
65	15.9	19.0
66	15.2	18.2
67	14.5	17.4
68	13.8	16.7
69	13.1	15.9
70	12.5	15.1
71	11.8	14.4
72	11.2	13.7
73	10.6	13.0
74	10.1	12.3
75	9.5	11.7
76	9.0	11.0
77	8.5	10.4
78	8.0	9.8
79	7.5	9.2
80	7.1	8.7

Government figures show that, in practice, fewer than 2 per cent of pensioners currently choose to defer their state pension.

However, from 2005 (assuming Parliament approves new laws that it is debating at the time of writing) the terms on which you earn extra pension are due to change. You will be able to earn an extra 10.4 per cent pension for each year in which you put off receiving it, and you will be able to defer the start of the pension for as many years as you like (not just the five years that are currently allowed).

Using 2004–5 figures as a guide, deferring your state pension for one year under the new rules would mean giving up £4,149. When the pension started, it would be increased by 10.4% x £79.60 = £8.28 a week or £431 a year. You would need to survive £4,149/£431 = 9.6 years to make this worthwhile. Referring back to Table 29.2, this suggests that on average deferring your state pension is worth doing up to age 78 if you are a woman and 74 if you are a man.

Under the new rules, you will also have the option to take your increase as a lump sum instead of a pension. To be eligible, you'll have to defer your pension for at least a full year. (You can defer your pension for less than a year but then you'll have to take the increase as extra pension not lump sum.) Similarly, where a husband has deferred and so increased his state pension and dies, if his widow is entitled to a pension based on his contributions, she can opt to receive a lump sum instead of extra pension.

The amount of lump sum you get depends on an interest rate to be set by the government. You earn this interest on the amount of your deferred pension. At the time of writing, the legislation was still being debated by Parliament and so no interest rate had yet been set, but in examples of how the new rules might work the government was using a rate of 6 per cent a year. If you reckon you can earn a better return than this by making your own investments, you might be better off starting your pension at the normal age and investing it rather than opting for deferral.

The lump sum, like the pension, will be taxable, but the government has indicated that some kind of relief might be available to prevent your being pushed into the higher tax band in the year you receive the lump sum.

CASE HISTORY: Iain

Iain, a confirmed bachelor, will be 65 in May 2005. He runs his own business and doesn't intend to stop working yet, so he's thinking that he might put off taking his state pension for a while. He'd be giving up £4,149 a year, in terms of today's money. In the event, he puts off drawing his pension for seven years until age 72. When his pension eventually starts, he can choose to receive a higher pension of £137.55 a week or to stick with his original pension of £79.60 a week, but also receive a lump sum of nearly £37,000 before tax. (The amounts of pension are expressed in 2004–5 money. The cash amounts will be higher since state pensions are increased each year in line with inflation, but the buying power will be the same as the amounts given here.)

Everyone in Iain's family has tended to live to a ripe old age, so Iain decides to opt for the higher pension rather than the lump sum.

Table 29.3 gives an idea of the amount of extra pension or lump sum you might get under the proposals as they stood in July 2004. (Parliament had yet to approve these, so they could be changed.)

Table 29.3: Extra pension or lump sum you might earn from deferring your state pension from April 2005 onwards

Number of years you defer your pension	Weekly increase for each £10 of deferred pension	Lump sum for each £10 of deferred pension [1]
1	£1.04	£537
2	£2.08	£1,106
3	£3.12	£1,709
4	£4.16	£2,348
5	£5.20	£3,026
6	£6.24	£3,744
7	£7.28	£4,505
8	£8.32	£5,312
9	£9.36	£6,168
10	£10.40	£7,075
11	£11.44	£8,036
12	£12.48	£9,055
13	£13.52	£10,135
14	£14.56	£11,280
15	£15.60	£12,493

[1] Assumes you earn interest at 6% a year on the pension deferred. This is the rate being used by the government in its examples of how the new rules might work. However, the government will be able to set a different rate and change it from time to time.

Deciding whether to take the lump sum or extra pension is not easy. If you turn out to live for a long time, the extra pension will with hindsight look the better deal. But, if you live only a short time, the lump sum would be better. As Table 29.3 shows, for each £10 of deferred pension put off for one year, you could earn either £1.04 extra pension or a £537 lump sum (both before tax). You would need to survive 9.9 years to receive the same amount in pension as the lump sum. So Table 29.2 suggests that, on average, if you are a woman aged 78 or over or a man aged 75 or over at the time you start your pension, you would probably do better to take the lump sum rather than extra pension.

More information

For more information about making Class 3 National Insurance contributions, see leaflet CA08 NIC – *Voluntary Contributions*, available from your local tax office★ or the Inland Revenue website★. From the same source, you can get leaflet CA13 *National Insurance for Married Women*, which contains guidance on switching from the married women's reduced rate to full-rate National Insurance contributions.

For details about deferring your state pension, see leaflet NP46 *A Guide to state pensions* and PMX *Update on your state pension options* from The Pension Service★.

Chapter 30

Boosting your occupational scheme pension

The Inland Revenue rules (see Chapter 10) allow you to pay up to 15 per cent of your earnings (which may be capped at £102,000 in 2004–5) for this purpose towards a pension from an employer's scheme on top of whatever your employer pays in on your behalf. Table 30.1 shows the maximum contributions that you can pay in 2004–5, given various levels of earnings.

In practice, most people pay far less than 15 per cent of their earnings towards their pension. Basic contributions are often set at around 3 to 5 per cent, so there is enormous scope for paying in extra. You can do this by making additional voluntary contributions (AVCs).

CASE HISTORY: Sean

Sean has pensionable earnings of £45,000 a year and pays 5 per cent of these into his pension scheme. This means that his contributions are 5% × £45,000 = £2,250 this year.

Under Inland Revenue rules he can also take into account the value of taxable fringe benefits when working out the maximum contributions he can pay. Including these, his earnings for pension purposes come to £48,500. The maximum that he can pay in contributions this year is 15% × £48,500 = £7,275.

Deducting his current contributions from the Inland Revenue maximum, Sean works out that he can pay a further £7,275 − £2,250 = £5,025 in AVCs this year.

Extra contributions can be used to boost your eventual pension and to increase other benefits, such as life cover and pensions for

Table 30.1: The maximum that you can pay towards an employer's pension scheme in 2004–5

Your earnings in 2004–5 [1]	Maximum contributions allowed	After tax relief, cost to you if you are a:	
		Basic-rate taxpayer	Higher-rate taxpayer
£10,000	£1,500	£1,170	£900
£15,000	£2,250	£1,755	£1,350
£20,000	£3,000	£2,340	£1,800
£25,000	£3,750	£2,925	£2,250
£30,000	£4,500	£3,510	£2,700
£40,000	£6,000	£4,680	£3,600
£50,000	£7,500	[2]	£4,500
£60,000	£9,000	[2]	£5,400
£70,000	£10,500	[2]	£6,300
£80,000	£12,000	[2]	£7,200
£90,000	£13,500	[2]	£8,100
£100,000	£15,000	[2]	£9,000

[1] Including the taxable value of most fringe benefits.
[2] Unlikely to be applicable.

dependants (see Chapter 15) or increases to your pension once it starts to be paid. But in most cases AVCs paid under an arrangement that you started on or after 8 April 1987 cannot be used to provide or increase a tax-free lump sum.

Note that you may have other options for boosting your retirement savings. In particular, since April 2001, many employees are eligible to save through a stakeholder pension scheme in addition to belonging to an occupational pension scheme. See page 290 for details.

Tax advantages

As with ordinary contributions, you qualify for tax relief at your top rate of tax on the amount that you pay in AVCs. Capital gains from investing the AVCs are tax-free. And part of the investment income is tax-free, but not any income from shares, unit trusts or similar investments. (These are paid since April 1999 with tax at 10 per cent already deducted; this cannot be reclaimed.)

Generally, there is no lump sum from AVCs to qualify for tax relief, as there is with your main contributions (though this is due to change from 2006 – see Chapter 9).

Choice of AVC schemes

Any employer who runs an occupational pension scheme must also offer an in-house AVC scheme to enable members to make extra contributions.

The in-house scheme usually works on a money purchase basis. The AVCs are invested to build up a fund which is used on retirement (or death) to purchase extra benefits. You typically have a choice of how to invest your AVCs: for example, on a unit-linked, with-profits or deposit basis.

Some in-house schemes (found mainly in the public sector) offer an alternative, 'added-years' AVC scheme. This is available only when the main pension scheme works on a final salary (or similar) basis. You pay AVCs, which buy added years in the main scheme. This means that you are credited with more years than you've actually been a member of the scheme. The enhanced number of years is used in the pension formula and feeds through to a higher pension and increases in the other benefits, too, including the tax-free lump sum. This is the one case in which post-1987 AVCs can increase the tax-free lump sum that you will get on retirement.

Your third AVC option is to pay into your own, independent AVC scheme, called a free-standing AVC (or FSAVC) scheme. This works like a personal pension plan to all intents and purposes, offering you the same investment choices, incurring much the same charges and so on.

Unlike in-house AVC schemes, your FSAVC scheme does not have to be used to buy benefits in your current employer's pension scheme. It can stay with you as you move from job to job and can eventually be used to buy benefits in whatever scheme you belong to at the point of retirement.

In general, saving through your employer's in-house AVC scheme will be a better option than saving through an FSAVC because:

- charges for the in-house scheme are likely to be lower
- sometimes the employer adds to your AVCs, for example, paying an extra 1 per cent contribution for every 2 per cent of AVCs which you make
- an added-years scheme (where available) is more tax efficient, because part of the AVCs goes towards a tax-free lump sum.

On the other hand, FSAVC schemes are more flexible if you expect to change jobs fairly often. But, if flexibility is important to you, you could instead consider saving through a stakeholder scheme (see page 290) or an Individual Savings Account (ISA), see Chapter 32.

The benefits from an added-years AVC scheme become inseparable from the benefits from the occupational scheme, so must be taken at the same time. The benefits from AVC and FSAVC schemes can be taken earlier or later than the benefits from the occupational scheme, but there are some complicated rules to be observed, so get advice before doing this.

CASE HISTORY: Peggy

Peggy went back to work as a teacher after taking a number of years off to bring up her three children. She's belonged to the pension scheme for 16 years and will have 21 years in the scheme by the time that she reaches normal retirement age.

In order to increase her eventual pension, Peggy is making AVCs to the in-house added-years scheme. These buy her extra years of membership, so that by retirement she will be credited with 25 years' membership instead of 21.

She currently earns £21,800 a year, and this is an 'eightieths scheme'. So, based on her current salary, Peggy will get an enhanced pension of $25 \times \frac{1}{80} \times £21,800 = £6,812.50$ instead of $21 \times \frac{1}{80} \times £21,800 = £5,722.50$. Her pension is increased by over £1,000 as a result of making the AVCs.

Inland Revenue limits apply

You can't use AVCs to boost your pension or other benefits beyond the Inland Revenue limits described in Chapter 10. If you've paid in more AVCs than are needed to bring your pension and other benefits up to the maximum level, the 'excess' AVCs can be repaid to you on retirement. But tax at a special rate of 33 per cent (in 2004–5) is deducted.

You cannot reclaim this tax. If you're a higher-rate taxpayer you'll be required to pay further tax on the refund. The amount that you must pay is found by 'grossing up' the net amount of your refund by the basic rate of income tax: this means finding the before-tax sum which would be reduced to the amount of the refund if tax at the basic rate were taken away. Higher-rate tax is then worked out, but you are treated as if you had already paid tax at the basic rate. The further tax due is the difference between tax at the higher and basic rates.

Bear in mind that the tax rules for pensions are due to change from April 2006 – see Chapter 9 for an outline of the new system.

CASE HISTORY: Samuel

Samuel retired in May 2004. It was found that if he used his whole AVC fund to buy benefits in the main pension scheme, his pension and other benefits would come to more than the Inland Revenue limits. Some of his AVCs therefore had to be repaid. The AVC refund would have been £1,000, but tax at the special rate of 33 per cent was deducted, so Samuel received 67 per cent of £1,000 = £670.

Samuel is a higher-rate taxpayer, so there was more tax to pay on the refund. It was worked out as follows. The £670 was grossed up at the basic rate of tax (22 per cent in 2004–5). This came to £670 ÷ (100% – 22%) = £859. Tax at the higher rate was 40% × £859 = £344. Samuel was treated as already having paid basic-rate tax of 22% × £859 = £189. So the extra tax due was £344 – £189 = £155.

Topping up your pension using stakeholder pension schemes

In addition to paying up to 15 per cent of your earnings into an occupational pension scheme and any AVC/FSAVC schemes, many employees can also pay up to £3,600 a year into personal pensions, including stakeholder schemes. However, you do not have this option if:

- you are a controlling director of a company or have been at any time during the previous five years, or
- your earnings from all sources in *all* of the previous five years have been more than £30,000 a year.

When looking back five years to see if these conditions apply to you, under transitional rules you cannot use any year earlier than 2000–1. For example, if you are checking the position in 2004–5, you will not be eligible for a stakeholder scheme if you have been a controlling director in any of the years 2000–1 to 2004–5 or your earnings in all these years were higher than £30,000.

Provided you do not fall foul of the controlling director test, if your earnings were £30,000 or less in even just one of the relevant years, you can use that year as the basis for being eligible to pay up to £3,600 into personal pensions and stakeholder schemes. This £3,600 is the before-tax-relief (gross) limit. In practice, you hand over your contributions after deducting tax relief at the basic rate. The maximum after-tax-relief contribution in 2004–5 is £2,808.

Provided you stay within the limit, you can have as many personal pensions and stakeholder schemes as you like but, given that the maximum is not very large, it would be usual to choose one scheme. Although you can choose non-stakeholder personal pensions, a stakeholder scheme will often be a good vehicle to choose in order to top up your pension, because a stakeholder scheme must meet certain conditions that ensure it offers value for money (see Chapter 20). The rest of this section assumes you consider making contributions to a single stakeholder scheme.

If you have enough money to spare, you can pay AVCs as well as contributions to a stakeholder scheme. But, if you have only limited amounts available for your retirement savings, you might need to choose between the two routes. The stakeholder route has the following advantages:

- part of the proceeds of a stakeholder scheme can be taken as a lump sum at retirement. Added-years AVCs can also provide a lump sum, but FSAVCs and most other AVCs cannot
- charges for a stakeholder scheme are capped at 1 per cent a year of your fund. Money-purchase AVC and FSAVC schemes typically have higher charges.

More information

In order to find out about the in-house AVC scheme, contact your pension administrator at work or the trustees of the main pension scheme. Your scheme booklet should have contact details.

In order to find out about FSAVC schemes or stakeholder schemes, either contact a scheme provider directly or talk to an independent financial adviser★. See Chapter 22 for the sorts of factors you should take into account when choosing the scheme. (Note that FSAVCs are essentially the same as personal pensions, so the guidance in Chapter 22 applies equally to FSAVCs.)

Chapter 31

Boosting your personal pension

Chapter 19 set out the maximum that you can pay into a personal pension plan or retirement annuity contract in any tax year. Especially if you've left starting your retirement savings until, say, your thirties or forties, you may find that you need to make contributions up to the maximum in order to catch up and stand a reasonable chance of hitting your pension target.

You can maximise the amount you are allowed to save by making careful use of the basis year rules (see Chapter 19). These let you base the contributions you make now on your level of earnings from any of the previous five tax years. Keep an eye on your yearly earnings and make sure you always have selected the year with the highest level as your basis year. (See the Case History on page194.)

If you have a retirement annuity contract, there is an extra way in which you can catch up on your retirement savings, if you haven't used up your full contribution limit in the past few years. That's by using the *carry forward* rules. Since 31 January 2002, these rules cannot be used with personal pensions. Bear in mind that the rules described in this chapter are due to be replaced from April 2006 by a new and simpler regime – see Chapter 9.

How the carry-forward rules work

You can use these rules only to make contributions to a retirement annuity contract. They may enable you to make contributions well in excess of the normal annual limit.

You can use the carry-forward rules if you have any unused contribution relief from the last six years. You can carry forward the unused relief, and use it now. You must carry forward from the earliest year first. But note that you get relief at the current tax rates – not the tax rates which applied in the earlier years.

In order to use carry-forward relief, you must first have used up the whole maximum relief available for the tax year to which you are carrying forward. For example, if you want to carry forward relief from 1998–9 to the tax year 2004–5, you must first have made the maximum possible contribution for 2004–5.

Bear in mind that, while you can only benefit from tax relief on your contributions to a retirement annuity contract if you pay income tax, the contributions themselves do not have to be paid out of taxed income. So, if you are carrying forward unused tax relief, you can use, say, a redundancy payment or inherited lump sum to use up that relief and invest in a contract.

Combining carry-forward and carry-back rules

You can combine the carry-back rules (see page 200) with the carry-forward rules, in which case you can scoop up unused relief from seven years ago rather than six. For example, if you make a contribution in 2004–5 you can opt to carry it back and have it treated as if it had been paid in 2003–4. You can then go as far back as 1997–8 and carry forward unused relief from that year and the following five years to 2003–4. Tax relief is given on the whole contribution at the 2003–4 tax rates.

Combining the rules in this way can be a good idea if:

- you have a large chunk of unused tax relief in the tax year seven years back. If you don't use it now that relief will be lost for good
- tax rates are lower in the current year than in the previous year and you want to maximise the relief that you get on your over-large contribution
- your marginal rate of tax was higher in the earlier years and you want to maximise the relief on your over-large contribution. This could apply when your earnings vary considerably from one year to another, so that, for example, one year you pay tax at the basic rate but in a good year you move into the higher-rate bracket. The timing and allocation of your pension contributions can be a useful tax-planning tool.

CASE HISTORY: Josh

Josh, aged 40, has more or less neglected his retirement savings for a number of years. He started a retirement annuity contract in 1982 but over the last ten years he has made only the occasional small *ad hoc* contribution. Having just inherited £50,000 and with his business flourishing, he decides to pay a £30,000 lump-sum contribution into his plan. He has unused contribution relief from the previous six years which he wants to carry forward and use up against a large contribution paid in the 2004–5 tax year. The position is set out in Table 31.1.

The £30,000 contribution uses up the current year's relief first and must then be set against the earliest years' unused relief, working one's way forward in time. In fact, it uses all the relief for the years 1998–9 to 2002–3 and part of the unused relief from 2003–4.

Tax relief is given at current tax rates. Making the £30,000 contribution reduces Josh's tax bill for 2004–5 dramatically from £7,408 to just £474.

Table 31.1: Josh's earnings and contribution limits

Tax year	Josh's earnings	Pension tax-relief limit	Josh's contributions	Unused relief for the year	How the unused relief is used by the 2004–5 contribution	Remaining unused relief
2004–5	£38,000	£7,600	£30,000	–	£7,600	
2003–4	£36,000	£7,200	–	£7,200	£1,425	£5,775
2002–3	£29,000	£5,800	–	£5,800	£5,800	–
2001–2	£26,000	£5,200	£100	£5,100	£5,100	–
2000–1	£24,000	£4,800	–	£4,800	£4,800	–
1999–2000	£18,000	£3,150	–	£2,650	£2,650	–
1989–9	£15,000	£2,625	£500	£2,625	£2,625	–
TOTAL					£30,000	

Personal pensions and retirement annuity contracts

If you have a retirement annuity contract you can choose whether to make contributions to the contract, a personal pension plan or both. But the choice that you make each year will affect the amount of carry-forward relief available to you for the retirement annuity contract.

The example below, set out in the form of a calculator, will help to illustrate how the rules work.

CASE HISTORY: Jayne

Jayne is 36 and self-employed. She started a retirement annuity contract 16 years ago. More recently, she has also started making contributions to a personal pension plan. Over the last three years she has contributed to both plans, as shown in Table 31.2.

The table also shows how the maximum contribution that she could make, taking into account carry-forward relief, is affected by the contributions that she makes to each plan.

Table 31.2: Jayne's contributions to her retirement annuity contract and personal pension plan

The sums	2002–3	2003–4	2004–5	Notes
Jayne's earnings	£93,000	£100,000	£90,000	A
Jayne's age at the start of the tax year	34	35	36	B
The personal pension plan				
Maximum contribution for the year as % of earnings	17.5%	17.5%	20%	C See Chapter 19
Earnings cap	£97,200	£99,000	£102,000	D
Maximum contribution in £s	£17,115	£17,325	£18,000	E Multiply percentage C by lower of amount A or D
Jayne's contribution this year to her personal pension plan	£500	£5,000	£5,000	F Contribution to personal penson plan cannot be more than amount E
The retirement annuity contract				
Maximum contribution for the year as % of earnings	17.5%	17.5%	17.5%	G See Chapter 19
Maximum contribution in £s	£16,275	£17,500	£15,750	H Percentage G multiplied by amount A
Jayne's contribution this year to her retirement annuity contract	£14,700	£10,000	£16,000	I Contribution to retirement annuity contract can exceed amount H provided that there is sufficient carry-forward relief (amount K) to set against the excess
Remaining retirement annuity contract limit for year	£1,575	£7,500	–£250	J Amount H less amount I

The sums	2000–1	2001–2	2002–3	Notes
Carry-forward retirement annuity contract relief available from the past six years	£500	£1,575	£4,075	K See amount N
Remaining relief available, including carry forward	£2,075	£9,075	£3,825	L Add amounts J and K. This amount cannot be less than zero. If it is negative, the retirement annuity contract contribution for the year must be reduced
Jayne's contribution this year to her personal pension plan	£500	£5,000	£5,000	M This contribution can exceed the relief available at L
Unused retirement annuity But contract relief available to carry forward	£1,575	£4,075	£0	N Amount L less amount M. if the result is negative, amount N is set to zero. This is the cumulative relief to be carried forward. Any unused relief from more than six years ago drops out of the total (not shown in this example)

More information

In order to increase the amount that you pay into an existing personal pension plan or retirement annuity contract, or to make an extra lump-sum payment, contact the plan provider or your independent financial adviser if you use the adviser regularly.

For more detailed information about using the carry-forward rules, see Inland Revenue Help Sheet IR330, available from the Inland Revenue Order Line*.

Chapter 32

Other ways of saving for retirement

This chapter is aimed largely at people who cannot join an occupational pension scheme (for example, because they are self-employed) and people who are in an occupational pension scheme but want to boost their pension. But, if you've been putting off starting your pension savings because you don't like the idea of tying up your money for a long time, then this chapter is for you, too.

Taxing decisions

If you can join an occupational pension scheme, this is, in most cases, the best way to save for retirement. The various advantages of occupational schemes have been outlined in Chapters 11 and 12, but the single factor that gives such schemes an unbeatable edge is that your employer must pay a substantial part of the cost of providing the pension and other benefits. Your pension savings are, in effect, heavily subsidised.

You could argue that this subsidy is really deferred pay, and that in the absence of the pension scheme you could have a higher salary today. This certainly holds true for a workforce as a whole, but few individuals are in the position of being able to demand a higher salary if they don't join the pension scheme. For most people, the only way that they can lay their hands on this deferred pay is by joining the pension scheme.

If you cannot join an occupational scheme you face a more difficult decision about how to save for retirement. The options that were open to you in the past have often proved a poor deal, though the position has improved considerably with the introduction of stakeholder schemes (see Chapter 20).

With no occupational scheme, the main pension vehicle available to you is a personal pension. The primary reason for choosing a dedicated pension vehicle used to be the tax advantages that it offered. But in its 1997 Budget the government withdrew an important tax perk. From 2 July 1997 onwards pension funds have no longer been able to reclaim the tax credit paid along with dividends from shares, distributions from share-based unit trusts and other income from similar, share-based investments. For pension funds, such income became taxable overnight.

Two other forms of investment were still able – for a little while longer – to receive this type of income tax-free: Personal Equity Plans (PEPs) and Individual Savings Accounts (ISAs). In terms of tax, personal pensions still had the edge. And, since 6 April 2004 onwards, this edge has increased because from that date income from shares, distributions from share-based unit trusts, and so on held within ISAs and PEPs is also taxed at 10 per cent. But when you also look at the disadvantages of pensions, saving through an ISA or a PEP could be the more attractive option. In particular, unlike personal pensions, ISAs and PEPs do not lock away your money for the very long term and are also extremely flexible.

A note about PEPs

From 6 April 1999 you can no longer start a new PEP, but if you already have PEP savings you could consider earmarking these for your pension target. For example, if your PEPs were originally linked to a mortgage but you then switch to a repayment mortgage, consider reallocating the PEPs to your pension target.

Boosting your pension

If you belong to an occupational scheme and you've decided to boost your retirement savings, making AVCs is an option (see Chapter 30). Your employer must offer an in-house scheme, and this may be the best deal, especially if your employer will add to your AVCs by matching or partially matching your contributions. And an added-years scheme (see page 288) may be an attractive deal, depending on how much you must pay for each year. However, if the in-house scheme does not offer any special advantages, or if you are considering making FSAVCs to a free-standing plan, you should also look at ISAs.

Unlike a personal pension plan, an AVC scheme (unless started before 8 April 1987) cannot be used to provide a tax-free lump sum on retirement. The tax-free lump sum is the key tax advantage which most pension vehicles have over ISAs. Without that, though, ISAs can have the tax edge, because they can also claim back the tax on income from shares and similar investments.

Together with the greater flexibility that ISAs offer compared with FSAVC and AVC schemes, investing through an ISA will often be the better option. However, since April 2001, many employees have been able to use personal pensions and stakeholder schemes to boost their retirement savings (see page 290). Personal pensions (particularly stakeholder schemes) are more tax-efficient than most AVC schemes, because they do let you take part of your fund as tax-free cash at retirement. Therefore, there is less reason to look at ISAs. But ISAs are more flexible than personal pensions and stakeholder schemes, because ISAs let you take your money out at any time and in any form you like.

Other approaches to retirement saving

This chapter focuses on tax-efficient ways in which to save for retirement. But you can, of course, use any other forms of saving and investment as a means of meeting your retirement target.

Retirement saving is, by definition, a long-term goal, so you should look at savings and investments that are suitable for the long term. In general, share-based investments, such as unit trusts, investment trusts and open-ended investment companies (OEICs) will be the most suitable. However, your choice also depends on your attitude towards risk, the amount that you have available to save, the degree of flexibility that you require and how close you are to retiring. In particular, if you are not comfortable with risk and/or you are within five years of retiring, you may want to have some of your savings in medium- to low-risk investments, such as unit trusts investing in corporate bonds, gilts, preference shares or money-market accounts. For more about these and other investments and how they can be used to meet your investment goals, see *Be Your Own Financial Adviser* from Which? Books★.

Another approach to retirement saving is open to you if you run your own business. This is to count on selling the business and using

Table 32.1: The pros and cons of personal pension plans versus ISAs and PEPs

	Personal pension/ stakeholder scheme	Free-standing AVC scheme [1]	ISA	PEP [2]
Tax features				
Tax relief on contributions	Yes	Yes	No	No
Tax relief on investment income from shares, share-based unit trusts etc.	No	No	No [3]	No [3]
Tax relief on income from other investments (e.g., bonds and deposits)	Yes	Yes	Yes	Yes
Tax relief on capital gains building up within the fund	Yes	Yes	Yes	Yes
Part of fund is largely tax-free because you had tax relief on contributions and there's no tax to pay on withdrawal	Yes	No	No	No
Rest of fund can be withdrawn tax-free	No	No	Yes	Yes
Other features				
Can impose a savings discipline, which could be useful if you find it hard to save regularly	Yes	Yes	No	No
Flexible payments	Sometimes [4]	Sometimes	Usually	Usually
High charges	Often [5]	Often	Sometimes	Sometimes
Your money is tied up for the long term (until at least age 50 – due to rise to 55 from 2010)	Yes	Yes	No	No
You make withdrawals whenever you like	No	No	Yes	Yes
Flexible withdrawals: e.g., you can choose partial withdrawal, as income, as a lump sum	No	No	Yes	Yes
Risk that you might use the money before retirement and end up with too little pension	No	No	Yes	Yes

[1] Can apply to some in-house AVC schemes too, but check carefully.
[2] From 6 April 1999 you can no longer start a new PEP.
[3] This type of income became taxable (at 10 per cent) from 6 April 2004.
[4] Yes, if the personal pension is a stakeholder scheme.
[5] No, if the personal pension is a stakeholder scheme.

the proceeds to provide your pension. Clearly, this is suitable only when you have substantial business assets to sell, but it can also be a risky strategy. When you reach retirement, you may find that no one wants to buy your business, or that the price that someone is willing to pay is less than you need. Consider making some savings for retirement to fund you at least for a delay of several years if you do face selling problems.

Similarly, some people hope to sell their family home, move to a smaller property and thus release funds to be used as a pension. Again, this is a risky strategy and is not recommended. You may not be able to sell the house, or it may fetch less than you had hoped. In addition, retirement is costly: as a rough rule of thumb you'd need to release at least £100,000 to fund a relatively modest retirement.

Even more risky is to rely on using an equity release scheme to provide the bulk of your retirement income. Equity release schemes let you unlock the capital tied up in your home without having to move house. They do this by you either taking out a mortgage against your home or selling part of your home and using the money raised either to provide an income or as a cash lump sum (or a mixture of the two). The company providing you with money eventually gets it back when your home is sold after your death (or if you permanently move into a care home). Since that may be many years away, the company wants some compensation for giving you the money now, so you get far less than the value of the part of your home you mortgage or sell. This makes it even less likely that you'll be able to raise enough this way to fund a decent pension. However, equity release schemes can be useful if, having retired, you need to supplement your income and really do not want to move house.

In recent years, some people have also been drawn to look on an investment in buy-to-let property as a way of saving for retirement or even as a way of providing income during retirement. This involves buying a property specifically to rent out to tenants. While you own the property, you earn rental income and, when you sell, you might make a profit. This is a high-risk strategy if you have to borrow to buy the property since, after all the costs including mortgage payments, you will not necessarily make much, if any, income from renting the place out. Moreover, you cannot be sure that when you sell you will realise enough to pay off any outstanding mortgage and leave yourself with enough profit to fund a reasonable pension. The investment looks more sound if you can afford to buy a property outright without borrowing, and better still if the property is just one of several investments you have, so that risks are spread across a range of different ways to save for retirement.

Individual Savings Accounts (ISAs)

Description

ISAs replaced PEPs from 6 April 1999. An ISA is not itself an investment: it is, in effect, a tax-efficient 'wrapper' within which you invest in a wide range of other investments, which can include deposits (including a special National Savings & Investments account), bonds, insurance, unit trusts, investment trusts, OEICs and shares. These are divided into three components: cash, insurance and stocks and shares. Each year you can take out a new ISA up to the investment limits for that year. The ISA must be run by an account manager and there are three types of ISA:

- **Mini-ISA** This invests in just one component: in other words, it can be a cash ISA, an insurance ISA or a stocks-and-shares ISA. You can take out all three types of mini-ISA in the same year, and each mini-ISA can be run by a different plan manager
- **Maxi-ISA** Instead of taking out separate mini-ISAs, you can instead take out one maxi-ISA in a given tax year. A maxi-ISA must have a stocks-and-shares component with, or without, a cash and/or insurance component, too. All components are offered by one plan manager
- **TESSA-only ISA** Tax-Exempt Special Savings Accounts (TESSAs) were tax-favoured deposit accounts that ceased to be available from 6 April 1999. They had a five-year life, and the capital from a maturing TESSA could be reinvested in a TESSA-only ISA (which is restricted to a cash component). The last TESSAs matured by 5 April 2004 and investors had six months – i.e. until 5 October 2004 at the latest – to reinvest the capital in this type of ISA.

Tax position

You don't receive any tax relief on the amount that you invest, but some income and all gains earned by the investment are tax-free.

Income from shares, share-based unit trusts, and so on, is paid into the ISA with tax at 10 per cent (in 2004–5) already deducted. The ISA manager used to be able to reclaim this tax so that the income was tax-free, but this ceased from 6 April 2004 onwards. Therefore, from 2004–5 onwards, income from shares, share-based unit trusts and similar income within an ISA is taxed at 10 per cent. This means that for many taxpayers there is no longer any advantage in holding these investments through an ISA rather than outright. However, advantages remain for higher-rate taxpayers and people who use up their full capital gains tax allowance each year.

The income from other types of investments held within an ISA – e.g. deposits, gilts and corporate bonds – is still tax-free.

Although you can in any case make substantial capital gains each year without paying tax (see page 309), the ISA wrapper could be useful in the long run, as it is possible to build up large gains within the account, which could exceed your annual tax-free limit.

There is no tax on withdrawals from your ISA, and you do not lose any of the tax reliefs already given.

How much you can invest

This depends on the type of ISA that you have.

- **Mini–ISA** Each tax year up to 5 April 2006 you can invest up to £3,000 in a cash ISA, up to £1,000 in an insurance ISA and up to £3,000 in a stocks-and-shares ISA. From the 2006–7 tax year onwards, the limit for cash ISAs is due to be reduced to £1,000.
- **Maxi–ISA** If instead of mini-ISAs you opt for a maxi-ISA, the following limits apply. Each tax year up to 5 April 2006 the maximum that you can put into a maxi-ISA is £7,000. If you choose, up to £3,000 of this can be put in a cash component and up to £1,000 in an insurance component. From 2006–7 the limits are £5,000 overall, with, if you choose, up to £1,000 in a cash component and up to £1,000 in an insurance component.
- **TESSA-only ISA** The maximum capital from a maturing TESSA is £9,000. Reinvesting this in a TESSA-only ISA does not affect the amounts that you can invest in mini-ISAs or a maxi-ISA.

How long you can invest

You can have your money in an ISA for as long or as short a period as you like. The government has guaranteed that ISAs will be available for ten years, up to 2009. It is impossible to say what may happen after that. Although governments have in general shown an enthusiasm for encouraging personal saving, the Labour government in power in

2004–5 was tending to target incentives more with the focus on lower-income households through, for example, the Savings Gateway pilot schemes and Child Trust Fund (which offers higher amounts to lower income households). Therefore, it is possible that generally available schemes, which give incentives perhaps unnecessarily to wealthier people who would probably save anyway, might not continue.

Risk

The risk depends on the underlying investments in your ISA (see Chart 32.1). See page 218 for an outline of the relationship between risk and return. For more information, see *Be Your Own Financial Adviser*, published by Which? Books★.

Access to your money

You can withdraw your money at any time without incurring any tax penalty. Dividend income can be paid out tax-free. Bear in mind that, if you have chosen investments whose price can rise and fall, you may get back less capital than you originally invested. Plan managers may impose their own restrictions and/or withdrawal charges.

Charges

In general, the charges depend on the investments inside your ISA. But in some cases – for example, if you use an ISA to invest directly in stocks and shares – there may be extra charges for the ISA wrapper. Make sure any extra charges do not outweigh the tax benefits you gain.

Personal equity plans (PEPs)

Description

A personal equity plan (PEP) is a tax-efficient wrapper around long-term investment in shares, gilts, bonds, unit trusts, investment trusts, and so on. It is offered by a plan manager, which might, for example, be an insurance company, unit or investment trust company, bank or stockbroker. There were originally two main types of PEP. With a general PEP, you invested in a spread of shares, bonds and/or collective investments (unit trusts and investment trusts). This can give you a balanced spread of risk, which is suitable for retirement saving. With a single-company PEP, your investment bought the shares of just one company. This is a high-risk strategy and less suitable for retirement saving. However, since April 2001, you can merge your different types of PEP if you want to.

You can buy and sell the investments within your PEP at any time. Either you can make the investment decisions yourself (a non-discretionary PEP) or you can leave them to the plan manager, in which case the plan is called a discretionary PEP.

Since 6 April 1999, you can no longer start a new PEP. But you can continue any PEPs you took out before then. The government has guaranteed that PEPs can continue until April 2009. It is not known what will happen after then.

Tax position

You did not get any tax relief on the amount you invested, but some income and all gains earned by the investment *are* tax-free. Investments within a PEP are taxed in the same way as investments within an ISA – see page 303.

Over the short term, the saving on capital gains tax is not very valuable. You can, in any case, make substantial capital gains each year without having to pay any tax (see page 309). But, if you're investing for the long term, you can build up very large gains within your PEP which, if cashed in from a non-PEP investment, would result in a hefty tax bill.

You can cash in part or all of your PEP at any time without losing the tax advantages and you can, if you like, just withdraw the income element on a regular basis. This makes PEPs very flexible in providing lump sums, income or a combination of both.

How much you can invest

You can no longer invest new sums in a PEP.

How long you can invest

You can leave your money in a PEP for as long or as short a period as you like.

Risk

The risk depends on the underlying investment in your PEP and can be broadly ranked as shown in Chart 32.1. Most PEPs are risk investments where the value of your capital can fall as well as rise. Choosing a spread of underlying investments is a way of reducing the risk. For more information, see *Be Your Own Financial Adviser*, published by Which? Books★.

Access to your money

You can withdraw capital at any time without any tax penalty. Dividend income can currently be paid out tax-free.

Drawbacks

Plan managers levy charges. These may take the form of an initial charge when you invest and possibly an annual charge. However, in recent years competition between unit-trust managers has been so intense that, with many unit-trust PEPs, there are no charges additional to the normal trust charges – in a few cases, it can even be cheaper to invest via a PEP than directly. PEPs offered by stockbrokers and some other investment managers tend to be the most expensive; as well as management fees, you'll also have to pay dealing charges when shares are bought and sold. You may be charged extra for services such as being sent the annual report and accounts of companies in which you hold shares. Charges vary greatly from plan to plan, so check carefully. In the worst cases, plan charges can swallow up most of the tax advantage.

A brief note about tax

Income tax

If you receive income from an investment that is taxable, whether or not you have to pay tax depends on the size of your income from all sources and what deductions you can make from it. The main deduction allowed is your personal allowance. The standard rates of allowances in the 2004–5 tax year are:

Personal allowance if you are aged under 65   £4,745
Personal allowance if you are aged 65 to 74   £6,830
Personal allowance if you are aged 75 or over   £6,950

Married couples, where one or both partners were born before 6 April 1935, can claim a married couple's allowance which is given at a rate of 10 per cent and reduces the tax payable. See Chapter 34.

You pay tax at the starting rate of 10 per cent on the first £2,020 by which your income exceeds your allowance(s) and any other deductions. On the next £29,380, you pay tax at the basic rate of 22 per cent. On anything above £31,400, you pay at the higher rate of 40 per cent.

Income from many taxable investments is paid with tax at the savings rate (20 per cent in 2004–5) already deducted. Non-taxpayers can reclaim the tax and may be able to arrange for the income to be

Chart 32.1: ISA and PEP investments, by risk

Least risky	A single gilt offering a fixed and guaranteed return provided you hold it until redemption
	A unit or investment trust investing in a range of gilts – note that, even though an individual gilt offers a fixed return, the trust provides a variable return
	A single bond issued by a very sound company offering a fixed and guaranteed return
	A unit or investment trust investing in a range of bonds – note that, even though the individual bonds offer fixed returns, the trust provides a variable return
	Your own selection of bonds
	A unit or investment trust investing in a broad range of UK shares
	A unit or investment trust investing in a broad range of international shares
	Your own broad selection of UK shares
	A unit or investment trust specialising in particular types of shares – e.g. recovery stocks, Asian markets or commodity companies
Most risky	Your own choice of specialist shares

paid gross. Starting-rate taxpayers can reclaim part of the tax. Basic-rate taxpayers have no further tax to pay. Higher-rate taxpayers have extra to pay.

However, dividends from shares and distributions from unit trusts and similar investments are paid with tax at 10 per cent already deducted. Non-taxpayers cannot reclaim this. Basic-rate taxpayers have no more to pay. Higher-rate taxpayers have extra to pay.

Capital gains tax

You make a gain on an investment when you sell it for more than you originally paid. Gains on some investments are tax-free but, even when this is not the case, all or part of your gain may not be taxable because you can make various adjustments and deductions. First, you can deduct any allowable expenses incurred in the process of buying or selling. Second, where you owned the asset before 6 April 1998 you can deduct an indexation allowance, which reflects the fact that part of the gain arose as a result of general price inflation over the period up to April 1998. For periods of ownership from April 1998 onwards, you may be able to claim taper relief. You can also deduct allowable losses made on other assets you've sold or otherwise disposed of.

After allowing for these deductions, you can make gains up to your annual tax-free allowance (£8,200 in the 2004–5 tax year). If you have gains above this amount, tax is worked out by adding your gains to your taxable income and taxing them as if they were savings income. So if, when the gains are added to your other income, your top rate of tax is the starting rate, your gains are taxed at 10 per cent. If your top rate is the basic rate, your gains are taxed at 20 per cent. If your income plus gains put you into the higher-rate tax bracket, your gain is taxed at 40 per cent. If adding the gain to your income takes you over a tax threshold, part of your gain will be taxed at one rate and part at the other.

Part 6

Reaching retirement

Chapter 33

What happens when you reach retirement

Retirement should be a time for relaxing a little, but you may find there's quite a lot of paperwork to be done before you can be sure that your pension income is properly arranged. Here are a few general rules which should help you:

- keep all the documents that you get throughout your working life concerning your pension rights. Don't discard documents relating to your earlier pension schemes and plans
- keep all the papers relating to your pensions in one place – start a file for them, if you don't have one already
- start sorting out your pensions well before your intended retirement date – three to four months before should be adequate in most cases, but allow longer for pensions from any schemes that you left on changing jobs
- always quote relevant reference numbers – for example, your National Insurance number in the case of state pensions, your works number or other scheme reference for an employer's scheme, and your policy or plan number with a personal plan – whenever you contact the Department for Work and Pensions (DWP), a scheme or a plan provider
- keep copies of letters you send
- make notes of telephone calls – include the date, who you spoke to and the main points of the conversation
- once your pensions start to be paid, keep counterfoils, payslips, and so on, in a handy place. You'll need them when you sort out your tax, and you may want them if you have any queries about your pensions.

It's important to keep in touch with old pension schemes and plan providers: if you move or change your name, contact all the relevant schemes and plan providers to give them your new details – it's all too easy to lose touch, only to find you have no idea who'll be paying your pension when you retire.

If you can't track down an old employer from whom you think a pension is due, you can turn to the Pension Schemes Registry for help. The Registry was set up by the government in 1990 to help people trace 'lost' pensions. If you need help, complete a Form PR4 which you can get from the Pensions Advisory Service (OPAS)★ or the Pension Schemes Registry★.

Your state pension

How to claim your pension

About four months before you reach the state pension age (currently 60 for women, 65 for men), you should receive a letter from The Pension Service telling you how much state pension you're entitled to. The pension is *not* paid automatically – you have to claim it. Do this either by phoning the Pensions Claims Line number included with the letter – someone will then take down all the required details over the phone – or, if you prefer, ask to be sent a claim form (Form BR1) that you fill in yourself. If you are a married man and your wife will be claiming a pension based on your contributions, you will need Form BF225 as well. Fill this in and return it to the DWP. If you decide to defer your pension (see Chapter 29) and haven't already written to The Pension Service about this, do so now.

If you haven't heard from The Pension Service within, say, three months before your birthday, get in touch with them yourself by visiting or writing to your local office or contacting The Pension Service★. Always quote your National Insurance number on any letters you send, and have a note of it with you if you visit A Pension Service Office in person. Alternatively, you can download the claim forms from the DWP website★.

If you haven't claimed your pension in time for your birthday, don't worry. You can still make your claim after reaching state pension age. A pension for yourself can be backdated up to 12 months. But, if you're a man and you're claiming a pension for your wife based on your own National Insurance (see Chapter 4), the pension for your wife can be backdated only *six* months – so don't delay too long before making your claim.

CASE HISTORY: George

George will be 65 in three months' time, but he hasn't had any communication from The Pension Service about his retirement pension yet – he has moved around a bit during the last ten years, so it's possible that the Service doesn't have his current address. He decides to make the first move. George is a 'silver surfer' and goes onto The Pension Service website at www.thepensionservice.gov.uk. By keying in his postcode, he finds the phone number of The Pension Service office for his area; alternatively, he could have looked in the phone book. But not all of these have yet been updated for the introduction of The Pension Service, which is fairly new, so he might have needed to look under Jobcentre Plus (a sister organisation that handles benefits for people of working age) for a suitable number to ring.

George rings The Pension Service office and they help him make his claim over the phone. They also suggest he claims pension credit (see Chapter 2).

Postponing your pension

If you decide to put off the start of your state pension (see Chapter 29), inform The Pension Service. When you want your pension to start, contact The Pension Service and ask for a claim form. Assuming legislation before Parliament at the time of writing goes ahead, for periods of deferment from 6 April 2005 onwards that last at least 12 months, you will need to tell The Pension Service whether you want to receive an increased pension or a lump sum. If you fail to make a choice, you will be paid a lump sum. If your deferment lasted less than 12 months, you'll have no choice but to receive a higher pension.

How your pension is paid

You used to be able to choose to have your pension paid weekly by order book, or credited monthly or quarterly to your bank or building society account. However, the DWP is part way through a programme of converting everyone to 'direct payment' of their state pension and other state benefits direct to a bank account or to a special Post Office Card Account (POCA). The POCA is an account that only accepts state pensions and benefits and lets you withdraw them in cash from post offices by presenting your POCA card and keying a personal identification number into a key pad.

If you cannot manage to operate a POCA, you can receive your pension or other benefits by girocheque sent to you each week.

To find out more about direct payment of state pensions and other state benefits, contact the DWP Direct Payment Information Line★.

It's important that you let the DWP know if your circumstances change – for example, if you move, marry or become widowed.

Going abroad

If you go abroad for less than six months, you can simply carry on receiving your pension in the normal way. If you'll be away for longer, let The Pension Service know your plans and choose one of the following arrangements for your pension:

- have it paid into a personal bank account (see above) while you're away
- arrange for it to be paid into a Post Office Card Account, or
- arrange to have the money paid to you abroad.

If you intend to live abroad in your retirement, then you'll definitely want to arrange to have your pension paid to you in the country in which you choose to live. There is no difficulty in doing this, but if you're abroad at the time of the annual increase in state pensions, you won't qualify for the increase unless you're living in a country which is a member of the European Union or a country with which the UK

Table 33.1: Retiring abroad: useful DWP leaflets

Leaflet number	Leaflet name
NI38	Social security abroad
SA4 to SA43	These leaflets outline the special agreements which the UK has with other countries regarding social security payments and state benefits. Leaflets include one each for Jersey and Guernsey, Australia, Switzerland, New Zealand, Sweden, Malta, Cyprus, Israel, Norway, Yugoslavia, Finland, Canada, Turkey, Bermuda, Iceland, Austria, Jamaica, the European Union, the USA, Mauritius, The Philippines and Barbados

has an agreement for increasing pensions. The latter include, for example, the Channel Islands, USA and Cyprus, but do not include some popular retirement choices, such as Australia, New Zealand, South Africa and Canada.

It's very important, therefore, that you check what will happen to your state pension (and entitlement to other state benefits, such as health treatment) before committing yourself to a decision to move abroad. Get in touch with the DWP International Pension Centre★ for more help.

A pension from an occupational scheme

How to claim your pension

Different schemes will have different arrangements, but here is a rough guide to what to expect and what action you should take.

About three months before you reach the normal retirement date (or dates) for any occupational schemes that will be paying you a pension, you'll need to be in touch with them. If the schemes haven't contacted you by then, make the first move. Either telephone or write to each scheme asking them to give you the details you need and any forms you must complete. If you're not sure who to contact, telephone and ask who deals with pension matters, or failing that you could address any correspondence to 'The Pensions Administrator' and send it to the employer's normal address (or through the internal post system in the case of your current employer). On your letters, always quote any reference number (check your last benefit statement for this), and have your reference number to hand if you telephone. If you can, it's a good idea to arrange a meeting with the pensions administrator so that you can discuss your position in detail. Don't be afraid to ask for extra information or advice.

At this stage, you'll need to ask the following questions about the employer's scheme providing your main pension:

- what pension are you entitled to?
- what lump sum are you entitled to?
- will taking a lump sum reduce your pension and, if so, by how much?
- how will the pension be paid; do you have any choices to make about the frequency and method of payment?

- is there a widow's or widower's pension, and, if so, how will that affect your retirement pension?
- are there pensions for any other dependants in the event of your death, and, if so, how much are they?

If you've been making additional voluntary contributions (AVCs), you'll need to know how much has built up in your fund. If you've been paying into your in-house AVC scheme, then you can ask staff there how much has built up and how you can use it to enhance your benefits from the main scheme. If you've been paying into a free-standing AVC scheme, you'll have to contact the company or society running the scheme as well as the administrators of your employer's scheme.

If you're entitled to a preserved pension from a previous employer's scheme, check the documents you have kept to find out who you should contact: this may be the old scheme, or it may be an insurance company if, say, the old employer's scheme no longer exists. You'll need to ask what preserved pension you're entitled to, what other benefits there are (if any), what options you have, and how the pension will be paid.

Retiring early

If you retire earlier than the normal age for your employer's scheme you may be able to start receiving a pension even at this earlier date. Get in touch with the scheme administrator, relating what you intend. He or she will advise what pension, if any, you qualify for, and any options you have.

If you're intending to retire early because of ill-health, first check the rules of your scheme to see if you might qualify for an ill-health pension – you'll probably need to look at the detailed rules (ask the pensions administrator or trustees) since scheme booklets often give insufficient detail. Contact the scheme authorities – if possible, *before* your employment stops – to find out what action you'll need to take and what information you'll need to provide. You'll certainly need to provide the scheme with medical evidence – perhaps from the scheme's choice of doctor rather than your own – before a pension can be approved.

Retiring late

Depending on the rules of your employer's scheme, you may be able to put off the start of your pension until after the normal retirement age for the scheme. If you want to do this, contact the scheme administrators, telling them what you intend. Ask them to give you details about how long you can defer the pension, and how it will be increased in the interim.

How your pension is paid

Depending on how the pension scheme is arranged, you may get a pension direct from the scheme, or your pension might be provided by an insurance company.

Usually, you'll be able to choose the method of payment that is most convenient for you – for example, a regular cheque through the post or payment direct into a bank or building society account. The scheme rules will generally dictate how often the pension is paid – monthly in advance is common – and when any increases are made. A trivial (i.e. very small) pension – taken to mean less than £260 a year – will generally be converted to a single lump sum at retirement instead of being paid out year by year. In that case, tax at a special rate of 20 per cent will usually be deducted and can't be reclaimed.

Pensioners' associations

Retirement does not necessarily mark the end of your relationship with your employer. Increasingly, the link continues through a pensioners' association. In essence this is a club for retired members which either you can choose to join or to which you automatically belong once you retire. Typically, membership extends to husbands, wives and unmarried partners, and their membership continues even if you die before them. The aims of pensioners' associations vary and may encompass some or all of the following:

- a social group organising parties, lectures and outings
- a support group giving advice and even financial help
- a source of training in matters particularly pertinent to the retired – e.g. how to make a will, paying for long-term care, and so on
- a lobbying group putting pressure on local and central governments to implement policies which benefit retired people.

Pensioners' associations may also become involved in putting forward member-nominated trustees to help run the pension scheme (see Chapter 17). During the passing of the member-nominated trustees legislation, there were calls for the law to require all schemes to have at least one pensioner on their trustee boards. It is certainly to be hoped that pensioners will take an active role in running their schemes, since they have a wealth of experience and a different perspective to bring to the role. However, it should be borne in mind that trustees are required by trust law to act in the interests of all the beneficiaries of the scheme and are not there to represent any particular group.

If there is no pensioners' association attached to your employer (or perhaps run through a union), consider setting one up. Approach your employer and ask whether it would be willing to promote such a group by providing office facilities, meeting places and so on.

A pension from a personal plan

How to claim your pension

About three months before you want your pension to start, get in touch with the pension provider, asking for the details you need and any forms that you must complete. If you had previously selected a retirement date, the provider may contact you; otherwise, you should make the first move. Provided you are within the age limits for receiving a pension from your plan (see Chapter 19), you don't have to actually retire – you can receive a pension but still carry on working. In any letters, always quote any plan or policy reference number that you've been given. And have the number to hand, if you make contact by telephone. These are the main questions you need to ask the plan provider:

- how much is your pension fund worth?
- how much pension would the plan provider offer?
- can you arrange for your pension to increase each year, and by how much? By how much will your starting pension be reduced to pay for the later increases?
- what's the maximum lump sum you could have, and how much pension would remain? How much of a lump sum do you get for each £1 of pension you give up?
- is there a widow's or widower's pension (or pension for another dependant)? How much must you give up to provide, or increase, a widow's or widower's pension?

- what other options do you have?
- can you defer buying an annuity but still draw an income?

When you come to take your pension, you don't usually have to stay with the plan provider with whom you have been saving up until then. Most personal plans include an open market option, which gives you the right to transfer your pension fund to a different plan provider. Pensions can only be paid by an insurance company or a friendly society – so, if your earlier saving had been made with a unit trust, building society, or bank (unless you dealt with an insurance subsidiary of the society or bank), you will *have* to switch plan provider at retirement. Some insurance companies choose not to concentrate on the actual payment of pensions; their terms tend to be unattractive compared with companies who do specialise in this area, so it's sensible to shop around at retirement and use your open market option if you find a better deal elsewhere.

If you have protected rights (see Chapter 23) from a contracted-out personal plan, these can be – and may have to be – treated quite separately from the rest of your pension. Protected rights from a personal pension can't be paid out until you reach age 60, so you'll have to wait for this part of your pension to start if you retire at an earlier age. You must, by law, have an open market option enabling your protected rights pension to be paid by another provider, if you wish.

Choosing the right annuity

It is very important that you do exercise your open market option at retirement. Many plan providers, which are a perfectly good choice while you are building up your pension fund, do not even pretend to specialise in annuities, whereas other companies are very active in the annuity market. When you come to retire, you need to check the rates on offer at that time and the annuity which best suits your particular situation. Consider getting advice from an independent adviser that specialises in annuities*.

If you have a husband or wife, you should seriously consider taking out a joint annuity, which will carry on paying an income until the last partner dies, otherwise your widower or widow could be left in financial hardship. Some joint annuities carry on paying the same income after the first death; others pay a reduced amount.

An option that is popular is an annuity guaranteed for five years. In the normal way, an annuity pays an income for your lifetime and stops

321

on your death. This makes investing in an annuity a bit of a gamble: if you live a long time, you're on to a winner; but, if you die soon after the annuity starts, the return on your investment will be very poor indeed. To guard against a total loss, you can buy an annuity which is guaranteed to pay out for five years, even if you die before then. If you do die within five years, the remaining payments are usually rolled up into a lump sum and paid to your heirs. However, this type of annuity is not a good substitute for a joint annuity, if you are concerned about dependants.

Another option is to take out an increasing annuity. This is compulsory for contracted-out pension rights, but optional otherwise. An annuity increasing in line with inflation or by 5 per cent a year starts at a dramatically lower income than a level annuity – see Table 33.2 – and you'll generally need to survive for at least the average life expectancy for someone of your age before you recoup the income initially given up. You might do better to choose the level annuity, but invest part to boost your income in later years.

Annuity rates have fallen greatly over the last decade or so. This means that someone retiring now stands to receive a lot less pension than someone retiring ten years ago with the same-sized pension fund. In order to avoid being locked into the currently low annuity rates, a further option, which is gaining some popularity, is the with-profits

Table 33.2: Starting income from different types of annuity

Type of annuity	Income in the first year for each £10,000 invested for		
	A man aged 65	A woman aged 60	Joint annuity for man aged 65 and woman aged 60 (no reduction on first death)
Level annuity, no guarantees	£742	£612	£552
Level annuity with 5-year guarantee	£732	£609	£551
Increasing with inflation, no guarantee	£520	£391	£350
Increasing by 5% a year, no guarantee	£446	£317	£268

Source: *Money Facts Life and Pensions*. Rates in June 2004.

annuity. This is a higher-risk option than taking out an annuity that provides a guaranteed income, but offers the chance of a better return.

With-profits investments have already been described in Chapter 21. The concept has to be adapted when applied to annuities, mainly because a terminal bonus cannot be paid at the end of the investment (which, with an annuity, is the point at which the annuity-holder dies). However, in other respects the with-profits approach is little different, and relies on the idea of adding bonuses from time to time, which reflect the performance of underlying investments, business conditions, costs and so on.

Income from a with-profits annuity may be made up of two parts: a guaranteed basic payment and bonuses. At the time that you take out the annuity you must choose the starting income which the annuity will provide. Your choice depends on your view of the likely level of future bonuses (the assumed bonus rate, or ABR) and the degree of risk that you are willing to take. You can choose between:

- **low ABR (minimum 0%, that is, no bonuses)** The annuity income will start at a very low level. But as long as any bonus at all is declared the income will increase. This means that you are virtually guaranteed some increase in your income each year
- **higher ABR (maximum, say 5%)** Your starting income will be higher: the higher the ABR you choose, the greater the starting income. Each year, provided the bonus that is declared is greater than the ABR you chose, your income will increase. But if the declared bonus is lower than your ABR, your income will fall back.

The ABR that you choose at the outset stays the same throughout the annuity's life.

The maximum ABR that you are allowed to choose is set by the annuity provider in line with current market conditions. It is pitched at a level that makes it likely that your income will at least be stable, and will, it is hoped, increase.

As market conditions change, the maximum ABR that new annuity purchasers can choose will also change. So, if bonus rates are falling, the maximum ABR will be reduced. But that changed ABR applies only to new annuity customers. If you have already bought your annuity, you are locked into the ABR that you originally chose.

If bonus rates are tending to fall, the ABR that you originally chose can start to look very high. For example, if you chose an ABR of 10 per cent some years ago, that figure looks very optimistic when compared with bonus rates in, say, 2004. If bonuses of less than 10 per cent are declared your income will fall back.

The higher the ABR that you choose at the outset, the greater the risk that bonuses will fall short at some stage, and that your income will fall. On the other hand, the starting income from an annuity based on a 0 per cent ABR is very low, and unless extremely good bonuses were declared it would take many years before you caught up with the income from a traditional-level annuity. A sensible compromise can be to choose a mid-range ABR.

Annuity deferral and income withdrawal

A major problem with all money-purchase-type pension arrangements is that annuity rates may be low at the time you come to retire. Once you buy an annuity, you are locked into that income for the rest of your life. Retiring when annuity rates are low commits you to a lower retirement income than would have been available if annuity rates had been more buoyant. You could, of course, put off retiring in the hope that rates will improve, but that's not realistic if you need a pension income now.

Pension plans set up on or after 1 May 1995 can offer another option: annuity deferral and income withdrawal. This allows you to start taking an income from your pension plan but without buying an annuity. Instead, the income is drawn direct from the pension fund. You must, however, use the remaining fund to buy an annuity by the time you reach age 75. At the time the income starts, you have to make the normal decision about whether to take a tax-free lump sum – you can't change your mind about this later on. The maximum income is the amount which a single-person annuity would have provided, as set out in tables published by the government. The minimum is 65 per cent less than that maximum. For example, if the maximum is £10,000 a year, the minimum would be £3,500.

The income must be reviewed every three years to ensure that your pension fund is not being run down too fast. The position will depend crucially on the investment return on the remaining fund. Here is a dilemma: do you invest in share-based investments (which over the long term tend to outpace inflation, bond-based investments and deposits but carry the risk that your capital can fall in value), or do you opt for investments that expose your capital to less risk but produce investment returns that are unlikely to be sufficient to make the annuity deferral worthwhile?

The annuity deferral and income withdrawal option is available only with personal pensions, not the retirement annuity contracts – and then only if the terms of the plan allow for it. You can use your open market option to switch to a plan which does have this option. Occupational money purchase schemes are also allowed to offer this option, though few, if any, do. However, you could transfer your pension fund at retirement from the occupational scheme to a personal plan that does include annuity deferral and income withdrawal.

So is annuity deferral and income withdrawal a good idea? The pros and cons can be set out as follows:

- **pro** Useful option if annuity rates are historically low at the time you want to retire
- **pro** Lets you vary your income within the upper and lower limits
- **pro** You can release the tax-free lump sum (e.g. to pay off a

---

Mortality drag

'Mortality drag' basically means the later you leave buying an annuity, the less you benefit from the effects of averaging.

What you pay for an annuity is based on the average life expectancy for a pool of people of your age. The average life expectancy for a relatively young group of people is damped down because some people will die soon. As you age, those people drop out of the annuity pool because they have indeed died. This pushes up the relative price of the annuity (i.e. pushes down the annuity rate) because you are losing the cross-subsidy you enjoyed from the people who die earlier than average.

In addition, the survivors are those people who personally have a higher life expectancy, so an annuity taken out at a later age is expected on average to run to a higher age than an annuity taken out at a younger age. For example, using the life expectancy figures on page 11, an annuity for men aged 60 would be based on them living on average to age 79, but an annuity for men aged 70 would be based on them living to age 82. This too pushes up the relative price of the annuity (i.e. pushes down the annuity rate).

---

mortgage or meet a divorce settlement) while keeping the pension income to a minimum until needed

- **pro** If you die, your dependants can benefit from the whole of the remaining fund, paid either as income direct from the fund or from an annuity or, less attractively, as a lump sum after deduction of tax at a special 35 per cent rate
- **pro** Useful if you are in poor health, in which case an annuity would usually look like a poor deal
- **con** Charges levied by the plan provider for administering the remaining fund can make this route uneconomic if you have only a small fund
- **con** Income withdrawal is risky if you can't afford to lose any of the capital in your pension fund – really, you do need other income which you can fall back on
- **con** It is hard to tell when annuity rates are favourable enough to warrant switching to an annuity
- **con** You lose out if annuity rates are still low when you reach age 75 and must switch to an annuity
- **con** The later you leave the purchase of an annuity, the more you suffer from 'mortality drag' (see box). This means, the older you are, the higher the relative cost of buying an annuity. To compensate for this price rise, your investments need to grow extra fast during the period of annuity deferral.

How your pension is paid

You can usually choose the most convenient method of payment – e.g. direct into a bank or building society account, or by cheque through the post. You may be able to choose whether to have the pension paid, say, monthly, quarterly or only once a year. The pension may be paid in advance or in arrears. You may get slightly more pension if it is paid less frequently, since the pension provider can invest your money in the interim.

From 6 April 1996 onwards, a very small pension may be paid to you as a single lump sum at retirement. This is allowed where your pension fund is less than £2,500 or it is too small to buy at least £260 annuity income (before taking into account any tax-free lump sum). The pension plan must be your only one.

Chapter 34

Tax in retirement

This chapter looks at the tax details in retirement.

How your pensions are treated for tax

Your state pension

State retirement pensions count as part of your income for tax purposes, and you may have to pay tax if your income is high enough (see 328). The exception is the £10 Christmas bonus, which is tax-free. You might be eligible for other benefits in retirement – for example, pension credit (see Chapter 2) – that are tax-free.

State pension is paid without any tax having been deducted, which is convenient if you're a non-taxpayer. If you're a starting-rate, basic-rate or higher-rate taxpayer, there will be tax to pay. If you're receiving a pension from elsewhere, or you have a job, the tax on your state pension will usually be deducted from the other pension or your earnings through the Pay-As-You-Earn (PAYE) system. If you don't pay the tax due through PAYE, it will be collected in instalments in January and July (see page 330).

Occupational scheme pensions

A pension from an occupational scheme is treated as your income for tax purposes, and there will be tax to pay if your income is high enough. Usually, the pension will be paid with tax already deducted through the PAYE system.

PAYE may also be used to collect tax on other parts of your income – for example, tax on your state pension or on income from your investments. This may take you by surprise, because it will look as if you're paying too much tax on your occupational pension – see the case history of Charlotte on page 331. If you're in any doubt about the deductions being made, first check your tax position – ask the scheme administrators to help you do this. If you still think you're being over-taxed, contact your tax office.

If, at retirement, you receive a refund of 'excess' additional voluntary contributions (AVCs), tax will have been deducted at a special rate of 33 per cent and there will be extra tax to pay if you're a higher-rate taxpayer – see page 290.

Personal pensions

A personal pension counts as your income for tax purposes, so there will be tax to pay if your income is high enough. The pension provider will usually deduct tax through PAYE before handing over the pension to you.

Using the PAYE system, tax on any other income you have – for example, a state pension – may also be deducted from your personal plan before it is paid. This may mislead you into thinking that you're paying too much tax on your personal plan. Before taking any other action, check your full tax position (see below) and the total tax you're paying. If you still find that your tax bill is too high, contact your tax office.

Your tax in retirement

In retirement, your tax bill continues to be worked out in the normal way, but you may benefit from higher tax allowances, so there may be less tax to pay than when you were working, even if your income stays the same. The calculations below are carried out for each tax year, which runs from 6 April in one year to 5 April in the next. Your tax bill is worked out like this:

- **income** from all sources is added together. This will include your pensions, interest earned by any investments, earnings from any work you do, and so on. But you do not include any tax-free income – this includes, for example, the proceeds from National Savings certificates, withdrawals from ISAs and the pay-out on maturity of most regular-premium insurance policies
- **outgoings** that you pay in full are subtracted from your income. 'Outgoing' is tax jargon for any expense which qualifies for tax

relief. With some – such as donations to charity through Gift Aid and contributions to personal pensions – you get relief by paying a 'net' amount from which basic-rate tax relief has already been deducted. Income less outgoings is called your *total income*

- **allowances** are then subtracted. Traditionally, an allowance has been a slice of income on which you don't pay tax, but some allowances are taken into account later as a deduction from your tax bill. Everyone (even a child) has a personal allowance
- what's left is your **taxable income**. This is divided into three slices. On the first slice you pay tax at 10 per cent. On the second slice, called the basic-rate band, you pay tax at the basic rate. On anything more, you pay tax at a higher rate. In the 2004–5 tax year, the starting-rate band of 10 per cent covers the first £2,020. The basic-rate band runs from taxable income of £2,021 to £31,400; the tax rate is 22 per cent. The higher tax rate is 40 per cent
- **married couple's allowance.** This is a reduced-rate allowance, given at a rate of 10 per cent as a reduction in your tax bill. Married couple's allowance is given only where you or your husband or wife were born before 6 April 1935. If you are single now but born before that date, you can claim the allowance if you marry later on.

How tax is collected

With many types of investment, you receive taxable income with tax at the savings rate (20 per cent in 2004–5) already deducted. This applies, for example, to interest from bank and building society accounts, corporate bonds and gilts. The main exception is various National Savings investments, such as the investment account and pensioners' guaranteed income bonds, where the income is paid gross (i.e. without any tax deducted). With gilts, you can choose to receive the interest either gross or after deduction of tax at the savings rate.

Assuming you are a basic-rate taxpayer, there is no further tax to pay if income is net of the savings rate. If you are a higher-rate taxpayer, there is a further 20 per cent tax to pay (on the gross amount, rather than the amount you receive). If you are a non-taxpayer, you can with some investments – e.g. bank and building society accounts and annuities – arrange to receive the income gross. This is convenient, because it saves you the trouble and delay of reclaiming tax. If you hold a bank or building society account jointly with someone who is a taxpayer, you can still usually arrange to receive your half of the interest without tax being deducted. If you are a starting-rate taxpayer, you can reclaim half of the tax already deducted.

Dividends from shares, distributions from unit trusts and income from similar investments are paid to you with tax already deducted at a rate of 10 per cent. If you hold the shares directly, since 6 April 1999 you are no longer able to reclaim this tax if you are a non-taxpayer.

If you are a basic-rate or starting-rate taxpayer there is no further tax to pay on income from shares, unit trusts or similar investments. If you are a higher-rate taxpayer tax is due at a rate of 32.5 per cent (less the 10 per cent already paid).

If part of your income comes from an employer or a pension provider, any tax due on income received gross will usually be collected through the PAYE system operated by that person or organisation.

CASE HISTORY: Jennifer

Jennifer is a higher-rate taxpayer. In 2004–5 she received income of £8,031 from her UK equity income unit-trust holding. This is income net of tax at 10 per cent. Before working out the higher-rate tax due, Jennifer must gross up the income received. She does the following sum: £8,031 ÷ (100% − 10%) = £8,923. Higher-rate tax is charged at a special rate of 32.5 per cent and comes to 32.5% × £8,923 = £2,900. From this she can deduct the 10 per cent tax already paid, leaving a tax bill outstanding of £2,900 − £892 = £2,008.

If any income tax remains to be collected, it is collected under the self-assessment system, which works as follows. Information about untaxed income for 2004–5 will be collected through the tax return you receive in April 2005. If you want the Inland Revenue to work out your tax bill for you, you must complete and send back this return by 30 September 2005. Alternatively, you can work out your own tax bill, in which case you have until 31 January 2006 to send in your tax return together with your calculations. In the meantime you will have paid tax for 2004–5 in two equal instalments, on 31 January 2005 and 31 July 2005, the amounts being based on your tax bill for the previous year. On 31 January 2006 there is a final payment or refund to square the books. On the same date, any capital gains tax is also payable.

CASE HISTORY: Charlotte

Charlotte, who is aged 66, has the following income in 2004–5:

State pension	£4,139
Occupational pension	£3,200
National Savings & Investments Pensioners Bond	£3,400
National Savings & Investments Income Bonds	£1,600
	£12,339

She has no outgoings. Charlotte claims her personal allowance of £6,830 (see below), which leaves her with a taxable income of £5,509.

Charlotte pays tax at 10 per cent on the first £2,020. This leaves £5,509 – £2,020 = £3,489 to be taxed at the basic rate. Her total tax bill is (10% × £2,020) + (22% × £3,489) = £969.58.

She receives her state pension and savings income without tax having been deducted, so the whole tax bill is collected from her occupational pension through the PAYE system. This makes it look as if her employer's pension is being taxed at a rate of 30 per cent (£995.22 ÷ £3,200). But this isn't really the case, because the amount deducted is the tax due on her whole income, not just the employer's pension.

Your tax allowances in retirement

Everyone has a personal tax allowance. In the 2004–5 tax year, the personal allowance for most people is £4,745. But, if you will be age 65 or more at any time during the tax year, you qualify for a higher personal allowance, the age allowance. There are two rates: in the 2004–5 tax year, the allowance is £6,830 for people reaching ages 65 to 74, and the higher-age allowance is £6,950 for people reaching age 75 or more.

A husband and wife each get a personal allowance to set against their own income. But they might also get an extra allowance called the married couple's allowance if either husband or wife (or both) were born before 6 April 1935. In 2004–5, this is £5,725 if the older partner is aged up to 73 at the start of the tax year, and £5,795 if the older partner is aged 74 or over.

CASE HISTORY: Christian

Christian, who is a higher-rate taxpayer, receives £4,000 interest from his building society account in the 2004–5 tax year. This is 'net' interest – i.e. the amount left after tax at the savings rate of 20 per cent has been deducted. To find the 'gross' (before-tax) amount of interest which this is equivalent to, he must work out the following sum: £4,000 ÷ (100% − 20%) = £5,000. The higher rate of tax is 40 per cent, so tax on £5,000 is 40% × £5,000 = £2,000. However, Christian has already paid tax of 20% × £5,000 = £1,000, so he has only to pay the remaining £2,000 − £1,000 = £1,000.

While the personal allowance saves you tax at your highest rate, the married couple's allowance only gives you tax relief at a rate of 10 per cent in the 2004–5 tax year (regardless of your top rate of tax).

If the husband's income is above a certain level (see below), the married couple's allowance is reduced, but never to less than a basic amount (£2,210 in 2004–5).

A wife can elect to have half the basic amount of the married couple's allowance (but not any of the age-related addition) set against her own income. Alternatively, the husband and wife can jointly elect for the whole basic amount to be transferred to the wife. This would be worth doing if the wife pays tax but the husband is a non-taxpayer.

Income limit for age allowance

Age allowances are reduced for people with earnings above a certain level. The personal age allowance is reduced if you have 'total income' (see page 329) of more than £18,900 in the 2004–5 tax year. The married couple's age allowance is also reduced if the husband has income over £18,900 in the 2004–5 tax year. In either case, the allowance is reduced by £1 for every £2 of income above the limit. Where the husband is receiving both age-related personal allowance and age-related married couple's allowance, his personal allowance is reduced first and then the married couple's allowance. The reduction stops once the allowances have fallen to a basic amount. So, whatever your income, in the 2004–5 tax year, your personal allowance could not be less than £4,745, and the married couple's allowance could not be less than £2,210.

CASE HISTORY: Mary and Denis

Mary and Denis have been married for nearly 40 years. Mary was born on 8 September 1933. She qualifies for a personal age allowance of £6,830 in the 2004–5 tax year. Denis is 62. He's too young to get personal age allowance and gets the normal personal allowance of £4,745. But he also receives the married couple's allowance because Mary was born before 6 April 1935. The allowance is set initially at £5,725.

Denis, however, hasn't retired yet and earns £19,400 a year – £500 above the £18,900 limit for age allowance. This means that the married couple's age allowance is reduced by £250 (£1 for each £2 of the excess income). Denis's married couple's age allowance becomes £5,725 – £250 = £5,475.

Mary's personal age allowance is not affected by Denis's earnings, and her own income is less than the £18,900 limit.

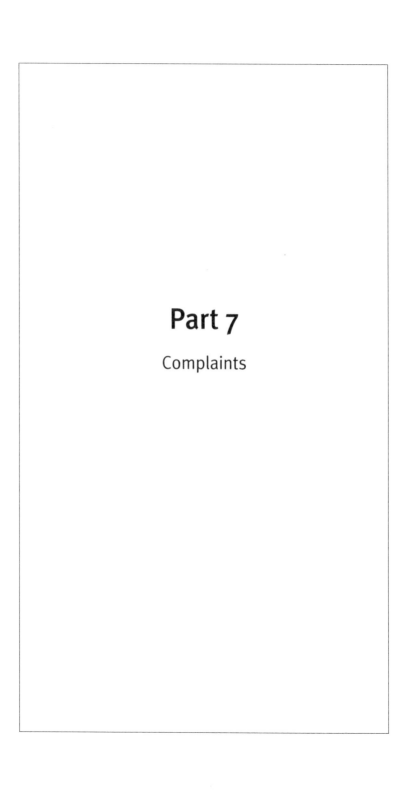

Part 7

Complaints

Chapter 35

What to do if things go wrong

If you have a problem or complaint concerning your pension arrangements, you can take steps to resolve it.

Problems with your state pension

If your complaint concerns your National Insurance contributions record – e.g., you believe that your record is wrong – contact your local tax office★; you may be given a form to complete.

With most other complaints concerning your state pension, you should contact The Pension Service★. Explain your problem and don't forget to quote your National Insurance number.

If you are disputing the amount the The Pension Service is paying you or plans to pay you, see the DWP leaflet GL24, *If You Think our Decision is Wrong* available from The Pension Service★ or Department for Work and Pensions★.

If your complaint concerns the way you have been dealt with or poor administration and you are not happy with the response from The Pension Service, If still not satisfied, write to your Member of Parliament (MP)★ with your complaint and the response from the DWP. Your MP may refer your case to the Parliamentary Commissioner for Administration (the 'Parliamentary Ombudsman'). You can't contact the Ombudsman yourself.

You can find out more about the Parliamentary Ombudsman from a leaflet, *The Parliamentary Ombudsman: How to Complain to the Ombudsman*, available from the Parliamentary Ombudsman's★ office.

Problems with personal pensions, stakeholder schemes or occupational schemes

If you have a complaint concerning a personal pension or stakeholder scheme, or the advice you were given, you should first contact the manager of the provider or the financial adviser with whom you dealt. If you're not satisfied with the response, ask for details of the formal complaints procedure – the firm must have one. If you are not happy with the response from the firm, you can take your complaint to the Financial Ombudsman Service★ (see below). For more information about making a complaint, see the *FSA guide to making a complaint* from the Financial Services Authority★.

If you have a complaint concerning your occupational pension scheme, contact either the pension scheme administrator or the trustees of the scheme. Details of who to contact and the address must be included in the basic information about the scheme which you should have been given, and may be displayed on a notice board at work. From April 1997 onwards, all employers' schemes are required to have a formal complaints procedure. If you are not happy with the response, you can take your complaint to the Pensions Advisory Service (OPAS)★ – see below. For more information about complaining to your scheme, see the leaflet, *Pensions Disputes Procedure*, from OPAS.

An advisory scheme

The Pensions Advisory Service (OPAS)★ was originally set up as a voluntary body to help people who were having problems concerning their occupational pension scheme. It has now evolved into a state-backed service with a much wider remit, offering its services to people having problems with either occupational schemes, personal pensions or stakeholder schemes. The service won't make any judgements about your case, but it can investigate the situation and advise you on the facts relevant to your case. It will often contact the occupational scheme trustees or administrators or plan provider on your behalf and will try to help you and the scheme or plan provider reach a solution.

Independent complaints bodies

If the firm does not deal with your complaint to your satisfaction and you have suffered a loss because of its actions, you could take your case to court. But a speedier option – and one which is free – is to take your case to an ombudsman.

If your complaint concerns the selling of a personal pension or stakeholder scheme or advice you were given, and either OPAS could not resolve the matter or you decided not to go to OPAS, you can take your case to the Financial Ombudsman Service (FOS)★. Initially, FOS will probably try to help you and the company concerned reach an acceptable compromise, but, if that fails, FOS can make a determination which is binding on the company but not on you. FOS can order the company to take the necessary steps to put the matter right. This could involve, say, reinstating a pension plan or paying you compensation. The maximum award is £100,000.

If your complaint concerns an occupational scheme or the way a personal pension or stakeholder scheme is run, you can take your case to the Pensions Ombudsman★. But first, you *must* have given OPAS a chance to try to resolve the matter. This is a sensible requirement. Pension schemes are complicated, and many disputes centre round a misunderstanding rather than an out-and-out grievance. OPAS has a good track record in clarifying issues and helping members understand the way their scheme works. The Pensions Ombudsman will examine all the evidence and make a determination which is binding on both you and the pension scheme.

Going to court

If you are unhappy with the decision of the Pensions Ombudsman, there is not usually any more you can do. But, if you are unhappy with the decision of FOS, you can, if you choose, still take your case to court.

If the actions of a plan provider, agent or adviser caused you to lose money, you could try to recover your loss in court by suing for, say, negligence, misrepresentation or breach of the Financial Services and Markets Act rules. Similarly, it is possible to take the trustees of an occupational pension scheme to court if you believe they have acted against the interests of the scheme members.

If the amount you are claiming is reasonably small, you can use the relatively quick and not-too-expensive small claims track. This procedure is fairly informal, and you should not need a lawyer. To use the small claims track, the amount you are claiming should be no more than:

- £5,000 in England and Wales
- £2,000 in Northern Ireland
- £750 in Scotland.

To find out more, contact your local county court★ in England, Wales or Northern Ireland, or the sheriff court★ in Scotland. You can also find useful information on the Courts Service website.★

Court cases are generally lengthy, costly and may be difficult to prove, so you'd be wise to look on this course of action as a last resort. If there are other people in the same position as you, you may be able to join together to bring a court action. In a case concerning an employer's scheme, you should find out whether a trade union or staff association would be willing to fight the case.

Compensation

If your complaint against a plan provider, agent or adviser is successful and an award is made in your favour – either by the firm itself, through the regulatory body, a specialist complaints procedure, or by a court – you'll usually recover your money from the firm. But, sometimes, the firm is broke and can't pay up. In this situation, you may qualify for compensation. Provided the firm is authorised by the FSA, you might be eligible for compensation from the Financial Services Compensation Scheme (FSCS★). The FSCS can pay compensation where you have lost money due to an authorised firm's fraud or negligence and the firm has gone out of business. The maximum compensation payable depends on the type of financial product involved – see Table 35.1.

At the time of writing, a compensation scheme exists to ensure that members of occupational pension schemes get at least some of their benefits back if their employer is insolvent and occupational pension scheme assets have gone missing because of fraud or some other crime. Basically, the scheme replaces 90 per cent of the lost assets, sometimes less. The compensation is paid to the scheme, which then distributes

Table 35.1: Maximum compensation payable from the Financial Services Compensation Scheme

Type of financial product involved	Level of cover	Maximum payment
Deposits (e.g. bank and building society accounts, cash ISAs)	100% of the first £20,000 90% of the next £33,000	£31,700
Investments (e.g. unit trusts, stocks-and-shares ISAs, shares)	100% of the first £30,000 90% of the next £20,000	£48,000
Long-term insurance, including most personal pensions	100% of the first £2,000 At least 90% of the remainder (including future benefits already declared)	Unlimited

all the available assets in accordance with the winding-up priority outlined on page 169. This means that individual members might still face some significant loss of benefits. Under the new laws going through Parliament at the time of writing, this scheme is to be replaced with a broadly similar scheme called the Fraud Compensation Fund.

Neither of these compensation schemes helps in cases where no crime has been committed but, nevertheless, the employer has gone bust, leaving a gaping hole in the pension scheme assets. To address this, the new laws will set up the Pension Protection Fund. This will cover defined benefit schemes (such as final salary schemes) and will step in to cover shortfalls left once the winding-up provisions (see page 169) have shared out what funds are available. The Pension Protection Fund will ensure that pensions in payment continue to be paid in full (though increases will not be fully protected) and that, for people still working, 90 per cent of their benefits up to a set limit are protected.

The government estimates that some 65,000 people have lost large amounts of pension in recent years, but the Pension Protection Fund will not be able to consider cases that occurred before it starts up. To help people who have lost out before then, the government plans to set up a £400 million assistance scheme. The plans are subject to parliamentary approval and details of how the scheme will work had not been announced at the time of writing.

Complaints to the regulator

If you are worried about the way a firm or an occupational scheme is behaving – for example, you think it is breaking regulations or might be acting fraudulently – you should report your concerns to the regulator. If the problem concerns a personal pension or financial adviser, contact the FSA★. If the problem concerns an occupational scheme, contact the Occupational Pensions Regulatory Authority (OPRA) (due to be replaced by a new Pensions Regulator★).

Addresses

Association of Consulting Actuaries
1 Wardrobe Place
London EC4V 5AG
Tel: 020-7248 3163
Website: www.aca.org.uk

Consulting actuary
For details of a consulting actuary in your area, see entries for Association of Consulting Actuaries and Society of pension Consultants.

County Court
See The Phone Book under 'Courts'.

Courts Service websites
- England and Wales:
  www.courtservice.gov.uk
- Scotland: www.scotcourts.gov.uk
- Northern Ireland:
  wwwcourtsni.gov.uk

Department for Work and Pensions (DWP)
- For information about state pensions and state benefits if you are over state pension age, see entry for The Pension Service.
- For information about most state benefits if you are of working age, see entry for Jobcentre Plus.
  For information about National Insurance contributions, tax credits and child benefit, see entry for Inland Revenue.

- DWP Direct Payment Information Line
  Tel: 0800 107 2000
  Website:
  www.dwp.gov.uk/directpayment
- DWP Public Enquiry Office
  Tel: 020-7712 2171
  Website: www.dwp.gov.uk

Designated Professional Bodies
- Association of Chartered Certified Accountants
  29 Lincoln's Inn Fields
  London WC2A 3EE.
  Tel: 020-7396 7000
  Website: www.acca.co.uk
- Institute of Chartered Accountants in England and Wales
  Chartered Accountants' Hall
  PO Box 433, Moorgate Place
  London EC2P 2BJ.
  Tel: 020-7920 8100
  Website: www.icaew.co.uk
- Institute of Chartered Accountants in Ireland Chartered Accountants' House
  83 Pembroke Road,
  Dublin 4
  Republic of Ireland
  Tel: (00 353) 1 637 7200
  Website: www.icai.ie

- Institute of Chartered
  Accountants of Scotland,
  CA House
  21 Haymarket Yards
  Edinburgh EH12 5BH
  Tel: 0131-347 0100
  Website: www.icas.org.uk
- Law Society
  113 Chancery Lane
  London WC2A 1PL
  Tel: 020-7242 1222
  Website: www.lawsoc.org.uk
  Law Society of Scotland
- 26 Drumsheugh Gardens
  Edinburgh EH3 7YR
  Tel: 0131-226 7411
  Website: www.lawscot.org.uk
- Law Society of Northern Ireland
  98 Victoria Street
  Belfast BT1 3JZ
  Tel: 028 90 231614
  Website: www.lawsoc-ni.org
- Institute of Actuaries
  Staple Inn
  High Holborn
  London WC1V 7QJ
  Tel: 020-7632 2100
  Website: www.actuaries.org.uk

Financial Ombudsman Service
South Quay Plaza
183 Marsh Wall
London E14 9SR
Tel: 0845 080 1800
Website: www.financial-
ombudsman.org.uk

Financial Services Authority (FSA)
25 The North Colonnade, Canary
Wharf
London E14 5HS
- Consumer Helpline:
  0845 606 1234
  Website: www.fsa.gov.uk
- FSA Comparative Tables:
  0845 606 1234
  Website: www.fsa.gov.uk/tables
- FSA Register: 0845 606 1234
  Website:
  www.fsa.gov.uk/consumer

Financial Services Compensation Scheme
7th Floor
Lloyds Chambers
Portsoken Street
London E1 8BN
Tel: 020-7892 7300
Website: www.fscs.org.uk

IFA Promotion
For a list of IFAs in your area, contact:
Tel: 0800 085 3250
Website: www.unbiased.co.uk

Independent financial adviser (IFA) (to find one)
See separate entries for the following organisations:
- IFA Promotion
- The Institute of Financial
  Planning
- Matrix Data UK IFA Directory
- Society of Financial Advisers
  (SOFA)

Independent financial advisers who specialise in annuities
- The Annuity Bureau
  The Tower, 11 York Road
  London SE1 7NX
  Tel: 0845 602 6263
  Website: www.bureauxltd.com
- Annuity Direct
  32 Scrutton Street
  London EC2A 4RQ
  Tel: 0500 65 75
  Website:
  www.annuitydirect.co.uk
- Hargreaves Lansdown Annuity
  Supermarket
  Website:
  www.hargreaveslansdown.co.uk/
  pensions
- WBA Ltd
  Tel: 020-7421 4545
  Website:
  www.williamburrows.com

Inland Revenue
- For local tax enquiry centres look in phone book under 'Inland Revenue'.
  Orderline: 0845 9000 404
  Website:
  www.inlandrevenue.gov.uk
- For your own tax office, check your tax return or other correspondence or ask your employer or the scheme paying your pension.

The Institute of Financial Planning
Whitefriars Centre
Lewins Mead
Bristol BS1 2NT
Tel: 0117 9345 2470
Website:
www.financialplanning.org.uk

Jobcentre Plus
For local office, check website or see Phone Book.
Website: www.jobcentreplus.gov.uk

Matrix Data UK IFA Directory
www.ukifadirectory.co.uk

Member of Parliament
- To find out who is your local MP, contact your local public library or look on www.locata.co.uk/commons.
- To contact your MP, write to:
  [your MP's name]
  House of Commons
  London SW1A 0AA

Money Management
- Current issue, from newsagents.
- Back issues from:
  WDIS
  Units 12-13 Cranleigh Gardens
  Industrial Estate
  Southall
  Middlesex UB1 2BR
  Tel: 020-8606 7545

Money Management National Register of Fee-Based Advisers
c/o Matrix Data Ltd
FREEPOST 22 (SW1565)
London W1E 1BR
Tel: 0870 013 1925

Occupational Pensions Regulatory Authority (OPRA)
Invicta House
Trafalgar Place
Brighton BN1 4DW
Tel: (01273) 627600
Website: www.opra.gov.uk

Parliamentary Ombudsman
Millbank Tower
Millbank
London SW1P 4QP
Tel: 0845 015 4033
Website: www.ombudsman.org.uk

Pensions Advisory Service (OPAS)
11 Belgrave Road
London SW1V 1RB
Tel: 0845 601 2923
Website: www.opas.org.uk

Pension Schemes Registry
PO Box 1NN
Newcastle upon Tyne NE99 1NN
Tel: 0191 225 6316
Website:
www.opra.gov.uk/traceAPension/

Pension Service (The)
- For local office, check website or see phone book.
  Tel: 0845 60 60 265
  Pensions Information Line:
  0845 31 32 33
  Pensions Forecasting Service:
  0845 3000 168
  Pension Credit Application Line:
  0800 99 1234
  Website:
  www.thepensionservice.gov.uk
- International Pension Centre
  Tyneview Park
  Newcastle upon Tyne NE98 1BA.
  Tel: +44 (0) 191 218 7777

Pensions administrator (occupational pension scheme)
Usually located in your Human Resources (Personnel) Department. Contact details will also be in any booklet and correspondence about the scheme and on any pensions noticeboard at work.

Pensions Management
• Current issue, from newsagents.
• Back issues from:
WDIS
Units 12-13 Cranleigh Gardens Industrial Estate
Southall
Middlesex UB1 2BR
Tel: 020-8606 7545

Pensions Ombudsman
11 Belgrave Road
London SW1V 1RB
Tel: 020-7834 9144
Website: www.pensions-ombudsman.org.uk

Sheriff Court
See Phone Book under 'Courts'.

Society of Financial Advisers (SOFA)
For a list of independent financial advisers who all have more than just the basic qualifications, contact:
20 Aldermanbury
London EC2V 7HY
Tel: 020-8989 8464
Website: www.sofa.org

Society of Pension Consultants
St Bartholomew House
92 Fleet Street
London EC4Y 1DG
Tel: 020-7353 1688
Website: www.spc.uk.com

Tax Office
See entry for Inland Revenue.

Which? and **Which? Books**
Freepost
PO 44
Hertford X
SG14 1YB
Tel: 0800 252 100
Website: www.which.net

Index